Intentionality Deconstructed

Intentionality Deconstructed

An Anti-Realist Theory

AMIR HOROWITZ

OXFORD
UNIVERSITY PRESS

Great Clarendon Street, Oxford, OX2 6DP,
United Kingdom

Oxford University Press is a department of the University of Oxford.
It furthers the University's objective of excellence in research, scholarship,
and education by publishing worldwide. Oxford is a registered trade mark of
Oxford University Press in the UK and in certain other countries

© Amir Horowitz 2024

The moral rights of the author have been asserted

All rights reserved. No part of this publication may be reproduced, stored in
a retrieval system, or transmitted, in any form or by any means, without the
prior permission in writing of Oxford University Press, or as expressly permitted
by law, by licence or under terms agreed with the appropriate reprographics
rights organization. Enquiries concerning reproduction outside the scope of the
above should be sent to the Rights Department, Oxford University Press, at the
address above

You must not circulate this work in any other form
and you must impose this same condition on any acquirer

Published in the United States of America by Oxford University Press
198 Madison Avenue, New York, NY 10016, United States of America

British Library Cataloguing in Publication Data

Data available

Library of Congress Control Number: 2023946101

ISBN 978–0–19–889643–2

DOI: 10.1093/oso/9780198896432.001.0001

Printed and bound by
CPI Group (UK) Ltd, Croydon, CR0 4YY

Links to third party websites are provided by Oxford in good faith and
for information only. Oxford disclaims any responsibility for the materials
contained in any third party website referenced in this work.

To my parents,
Reuven Horowitz and Varda Horowitz

Contents

Preface	ix
Acknowledgments	xi

1. Introducing Intentionality | 1
  1.1 First Acquaintance with Intentional Anti-Realism | 1
  1.2 What Is Intentionality? What Is Its Source? | 3
  1.3 Intentionality as Transcendence, Intentionality as Relational | 7
  1.4 Against Intentional Primitivism | 11
  1.5 Functional Role, the Transcendence of Intentionality, and Narrow Content | 20
  1.6 The Plan for the Remainder of the Book | 25

2. How to Settle Issues of Intentionality, and a Tentative Argument for Intentional Anti-Realism | 29
  2.1 Referential Diversity? | 29
  2.2 Do Philosophers Intuit Reference? | 33
  2.3 Can Theoretical Considerations Settle Issues of Reference Determination? | 38
  2.4 A Lesson for Experimental Philosophical Semantics? | 42
  2.5 An Argument for Intentional Anti-Realism | 45

3. Against Phenomenal Intentionality as Intrinsic Reductive Intentionality | 49
  3.1 Preliminaries for Phenomenal Intentionality | 49
  3.2 The Phenomenal Intentionality Thesis | 54
  3.3 Phenomenal Intentionality as Grounding Intentionality | 55
  3.4 Arguments for the Phenomenal Intentionality Thesis | 60
    3.4.1 The Accuracy Conditions Argument | 60
    3.4.2 The Empirical Adequacy Argument | 61
    3.4.3 The Argument from Introspection | 62
    3.4.4 Disquotation and the Sense of First-Person Content Ascriptions | 73
  3.5 Conceptual Connections between Consciousness and Intentionality | 78
    3.5.1 Searle's Argument | 78
    3.5.2 McGinn's Argument | 81
    3.5.3 Against Conceptual Reductions of Intentionality to Phenomenality | 84
  3.6 Against Synthetic Reductions of Intentionality to Phenomenality | 86
  3.7 Against Intrinsic Reductions of Intentionality | 90
  3.8 Indeterminacy Again | 92
  3.9 What Has Been Shown and What Has Not Been Shown regarding the Intentionality of Phenomenal States | 95

viii CONTENTS

4. Against Naturalistic Reductions of Intentionality 96
   4.1 The Idea of Intentional Naturalistic Reduction 96
   4.2 The Naturalistic Reduction of Intentionality as a Scientific
      Reduction 99
   4.3 Naturalistic Reduction and the Concept of Reference 104
   4.4 Naturalistic Reduction and Indeterminacy 107
   4.5 Extending the Arguments' Applicability 111
   4.6 Naturalism and Content Ascription 113

5. Intentional Anti-Realism I 115
   5.1 Intentional Anti-Realism—The Negative Thesis 115
   5.2 Practice-Dependence Intentional Anti-Realism 118
   5.3 Intentional Anti-Realism, the Existence of So-Called
      Intentional States, and Logico-Syntactic Structures 125
   5.4 Intentional Anti-Realism and Truth (or Epistemic Worth)
      without Meaning 134
   5.5 Coherence and the Status of Content Ascriptions 138
   5.6 Two Implications of Intentional Anti-Realism 144
      5.6.1 Thought and Language 144
      5.6.2 The Turing Test and the Alleged Ubiquity of Intelligence 146

6. Intentional Anti-Realism II: Objections and Further Developments 148
   6.1 Intentional Anti-Realism and the Success of Content Ascription 148
   6.2 Intentional Anti-Realism and Naturalistic Patterns 152
   6.3 Back to the Success Argument 159
   6.4 Explananda, Intentional Characterizations, and Roles of Content
      Ascription 165
   6.5 Intentional Suicide, and Intentional Anti-Realism as Radical
      Philosophy 170
   6.6 Still Another Argument for Intentional Anti-Realism 180

References 183
Index 199

Preface

This book is the product of many years of thinking about intentionality, during which I have changed my mind several times—from taking this (alleged) phenomenon to be an irreducible distinguishing mark of the mental, to considering it to be naturalistically reducible, to finally denying its existence and even possibility. This denial is the central claim of the theory to be presented on these pages, intentional anti-realism.

John Collins, Frances Egan, Yuval Eylon, Eugen Fischer, Angela Mendelovici, David Papineau, Steve Stich, Ruth Weintraub, and Assaf Weksler gave me very useful comments on drafts of chapters of the book, and following suggestions of two anonymous readers for Oxford University Press also made the book significantly better than it would have been otherwise. I extend my gratitude to all of them. I owe special thanks to Arnon Cahen for reading the whole manuscript and making excellent comments with respect to both content and style. I have also benefited from conversations with Yuval Eylon, David Papineau, Assaf Weksler, and Steve Stich. The influence of Stich's views on mine is greater than the references reflect. The title of this book draws inspiration from his *Deconstructing the Mind*.

Acknowledgments

I thank the Israel Scientific Foundation for grant number 419/11, and the Open University of Israel for grant number 507444.

Most parts of Chapter 2 are taken from "Experimental Philosophical Semantics and the Real Reference of Gödel," in *Experimental Philosophy, Rationalism and Naturalism: Rethinking Philosophical Method*, ed. by Eugen Fischer and John Collins, pp. 240–258, copyright 2015 by Routledge. Reproduced by permission of Taylor & Francis Group.

Parts of Chapter 4 are taken from "On the Very Idea of a (Natural) Intentional Relation," in *Intentionality and Action*, ed. by Jesús Padilla Gálvez and Margit Gaffal, pp. 139–157, copyright 2017 by De Gruyter. Reproduced by permission of De Gruyter.

1

Introducing Intentionality

1.1 First Acquaintance with Intentional Anti-Realism

This book is about intentionality. Its main purpose is to argue for the thesis of intentional anti-realism, according to which nothing is, and nothing can be, about anything.[1] More precisely, there is no intentionality and there cannot be intentionality in the concrete world. No concrete entity—a mental state, a linguistic object or act, a picture, a computer, a robot, a thermometer, or any of their states, etc.—can be intentional. So, this book denies what Galen Strawson (2010, p. 345) calls "concrete intentionality" (though the term "concrete" will be henceforth omitted). It is not committed to a view about whether abstract intentional entities such as concepts (in the semantic sense, in contrast with the psychological sense) and propositions exist. Denying that mental states can be intentional involves rejecting the claim that they can be propositional and denying that linguistic acts can be intentional involves rejecting the claim that they can express propositions, but these do not amount to denying the possibility of propositions.[2,3]

Propositions aside, denying intentionality neither amounts to nor entails denying that there are facts and states of affairs. Relatedly, intentional anti-realism is not as such committed to idealism or irrealism about the "external" world. Of course, not any version of realism about the external world is tolerated by intentional anti-realism, and intentional anti-realism has implications for our understanding of the "fact that" locution. In an important sense, intentional anti-realism also allows knowledge of facts and states of affairs, though the truth (or the alternative epistemic merit) that this knowledge involves is not that of faithfully representing facts or states of affairs. Some of these issues will be discussed in later chapters.

The denial of the thesis of intentional realism—the denial of the existence of intentional states and objects—usually takes the form of a contingent empirical

---

[1] Of course, these two sentences seem to be in tension with each other. This seeming tension is dealt with in Chapter 6, which details intentional anti-realism.

[2] I do not rule out the possibility that intentional anti-realism might leave no room for propositions, but I will not pursue this path here.

[3] My use of the expression "mental states" is not meant to be committed to a mental ontology of states in contrast to that of events.

Intentionality Deconstructed: An Anti-Realist Theory. Amir Horowitz, Oxford University Press.
© Amir Horowitz 2024. DOI: 10.1093/oso/9780198896432.003.0001

2 INTENTIONALITY DECONSTRUCTED

conjecture.[4] Thus, Stich (1983) argued that it is a plausible empirical conjecture that there are no propositional attitudes. Stich's view also includes, in addition to this ontological element, a methodological one—he recommends against appealing to intentional properties in cognitive science. Paul Churchland's (1979, 1981, 1988) eliminativism also includes two such (interrelated) components. He suggests empirical considerations against the existence of mental intentional states, and recommends against appealing to intentional properties in any science of behavior. The repudiation of intentional realism that I suggest differs from those of Churchland and Stich in a few respects. First, it is not a contingent and empirical thesis, but a necessary, conceptual, and a priori one; it concerns the integrity of the concept of intentionality. Relatedly, it is not only the existence of intentionality that the proposed view denies, but rather, also its possibility. The expression "intentional anti-realism" refers in this book to this stronger, conceptual, view, while the weaker, contingent, view is referred to as "intentional irrealism." (The literature often uses both to refer to the weaker view.) Second, my main concern here is ontological. The theory to be proposed here includes no methodological recommendation concerning how the sciences of behavior should proceed. (It is mainly for this reason that I refrain from referring to my view as "eliminativism," a term which I take to better express the methodological thesis.) I will refer, though, to roles that the employment of the intentional stance plays in folk psychology. Third, the theory to be proposed does not deny the existence of those mental states standardly considered intentional, notably the so-called propositional attitudes; it affirms it. That is, I defend the existence of those states with the properties usually attributed to them—be they epistemic, phenomenological, causal, or logico-syntactic properties—except for intentional properties.[5]

So according to intentional irrealism, there are no concrete intentional entities (or, in a softer version, there are not many); put differently, no concrete entities (or not many) instantiate intentional properties. According to intentional anti-realism, there also *cannot be* concrete intentional entities—no concrete entities can instantiate intentional properties, for the concept of intentional property is flawed. There are various examples in the history of philosophy of concepts that seem to be perfectly lucid and coherent, but that, upon philosophical reflection (or so it is argued), are revealed to lack clear sense and integrity (e.g., the concept of substance and that of self). On the version of intentional anti-realism to be defended in this book, the concept of intentionality (like that of reference, or that of think-about, etc.) is such a concept.

---

[4] Fodor (1985, 1987) characterizes intentional realism as committed not only to the existence of intentional states but also to the causal relevance of mental intentional properties. Since I deny their existence, I will ignore this characterization.

[5] While in his early work on the topic Stich (1983) rejects the existence of such states, he later develops an intricate pragmatist view on this issue (see Stich 1996).

INTRODUCING INTENTIONALITY 3

We may put the theses of intentional realism, intentional irrealism, and intentional anti-realism in terms of the truth of content ascriptions.[6] Intentional realism is the thesis that many of our actual content ascriptions—many of our folk psychological statements—are true (see, e.g., Fodor 1987). Intentional irrealism is the thesis that such ascriptions (or the majority of them, in the softer version) are, in themselves, false, whereas intentional anti-realism is the thesis that content ascriptions, in themselves, *cannot* be true and *cannot* be false (where the modality in question is conceptual)—they lack truth conditions. Nonetheless, on the latter view content ascriptions still have truth conditions and can be true (or have a related epistemic merit) relative to schemes or practices of content ascription. If the ascription of the content that it is raining to one who utters, or believes (or, perhaps, believes*), "It is raining," or "Es regnet," is true, then it is true in the sense (and only in the sense) that in the circumstances that obtain such an ascription accords with an assumed scheme of content ascription.

1.2 What Is Intentionality? What Is Its Source?

What is intentionality supposed to be? We often ascribe mental states to people (ourselves included), less often to animals of certain species, and, still less often, to various machines and other entities. Many of these ascriptions appear to be ascriptions of content or, as philosophers are used to say, of intentionality.[7] Thus, Sara ascribes to Sam the belief *that dogs are faster than cats*, Romi ascribes to Jonathan the desire *that Stephany will leave George*, and so on. The italicized clauses in these examples—those that-clauses—stand for the ascribed contents. Such ascriptions are so common and natural to us that it might take a philosopher to notice their peculiarity: they often describe states of one category—mental ones—in terms of states of another category—extra-mental ones. (The "often" was introduced since ascribed contents of mental states sometimes concern mental states. For example, we sometimes ascribe to one a desire regarding the emotions of one's beloved.) Once this fact is noticed, we may wonder how we manage to capture the former in terms of the latter. What, on earth, is the connection between Sam's belief and the alleged fact that dogs are faster than cats that allows us to describe this belief as the belief that dogs are faster than cats? Philosophers who believe that mental states such as beliefs and desires indeed possess contents

---

[6] For most purposes of this investigation, we can use "content" and "intentionality" interchangeably. Usually I will do so, though in certain contexts I find one more suitable than the other. I highlight their difference later in the chapter.

[7] Throughout this book, I present examples of alleged intentionality without mentioning that they are only alleged examples of intentionality, whose existence and possibility I deny. Relatedly, as I explain in Chapter 6, intentional anti-realists may legitimately employ intentional terms such as "believe that," "refer," or "about" when taking them to be rhetorical devices.

4 INTENTIONALITY DECONSTRUCTED

may ask, similarly, what makes Sam's belief that dogs are faster than cats have the content that dogs are faster than cats. The general question is: What endows mental states with their intentionality and contents? What constitutes the possession of content? Since the phenomenon of having content—the phenomenon of mental states being directed at various (usually non-mental) objects and states of affair, or their being about them—is referred to (following Brentano (1874), who himself followed a Scholastic tradition) as "intentionality," this general question is referred to as "the question of intentionality."[8] It is most often taken to be a very difficult question. Many philosophers believe that intentionality is an elusive phenomenon, and Russell (1912) even considered it a mysterious one. It isn't clear how one entity can "transcend" itself to, and be about, or represent, another entity.[9] Kant considered "the question of how anything in the mind can represent anything outside the mind" the most difficult philosophical question (see Kant 1772/1967). Note that in some contexts (we will encounter one in Chapter 3) it may be useful to keep this "how question" (which we may also call "the hard question of intentionality") and the above-mentioned "what question" ("the question of intentionality") distinct, for answering the latter is not necessarily answering the former.

The question of intentionality at least seems to concern the relation between intentional states and what these are said to be about—their intentional objects. Delilah's belief that Maputo is the capital of Mozambique is about (or represents) Maputo, but is also (so "about" is used in discussions of intentionality) about (or represents) Mozambique and the fact (or the state of affairs) that Maputo is its capital. (See Crane's discussion of the issue in Crane (2013, p. 7).) Relatedly, the expression "intentional object" is used in a broad sense, so as to refer both to objects in the strict sense and to facts or states of affairs (those facts or states of affairs intentional states are about).

Intentionality, as aboutness, appears to be a feature not only of mental states but also of linguistic entities, and perhaps of other entities. Delilah's belief that Maputo is the capital of Mozambique is about Maputo (and about Mozambique, etc.), but so is Delilah's saying that Maputo is the capital of Mozambique. The same property—that is, the same aboutness—is ascribed to the belief and to the saying. Many philosophers believe that whereas the intentionality of a mental state is original—that is, a mental state's having its intentional content is independent of any other entity's having the same (or any other) intentional content—the

---

[8] It is sometimes asked (see, e.g., Field 1978) how there can be intentionality *in a physical world*. This is often referred to as "the problem of intentionality." Brentano is standardly interpreted as maintaining that this problem is unsolvable, hence that physicalism is false. Most anti-physicalist arguments in contemporary philosophy revolve around phenomenal consciousness, and intentionality is usually not considered to have a bearing on the issue. For an intentionality-based anti-physicalist argument, see Plantinga (2006); for a reply, see Horowitz (2011). Trivially, if the thesis of this book is true, no such arguments can be sound.

[9] The characterization of intentionality in terms of transcendence is due to Husserl (1913).

intentionality of a linguistic act is derived—that is, a linguistic act's having some intentional content is determined by another entity's having the same intentional content; specifically, the linguistic act derives its intentional content from a mental state (one with the same content).[10] However, this distinction is not in conflict with the claim that when we ascribe to one both the belief that p and the saying that p, we ascribe to one not only different properties but also the same property. The issue of original versus derived intentionality concerns the source of the intentionality of entities, the enabling conditions for the possession of this property, its underlying metaphysics. It does not concern the identity of the possessed property. The property is simply that of being about something, and specifically (to stick to that example), that of being about Maputo. And if the ascriptions in question are true, then the belief and the saying share this property.

Referring to original versus derived intentionality may also help us realize the cogency of the question of intentionality. For the thesis that conditions the intentionality of language on the intentionality of the mind is a way of replying to that question when applied to language. That is, if it is asked what endows linguistic entities such as utterances of sentences with their intentionality, this thesis' reply is that such entities derive or inherit their intentionality from the intentionality of mental states by virtue of some relations that hold between them.[11] But for this reply to be complete, it must be supplemented with an account of how the mind acquires its intentionality. On such accounts, the mind's intentionality itself may

---

[10] The locution "having the same intentional content" is significant. In the usage of some philosophers (e.g., Bourget 2010), content is derived also in cases in which its possession by an entity is determined by the possession of contents (in the plural) by these entities' components. Such a "whole-parts derivation" is not derivation of content in my use of this expression. Similarly, accounts of the contents of non-experiential intentional states in terms of their causal or inferential connections with experiential intentional states and other mental states (such as those of Loar (1995), Horgan and Tienson (2002), and Horgan and Graham (2012)—see Kriegel (2011) for a critical discussion), and functional role accounts of the meaning of linguistic entities, are not accounts of content derivation in my usage. It is essential to content derivation in my sense that one entity's content be inherited, as a whole, from another entity. When the issue is whether mind or language (or anything else) is the ultimate source of intentionality, this is the relevant sense of "content derivation."

Note also, that derived content in my sense is supposed to be real content, and not merely ascribed content or as-if content. Aizawa and Adams use this expression differently, in the way I use "(merely) ascribed content": "derived content arises from the way in which items are handled or treated by intentional agents" (Aizawa and Adams 2005, p. 662).

[11] The most detailed program regarding how the mind endows language with meaning is Grice's Intention Based Semantics (in, e.g., Grice 1957); see also Lewis (1969) and Schiffer (1972). (Schiffer (1987) argues against Intention Based Semantics.) Philosophers of different persuasions endorse the mind–language priority thesis of intentionality, as well as the related idea that the mind endows intentionality upon all other entities that possess intentionality and is thus the source of intentionality. We can find them among those who take intentionality to be the mark of the mental (see Chisholm in Chisholm and Sellars (1958)); among tracking (reductive-naturalistic) theorists (see, e.g., Dretske 1988; Fodor 1981, 1987); among proponents of phenomenal intentionality (see, e.g., Kriegel 2011). Among proponents of the converse thesis, the language–mind priority thesis of intentionality, see Sellars in Chisholm and Sellars (1958), and Dummett (1973). Among those who treat the intentionality of the mind and that of language on a par, see Davidson (1975), Block (1986), Harman (1999), Horwich (2005), and Millikan (1984).

6 INTENTIONALITY DECONSTRUCTED

be either original or derived from some other entity, but be the case what it may—whether the chain of derivation stops with the mind or goes further (say to mother nature)—the alleged reality of intentionality implies that it must come to an end: that is, that there is original intentionality. Suppose, for the sake of simplicity, that it is the mind that has original intentionality. The question of intentionality then becomes the question of original mental intentionality. What endows the mind with it?

This question is usually understood as implying that the alleged original intentionality of the mind must be rooted in something else that is not itself intentional. In other words, the intentional is reducible to the non-intentional. Thus, according to Field, "There are no 'ultimately semantic' facts or properties, i.e., no semantic facts or properties over and above the facts and properties of physics, chemistry, biology, neurophysiology, and those parts of psychology, sociology, and anthropology that can be expressed independently of semantic concepts" (Field 1975, p. 386). And according to Fodor, "If aboutness is real, it must be really something else" (Fodor 1987, p. 97). Though not expressed in this citation, Fodor's reducibility conviction is, like Field's, naturalistic. For many philosophers, the idea that intentionality is reducible to something else, so that intentional facts are nothing over and above non-intentional facts, seems self-evident. But we may well wonder, and should wonder, whether it is true. Why can't it be that the intentional floats free of the non-intentional? Why can't intentional properties be among the basic properties of reality, ones that are instantiated by mental states without being metaphysically determined by the instantiations of non-intentional properties, whether mental or otherwise? What is wrong with such a primitivist approach to intentionality? I suggest what is wrong with it in section 1.4.

Note that the notion of *primitive intentionality* should be distinguished from the notion of *intrinsic intentionality*. Primitive intentionality is intentionality that cannot be reduced to something else: that is, to any non-intentional property. Yet the idea of intentionality as reducible or non-primitive is compatible with the idea of intentionality as intrinsic to its possessor. Consider, for example, the view of phenomenal intentionality, according to which intentionality is grounded in phenomenal consciousness. This view will be discussed at length in Chapter 3, but now note that while this view is, *ipso facto*, a reductive rather than a primitivist view of intentionality,[12] still, on the assumption (which is integral to this view) that phenomenal consciousness is an intrinsic property of mental states, this view

---

[12] Pautz (2013, 2021) takes the intentional relation of sensory experiences to be an irreducible relation and considers his view a version of the phenomenal intentionality view. For a similar approach, see Woodward (2019).

There are theories that take intentionality and phenomenality to be mutually dependent, and one may wonder whether they can be said to be reductive theories of intentionality. I argue (in Chapter 3) that such theories are not reductive in a sense that would have made them answer the question of intentionality and provide a non-circular explanation for this phenomenon. (David Chalmers (2004 and 2006) takes such theories to be non-reductive theories of phenomenality.)

is committed to the idea that intentionality is an intrinsic property of mental states. That is, this view takes various mental states to have intentionality in themselves, independently of the instantiation of any property by any *other* entity. The mind is intentional, on such a view, since the mind is conscious; and it is intrinsically intentional since it is intrinsically conscious.[13] So intrinsic intentionality need not be primitive. However, primitive intentionality is necessarily intrinsic intentionality. Intentionality that cannot be reduced to any property is, a fortiori, a property of the entity that possesses it independently of the instantiation of any property by any other entity.

The notions of intrinsic intentionality and primitive intentionality should both be distinguished from the above-mentioned notion of original intentionality. As noted, intentionality is original if, and only if, its possession by its possessor is independent of its possession by any other entity. Intentionality that is not original is derived: that is, its possession by its possessor is dependent upon its possession by another entity. We can see that intrinsic intentionality is necessarily original intentionality since, trivially, being independent of the instantiation of any property by any other entity is being independent of the instantiation of any intentional property by any other entity. Since the converse does not hold, original intentionality need not be intrinsic: an entity's having some intentional content may depend upon some other entity's possessing some non-intentional property (e.g., some causal property). Relatedly, original intentionality is not necessarily primitive. However, derived intentionality cannot be primitive—it is necessarily reducible to a relation to another entity's intentionality (and so, whether or not it is reducible to the non-intentional depends on whether or not the intentionality of the other entity is thus reducible).

1.3 Intentionality as Transcendence, Intentionality as Relational

According to Brentano (1874), intentional states' intentional objects need not exist. That is, an intentional state may have content and be about, be directed at, or represent, a certain object, even though this object—its intentional object—does not exist. Examples appear to abound: we take people to have beliefs about unicorns, angles, Santa Claus, and the like. In fact (construing "intentional

---

[13] Prima facie, proponents of the thesis that reduces intentionality to consciousness need not endorse the view that consciousness is an intrinsic property of the mind—they can endorse phenomenal externalism (which is usually presented as an intrinsicist view). But in Chapter 3 we shall see that phenomenal externalism is not an option for them.

"Intrinsic intentionality" is sometimes taken to refer to intentionality that is an essential (or necessary) property of its possessor. I need not discuss intrinsic intentionality in this sense, since by arguing against intrinsic intentionality in the sense of independence of the fate of other entities I also argue against it.

8   INTENTIONALITY DECONSTRUCTED

objects" broadly, so as to refer also to facts or states of affairs), any false belief and any frustrated (or not yet fulfilled) desire seem to have intentional objects that do not exist. Talk of states having intentional objects that do not exist may appear to involve a difficulty, perhaps even to be unintelligible (see, e.g., Russell 1919). On the assumptions that intentionality is essentially a relation and that a relation is instantiated only if all its relata are instantiated, the phenomenon of "intentional inexistence" creates a puzzle.[14,15]

One way to avoid the puzzle is to deny that the cases in question are cases of intentional states with non-existent intentional objects, and adopt, instead, the view that intentional objects (at least in such cases) belong to a different ontological category than that of standard objects (such as the physical objects that populate our environment). Specifically, they are mental objects, or abstract objects of some variety. However, as some philosophers have shown, no non-standard objects can be the intentional objects of our intentional mental states (insofar as we are not specifically concerned with such entities, as in philosophizing, for example); they cannot be what our intentional mental states are about. In rejecting the view that intentional objects are mental objects, Harman writes: "From the fact that there is no Fountain of Youth, it does not follow that Ponce de Leon was searching for something mental. In particular, he was not looking for an idea of the Fountain of Youth. He already had the idea. What he wanted was a real Fountain of Youth, not just the idea of such a thing" (Harman 1990, p. 36). If indeed I have a belief with the content that it is raining, then what makes my belief true, if it is, is the fact that it is raining—a standard non-mental and non-abstract regular fact. And in the case in which this belief is false—a case of intentional inexistence—it is the obtaining of this same fact that would have made it true, and it is its absence that makes it false. Had this belief been about mental rain (or about an abstract rain) then the absence of the fact that it is raining wouldn't have made it false (and at least the mentalist conception is committed to its being true also in this case—it is true by virtue of being thought). A similar reasoning applies to desires and their satisfaction and dissatisfaction.

The idea that intentional objects belong to a different ontological category than that of standard objects amounts to the idea that words do not retain their standard meanings when embedded in content ascriptions. Wittgenstein refers to the latter idea:

---

[14] Of course, the puzzle is dissolved if the view that intentionality is relational in the full-blown sense is rejected, a matter I address below. As I will argue, rejecting this view entails intentional anti-realism.

[15] The expression "intentional inexistence," which is usually used in the philosophical literature (and also in this book) to refer to the phenomenon of non-existing intentional objects, is taken from Brentano (1874). But Brentano used it to refer to the existence of intentional objects *in* mental states (see, e.g., McAlister 1970). Crane (2001, p. 29) explains that this "existence in" mental states is to be understood in terms of individuation: "different intentional object, different state of mind."

One may get the feeling that in the sentence "I expect he is coming" one is using the words "he is coming" in a different sense from the one they have in the assertion "He is coming." But if it were so how could I say that my expectation had been fulfilled? If I wanted to explain the words "he" and "is coming," say by means of ostensive definitions, the same explanations of these words would go for both sentences.   (Wittgenstein 1953, §444)

Thus, the idea that intentional objects belong to some different ontological category than that of standard objects is undermined. Intentional states are directed toward standard, real—and typically physical and extra-mental—objects.[16]

Another way to express the idea of intentionality as outward directedness is to say that intentionality is transcendence: it is one entity's transcending itself to another. Specifically, intentionality is the transcendence of the mind (typically) to the extra-mental, and, as we now saw, to standard real objects.[17] Turning to the relationality of intentionality, an issue that is important for its own sake, may further clarify this idea. A claim to the effect that there are intentional states with (existing) intentional objects is a claim to the effect that certain relations obtain. Intentional relations can be said to be the actualizations of "intentional functions"—those functions that take us from intentional states to their intentional objects. If there are cases of states that are about standard real (physical or other) existent objects, then these are cases in which intentional states maintain actual relations—"intentional relations"—with such objects. This is a significant "if." The main thesis of this book in fact denies that a sound reply can be provided to the question of whence comes the supposed relationality of intentionality, or, put differently, that sense can be given to the idea of intentional relations. This last claim amounts to the claim that the concept of intentionality is flawed.

The claim that there are cases in which intentional states maintain actual relations of aboutness with standard real (physical or other) existent objects is weaker than the claim that intentionality is *essentially* relational, and at this stage we are not entitled to the latter. In cases of intentional inexistence, whatever other truths hold, it is true (indeed, trivially true) that intentional states maintain conditional relations—and only conditional relations—with standard real (physical, in most cases) existing objects. This means that had such states had (standard) intentional

---

[16] Rejecting the idea that intentional objects belong to a special ontological category leaves intentional realists with the above-mentioned puzzle of intentional inexistence. Various ontologically innocuous analyses of intentional inexistence have been suggested (see, e.g., Crane 2013; Sainsbury 2018), but delving into them is not important for our discussion.

[17] This claim about intentional transcendence does not assume semantic externalism—it is a claim about the very idea of intentionality as outward directedness. Semantic externalism and semantic internalism disagree about the way mental states' extra-mental intentional objects are determined, or in other words, about the way intentional transcendence is determined. Relatedly, intentional transcendence does not require that intentional objects be extra-mental. The directedness of one thought toward another is also transcendence in the relevant sense.

10 INTENTIONALITY DECONSTRUCTED

objects, then they would have borne (actual) relations to them. Admittedly, as these very words suggest, bearing a conditional relation to an object in this sense is not bearing an (actual) relation to an object. However, there is a sense of "relation" in which such cases do exhibit (actual) relations (or at any rate relational properties). These are not relations in the sense in which, for example, being Dan's father is a relation—a relation the bearing of which by one depends on the existence of Dan. Call relations of this kind "relations in the strong sense." Philosophers who reject the idea that intentionality is essentially relational (e.g., Kriegel 2007, 2011, 2016; Mendelovici 2018) in fact reject the idea of intentionality as relational in the strong sense. According to them, the possibility of intentional inexistence entails that intentional states do not maintain these relations essentially.[18] But consider, for example, the property of a material being soluble in water (in contrast to any categorical property that is responsible for water's solubility), which is necessary for its ever being dissolved in water, although its possession by the material does not depend on the actual existence of any sample of H_2O. This is an example of what we can call "a relation [or a relational property] in a weak sense."

Now consider the notion of intentionality as purport-to-refer, or purport-to-represent, or, in other words, as potentially referring. The purport to refer may succeed or fail, depending on the cooperation of the world. Brian Loar, who introduces the notion of purporting-to-refer, takes it to stand for "a non-relational phenomenal feature" (Loar 2003, p. 239). Indeed, intentionality as purport-to-refer is not a relation in the strong sense, but it is essentially a relation, or relational property, in the weak sense. Were it not, then, since successful reference is a relation, there would be no sense to the idea of such a success, of the actualization of a potential to refer; in other words, there would be no sense to the idea of intentionality. The claim that intentionality is not essentially relational even in the weak sense entails that nothing can be intentionally related to anything; nothing can be about anything, under any circumstances. Were this claim true, the fact that snow is white would not make the belief expressed by "Snow is white" true, and my desire that is expressed by "The war will end" would not be satisfied by the ending of the war. Such a view disconnects alleged intentional states from their alleged intentional objects, and thus leaves intentionality out. Actual aboutness presupposes essential weak relationality precisely as actually dissolving in water presupposes water solubility.[19]

---

[18] According to other philosophers (e.g., the later Brentano (1911) is often taken to hold such a view), not only is intentionality not essentially relational, it is not relational period. Such a view is, on its face, opposed to intentional realism. The moderate claim that intentionality is not essentially relational also leads to a denial of intentional realism, but not as straightforwardly. See next paragraph.

[19] Note that the view that intentionality is essentially weakly relational suffices to dissolve the above-mentioned puzzle of intentional inexistence, since only one relatum of a dyadic relation in the weak sense must exist.

Thus, the view that intentionality is not even a relation in the weak sense is not a realist view of intentionality—it robs the notion of intentionality of its content.[20] One may present the question of intentionality as the question of whence comes intentional relationality. But the more general, basic, and challenging question is whence comes the weak relationality of intentionality. Give me this weak relationality, give me intentionality as purport-to-refer, and I will give you full-blown intentionality. And the meaningfulness of the latter presupposes the meaningfulness of the former. Intentionality is essentially weakly relational and contingently (when successful) strongly relational. It is not important whether what I call "a relation in the weak sense" merits the title of "relation."[21] What is important about it is that its characterizing intentionality has significant implications for our issue. One of them is that it stands in the way of a primitivist approach to intentionality, as we shall now see.

1.4 Against Intentional Primitivism

Consider the following reasoning: In order to represent anything, an entity must be used in some way by an agent who interprets it, or understands it, as having some intentionality. But this understanding or interpreting is an intentional attitude, and so there must be in the agent's head some homunculus who represents it in some way, and so on. That is, we are led into a vicious regress of representations and homunculi, whose import is that nothing can anchor intentionality, and nothing, in itself, can really be intentional (see Dennett 1978a; Searle 1983). Searle blocks this regress argument by denying the premise that in order to be a representation an entity must be used by an agent who understands it in a certain way. This claim is true, according to him, only as far as non-mental entities are concerned. Mental entities, in contrast, need not be used or interpreted, for intentionality is a primitive property of such entities, which they have intrinsically (Searle 1983, p. 22).

Searle does not consider the option that what endows mental states, or linguistic entities, with intentionality is their external connections (e.g., their causal connections with the environmental features they are supposed to represent).

---

[20] Let me clarify the dialectic. I argue here that the concept of intentionality is the concept of a property that is essentially relational (in the weak sense). Claims to the effect that intentionality is not essentially relational even in the weak sense robe intentionality of its content from the very beginning. In the final analysis, though, I argue that the fate of the view that intentionality is essentially relational is not better. The concept of intentionality, on my view, is flawed.

[21] In the 1911 appendix to Brentano (1874), Brentano wrote: "So the only thing which is required by mental reference is the person thinking. The terminus of the so-called relation does not need to exist in reality at all. For this reason, one could doubt whether we really are dealing with something relational here, and not, rather, with something somewhat similar to something relational in a certain respect, which might, therefore, better be called 'quasi-relational'" (p. 272).

12   INTENTIONALITY DECONSTRUCTED

For the sake of argument, let's remain in this framework.[22] If external connections are out of the picture, then indeed there seems to be a problem for the intentionality of linguistic entities, and an appeal to a user might appear to be called for. However, if linguistic intentionality requires a user, the reason for this requirement does not seem to concern any peculiarity of language (e.g., its notorious arbitrariness), and so it should equally apply to non-linguistic representations. Indeed, we have no difficulty understanding the applicability of this requirement to non-linguistic non-mental representations (such as pictures and drawings), but why should we assume that the mental evades it? (The claim that there is a difficulty with the idea of using a mental state does not entail that the mental evades this requirement; it only entails that it cannot fulfil it.) It is here that the threat of vicious regress comes in. As Searle's primitivist reply stands, it is more a denial of the problem than a solution to it. Searle is not entitled to simply declare that some mental states are intrinsically intentional. He must explain how intentionality can be a primitive property of mental states *but not of* non-mental entities, yet he doesn't. He cannot be satisfied with claiming that it is *in fact* a property of mental states, since in that case the idea of "gluing" intrinsic intentionality, and thus of primitive intentionality, to non-mental entities, such as linguistic entities, which supposedly lack it, should make sense, yet it doesn't. For it is unclear what the difference between a linguistic entity with non-intrinsic intentionality and one with intrinsic intentionality is. (And, of course, Searle would be the first to reject this "gluing" idea.)

As noted, intrinsic intentionality need not be primitive. Thus, one who believes that intentionality is an intrinsic property of mental states may try to avoid that vicious regress by pointing out some feature, peculiar of the mental, that allows the mental to be intrinsically intentional, and whose necessary absence from non-mental phenomena is responsible for the impossibility of intrinsic non-mental intentionality. In his later work Searle (who does not always keep clear the distinction between intentionality as a primitive mental property and intentionality as an intrinsic mental property) in fact attempts to do just that—to reduce intentionality to consciousness, which on his view is an intrinsic property of the mind, and so intentionality is an intrinsic property of the mind, although a non-primitive one. This view of Searle is discussed in Chapter 3, but here we are concerned with the very idea of primitive intentionality. We shall now see, then,

---

[22] In later work, Searle charges the reductive-naturalistic approach to intentionality with leaving out the subjective aspect of intentionality (see Searle 1992, ch. 2). This approach is also reflected in Searle's Chinese-room argument (Searle 1980), which Dennett (1987a) argues confuses being meaningful with being meaningful *for one*. I wholeheartedly agree with this criticism, and believe that this confusion is also reflected in the charge that Searle raised against the reductive-naturalistic approach. In Chapter 3, I will argue that intentionality is detached from any subjective dimension and discuss also Searle's view on the matter.

that what Searle must explain but does not cannot be explained, since it isn't true: intentionality cannot be a primitive property of anything.

It appears that an object has to be a certain way for being thought of (or desired, etc.) by a certain subject, and a subject has to be a certain way for thinking of (or desiring, etc.) a certain object. After all, something must distinguish between an objects one thinks of and an object one doesn't think of. Similarly, something must distinguish between one who thinks of a certain object and one who doesn't. And for the relation of think-of to obtain, given that the thinker is a certain way, the object must be a certain way (and, trivially, vice versa).[23] However, if the primitivist is asked what should happen between a subject S and an object O for O to be S's intentional object (e.g., for S to think about O), she would reply that all that should happen is that O be S's intentional object, or in other words, that S bear the intentional relation to O. Nothing more. The expectation that there be an additional answer to this question—that is, that there be another relation—simply ignores the primitivist position. Why, the primitivist would insist, should we reduce the intentional relation to another relation? On pain of infinite regress, we cannot require that all relations be reducible to other relations. Why require it in the case of intentionality?

Suppose for the moment that the primitivist's claim that S simply possesses the property of being intentionally related to O—that is, of being about O—indeed works for the case in which O exists. This seems to make sense, for something positive is attributed to S on such an occasion. What about the case in which O does not exist? In such a case S is supposed to have a weakly relational property, and then a modified version of the requirement presented above holds for it: S must be such that something about it—its being a certain way—makes it potentially referring to O; it must be such that its being a certain way rather than another would have made it refer to O had appropriate circumstances obtained. (Compare: given the relevant laws of nature, some property of a material makes it dissolvable in water.) But how should S be like? What (actual) positive thing can be said about it? If we reject the idea that S refers to a mental entity, or to a spooky Meinongian one, then S cannot be said to be intentionally related to O (or to anything else).

It might seem that we would get the relevant property that S possesses in such a case by subtracting O from being intentionally related to O. However, if S's being intentionally related to O is irreducible to any other relation, then subtracting O from this relation leaves us with nothing. If O drops out of the picture, then nothing that is true of S makes S have O-intentionality (i.e., even O-intentionality-as-purport-to-refer). No property possessed by it makes it such that had O existed, it would have been about it, in the way in which the property of a material makes

---

[23] "Being a certain way" as used here should be construed broadly to include, *inter alia*, relational properties, historical properties, and spatio-temporal properties (whether these are relational or not).

14   INTENTIONALITY DECONSTRUCTED

it such that had it been put in water, it would have dissolved. Such a subtraction makes no sense. There can only be such a weakly intentional property (purport-to-represent) if the intentional relation is reducible to another relation to which said subtraction can be applied, which relation connects the intentional state with O under the appropriate circumstances; yet primitivism opposes such reductions. It is tempting to think that in the case where O does not exist, S possesses the same intentional property (or the same weakly intentional property) she would have possessed had O existed. But in the primitivist picture the only relevant property of S is simply that of being intentionally related to O, and in the case where O does not exist this property is absent.[24] Finally, if the subtraction in question makes no sense and so nothing makes S intentional in the case where O does not exist, then nothing also qualifies S itself to be intentionally related to O in the case where O does exist. For if no sense can be given to S's being potentially about an object, then no sense can be given to S's being actually about O. No dissolving without solubility, and no (successful) reference without purport or potential to refer. The alleged intentionality vanishes altogether.[25]

One who shares the primitivist sentiment of avoiding the notion of intentionality as reducible to something else but is impressed by this predicament of intentional primitivism may suggest that intentionality is not a relation even in the weak sense. But, as noted in the previous section, if intentionality is not even weakly relational, then nothing is intentionally related to anything; nothing is such that it could have been about anything under any circumstances. Such a view detaches alleged intentional states from their alleged intentional objects and leaves out the supposed "hook up to the world." It is a form of intentional irrealism or of intentional anti-realism.[26]

It is worth stressing that the idea upon which my argument against the notion of primitive intentionality rests is that this notion cannot make room for the weak

[24] It would not do to posit an intermediate entity, such as an intension or sense, between S and O (whether O exists or not), for such an entity would inherit the said difficulty of failing to possess a property that enables it to bear the intentional relation.

[25] It might be thought that this reasoning presupposes the highest common factor assumption challenged by some disjunctivists and direct realists. But it does not. Suppose that there are mental states whose mental identity depends on what happens outside the heads of their owners, and, specifically, on the existence of their intentional objects (as argued by, e.g., Evans (1982); Peacocke (1981, 1983); McDowell (1977, 1984, 1986, 1994)). Suppose, that is, that such mental states do not have any phenomenal or other mental factor in common with mental states that do not have the same (or any) intentional objects. Still, it is logically, metaphysically, and plausibly nomologically possible that the neural correlates of these mental states occur without being intentionally related to the same objects. In such cases, these brain states possess weak relational properties—weak intentional properties (those that would have turned into intentional relations under the appropriate circumstances), and the argument to the effect that these properties cannot be primitive still prevails.

[26] It is sometimes objected to intentional primitivism on the grounds that unless we assume that intentional properties of mental states are determined by their standard (non-semantic) properties, the fact that intentional ascriptions are successfully used to predict and explain behavior would be unexplainable. However, in Chapter 6 we shall see that the predictive and explanatory success of content ascriptions does not at all depend on the existence of intentional properties.

relationality of intentionality in the sense explained above. Thus, claims to the effect that intentionality is not relational due to the possibility of intentional inexistence pose no threat to this argument, for they leave the idea of weak relationality intact. An example of such a claim can be found in Kriegel's treatment of objections to the non-relational view he attributes to Brentano. One objection is that

> One symptom of the fact that carrying is a relation is that the active-voice "Jimmy is carrying Johnny" seems to mean the same as the passive-voice "Johnny is carried by Jimmy." Remarkably, the same holds for intentional statements: "Jimmy is thinking of Johnny" means the same as "Johnny is thought of by Jimmy" (or indeed "Johnny is the object of Jimmy's thought"). This suggests that think-ing-of is just as relational as carrying.   (Kriegel 2016, p. 9)

Kriegel undermines this inference by relying on the claim that " 'I am thinking of Bigfoot' and 'Bigfoot is thought of by me' have different truth values: the first is true but the second untrue" (p. 9). Now this move on the part of Kriegel might be taken to undermine not only that argument for intentional relationalism but also the very view of intentional relationalism, for it implies that intentional attitudes— which might be non-veridical—do not essentially involve relations. However, this difference in truth value does not undermine the view that intentional attitudes (if there are such) are essentially weakly relational, or my argument to this effect.[27] Similar considerations apply to the way Kriegel defends the adverbialist approach to intentionality against the charge that it cannot connect us to the world. According to Kriegel, intentionality connects us to the world contingently and not constitu-tively, and so adverbialism's allowing veridical or successful intentional attitudes to connect us to the world delivers what it should (Kriegel 2011, pp. 165–166). But, again, the crucial point for my argument against primitive intentionality is that intentional states, as purporting-to-represent—which purporting might either succeed or fail—must essentially and constitutively possess weak relationality. Without even weak relationality, intentionality as directedness to the world is impossible even in the successful cases—intentionality vanishes altogether; suc-cessful reference depends on purporting-to-refer.

Mendelovici (2018) raises two worries regarding "the relation view" of inten-tionality. The first is that "Many relation views cannot plausibly accommodate all the diverse intentional states that we can manifestly enjoy. Relation views that avoid this problem are driven to ontological extremes, which suggests that the relation view is wrongheaded" (p. 200). The second worry is that "No relation we can bear to the items that are supposed to be identified with contents can make those items entertained or otherwise represented by us" (p. 200). I need not

---

[27] Kriegel's responses to other objections to later Brentano's non-relational view of intentionality do not target the view of weak relationality for which I argued above.

16 INTENTIONALITY DECONSTRUCTED

deny the cogency of these difficulties, since they are not difficulties for the relational view of intentionality as I characterize it. This view is concerned with *the concept* of intentionality. It is my claim that denying the essential (weakly) relational character of intentionality undermines intentionality itself. It is denying aboutness, that is, it is denying mental states' (or other entities') directedness to things in the extra-mental realm, and, correspondingly, the satisfiability of mental states (and of any other entities) by such things. Arguing that no possible theory makes room for this relational character is not arguing against my analysis of the concept of intentionality in terms of (weak) relationality, for the claim that this concept is or can be instantiated is no part of this analysis. Rather, if this analysis is correct, and this concept is not or even cannot be instantiated, then intentional anti-realism is correct. I charge the primitivist approach to intentionality with not being able to make room for that relational character (and thus for intentionality). If no other approach can make room for it, then the concept of intentionality is flawed. Indeed, I will argue that no approach can make room for it, and hence that intentional anti-realism is true.[28]

We saw that intentionality cannot be primitive. Thus, undermining the possibility of reducing the intentional to the non-intentional would undermine the possibility of intentionality and establish intentional anti-realism.[29] This will be done in later chapters. Notice that the case against the primitivity of intentionality was based upon the (weakly) relational nature of intentionality, which, in turn, was based upon the view that intentional objects are (typically) standard extra-mental objects, or, in other words, that intentionality is the mind's transcendence to the extra-mental.

Moreover, this transcendence to the extra-mental is not just an essential aspect of intentionality; rather it exhausts its nature: there is nothing in intentionality except for this transcendence to objects (and what transcendence to objects involves). Intentionality consists in "standard-object aboutness" and is nothing but directedness toward standard (typically extra-mental) objects or states of affairs. To see this, consider, first, the stronger claim that *content* is standard-object aboutness—that directedness or transcendence to the extra-mental exhausts the nature of *content*, and not only that of intentionality. Many philosophers distinguish between intentionality and content and take the notion of content to be more fine-grained. Some would agree that intentionality is standard-object aboutness but would take content to involve more. However, my claim that content is

---

[28] It might be suggested that while intentionality or content cannot be primitive, narrow intentionality or narrow content is primitive (and so intentionality—wide intentionality—is reducible to narrow content plus a relation to the environment). I discuss the notion of narrow content in section 1.5 and argue that it should be dismissed.

[29] This idea makes no room for intentional anti-constructivism like McDowell's (1986, 1994): the existence of intentionality requires that the gulf (which indeed exists) between supposed intentional states and intentional objects be, in principle, bridgeable.

standard-object aboutness—that it is transcendence to standard objects—is a conceptual claim about content as that which is ascribed by content ascriptions. Thus construed, this claim seems to me evident, since the content parts (in contrast to the attitude part) of content ascriptions are wholly expressed in terms of those extra-mental objects or states of affairs that the supposedly intentional states are supposed to be about. A fortiori, this reasoning applies to the less fine-grained notion of intentionality. Intentionality, too, is standard-object aboutness, or, in other words, standard-object directedness.

But note that among the terms by which the content parts of content ascriptions are expressed, there are, in many cases, terms of the properties the objects and facts are supposed to be represented as possessing, e.g., "Gal believes that *the tall blond guy who lives around the corner* is a spy." (The claim that the content parts of content ascriptions are wholly expressed in terms of those extra-mental *objects or facts* should not be construed as ruling this possibility out.) For this reason, I construe the view of content as standard-object aboutness as the view that content consists in directedness to objects *as possessing properties*. It is here that the fine-graininess of the notion of content is expressed. It then makes sense to say that the notion of content is the notion of directedness *as*, while the notion of intentionality is the notion of directedness *simpliciter*. Importantly, it is *the objects'* properties that count. It is only the identity of items (objects, properties, facts) in the represented realm, and not of items in the representing realm, that matters to content, to intentionality, and to intentional individuation. This is dictated by the concept of content as that which is ascribed by content ascriptions and the related concept of intentionality.[30]

Now there is a philosophical tradition, probably beginning with Frege (1892), that associates meanings and contents with modes of presentation of intentional

---

[30] Let me make a few clarifications. First, it is the opaque readings of content ascriptions that demonstrate that content consists in directedness to objects *as possessing properties*; transparent readings "bypass" the properties. Still, opaque readings of content ascriptions may differ among themselves with respect to their fine-graininess: that is, with respect to the extent to which they specify the properties objects are suppose to be represented as possessing, but we need not dwell on this issue and its complications for the purposes of this book.

Second, directedness as and directedness *simpliciter* are not mutually exclusive. Rather, any case of directedness as is necessarily a case of directedness *simpliciter*. There is a dispute over whether there are cases of directedness *simpliciter* without directedness as: that is, cases in which intentional states do not represent their intentional objects as possessing properties. If there are such cases (cases of "direct reference"), one may say either that they do not involve content, or that content consists in directedness to objects as possessing properties only in cases in which intentional objects are indeed represented as possessing properties, and in cases of direct reference content consists in direct reference. Nothing of importance hinges on this choice.

Third, we should distinguish between the claim that intentional states represent objects *as* possessing certain properties, and the claim that intentional states represent objects *in virtue of* the latter's possessing certain properties. (It is the former claim that direct reference theorists reject with respect to expressions of various kinds.) The properties in virtue of which objects are supposed to be represented may but need not be the properties objects are supposed to be represented as possessing, which are our present focus.

18 INTENTIONALITY DECONSTRUCTED

objects (e.g., the famous evening-star and morning-star modes of presentation of Venus). Does such an association conflict with the view of content as standard-object aboutness? That depends. Such an association may take various forms. If it takes "modes of presentation" to refer to features of mental vehicles of representations—such as how contents are experienced by subjects—so that representations with the same content may differ in such modes (e.g., due to differences in phenomenological mechanisms), then it is irrelevant to the issue of what content is, or what aspects content has. Such a view simply pertains to a different dimension from that of the view of content as standard-object aboutness, and a fortiori does not conflict with it. That association often takes the form of viewing modes of presentation as contents, or at least as aspects of contents: that is, it individuates them in terms of the properties intentional objects are represented as possessing. In this case, it simply amounts to the view of content as directedness to objects *as possessing properties.*

However, it seems that modes of presentation are sometimes taken to be both aspects of content and what appear to be elements of vehicles of representation, and specifically, of the agent's consciousness. A view that makes room for such entities may (but need not) respect the view of content as standard-object aboutness if it endorses a pure representationalist view of consciousness, according to which there is nothing in consciousness other than content. But if it rejects pure representationalism, then it does conflict with the standard-object aboutness view. Yet such an amalgam of content and consciousness involves a category mistake, for conflating the medium with the message.

This last point may be better realized by considering John Searle's discussion of modes of presentation as "aspectual shapes." According to Searle, every intentional state essentially has an aspectual shape under which its intentional object is represented. The desire for water, for example, is different from the desire for H_2O, due to their difference in aspectual shape, even though there is no way to satisfy the one without satisfying the other. The presence of aspectual shapes, according to Searle, implies (in a sense to be immediately qualified) accessibility to consciousness. "The link, then, between intentionality and consciousness lies in the notion of an aspectual shape" (Searle 1989, p. 52). The aspectual shape must matter to the agent and exist from her point of view. Searle asks what facts about intentional states give them their particular aspectual shapes, and provides different replies for the cases of conscious and unconscious intentional states. In the conscious cases, it is the way the agent is conscious of the intentional object. It is constitutive of the aspectual shape and essential to its identity, and hence to the state's intentional content. On the other hand, unconscious intentional states have aspectual shapes as "possible contents of consciousness." Ultimately, then, it is consciousness—whether actual or merely possible—that is responsible for the aspectual shape (see Searle 1989; 1992, pp. 155–160).

The connection between intentionality and consciousness, including Searle's approach to the matter, will be discussed at length in Chapter 3. Here I only wish to point out that a claim for a connection between intentionality and consciousness, understood so as to conflict with the view of intentionality as standard-object aboutness, must be based on a mistake. For the sake of argument, let's grant (*pace* direct reference theorists) that every intentional state has an aspectual shape. Let's focus on the claim that the way the agent is conscious of the intentional object is constitutive of the aspectual shape and essential to its identity. There is some temptation—perhaps stronger in the case of perceptual experiences—to identify the *aspect under which an intentional object is represented by an intentional state* with the way the agent is conscious of the intentional object. But this is a confusion. Intentional states represent their intentional objects under aspects *of the intentional objects*: that is, as possessing properties. Thus, Venus is sometimes represented as *being* the evening star, and sometimes as *being* the morning star; these are properties of Venus—after all, Venus *is* the evening star and the morning star. Insofar as intentional aspectual shapes are characterized in terms of the properties the intentional objects are represented as possessing, they are not the ways the agent is conscious of the intentional object and do not involve them: these two sets are conceptually distinct and cannot be identified with one another on purely analytic grounds. There may be various constraints on the experiential ways in which minds can represent objects as possessing certain properties, and perhaps also on the properties that experiences of certain sorts can represent (assuming that experience can represent anything), but no conceptual link connects kinds of phenomenally conscious states with aspects of intentional states that are characterized in terms of properties of the states' intentional objects. Whether or not they can be identified on substantial grounds is another matter (to be discussed in Chapter 3), but the standard-object aboutness view needs only to insist that they are conceptually distinct, for according to it there is nothing more in the concepts of intentionality and content than standard-object aboutness. Again, this view is a conceptual view about intentionality or content as that which is ascribed by content ascriptions, the content parts of which are wholly expressed in terms of those extra-mental objects or facts that the supposedly intentional states are supposed to be about (including in terms of the properties they are represented as possessing).[31] It seems, then, that we can

---

[31] It might be thought that while explicating modes of presentation in terms of properties objects are represented as possessing works for cases of contingent co-reference (such as the case of Venus), it does not work for cases of necessary co-reference, such as that of "equilateral triangles" and "equiangular triangles." It is so, according to this line of thought, since the property that is associated with both expressions in such cases is one and the same, while the expressions differ in content. However, whether or not such properties are one and the same is a matter of individuation, and all that is needed for the explication in question to work is that *there be* an individuation on which the properties are not one and the same, and this is trivially true in the cases under consideration.

20   INTENTIONALITY DECONSTRUCTED

adhere to the view of intentionality and content as exhausted by standard-object aboutness. This view is not committed to denying that the concept of content is also the concept of modes of presentation. Its only commitment in this regard is that if it is, then modes of presentation should be understood as consisting in directedness to objects as possessing certain properties.[32]

This conceptual view by no means presupposes that intentional states can exist. That a concept has its commitments does not mean that it is not flawed to the extent that nothing can satisfy it. So the analysis of this concept, according to which it is exhausted by standard-object aboutness, is in no conflict with the thesis of intentional anti-realism to be advanced in the following chapters.

1.5 Functional Role, the Transcendence of Intentionality, and Narrow Content

The foregoing discussion of the relational character of intentionality has implications for the functional role theory of content.[33] According to this theory, the content of an expression is determined by its functional role, which is "a matter of the causal role of the expression in reasoning and deliberation and, in general, in the way the expression combines and interacts with other expressions so as to mediate between sensory input and behavioral output" (Block 1986, p. 628). The main consideration in favor of such a theory is the need to explain the strong observed correlations that obtain between our content ascriptions to people's mental states and these states' psychological causal powers. These correlations, it seems, are best explained by assuming that contents are functional roles. The functional role theory, says Loar in such a context, "quite naturally imposes itself" (Loar 1982, p. 275).[34]

Versions of this theory differ from each other along several dimensions. One dimension that is important for our concern is that of long-armed versus short-armed functional roles. On long-armed functional role theories, the functional roles that determine content involve remote inputs and outputs. For example, what makes the concept "red" the concept that it is, is the way in which it figures in causal chains that include not only internal segments but also external ones,

---

[32] In the same vein, the view of intentionality and content as standard-object aboutness does not deny that intentionality may have "horizontal" dimensions, such as Husserl's (1913) horizontal intentionality, Searle's (1983, 1992) intentional network, or, for that matter, concepts of complex definite descriptions. These are all instances of directedness to objects as structured (in this or that way), and so are nothing but structured forms of standard-object aboutness.

[33] This theory and variations thereof are sometimes referred to as "causal role," "computational role," or "conceptual role" theories. For the present purpose, we can ignore different elements that are alluded to by these titles.

[34] Proponents of this consideration present these correlations in terms that presuppose intentional realism, whereas my presentation is neutral regarding this issue.

those segments in which red things figure and are thereby responsible for those chains forming perceptions of red things (see Harman 1982, 1987). Thus, the external links of some of the causal chains, which form only part of what constitutes content, are supposed to ensure the intentional relation to the extra-mental world. Such an approach to intentionality shares the main features of the tracking (reductive-naturalistic) approach, which suffices to make the former vulnerable to some of the difficulties to which the latter is vulnerable. Such difficulties will be highlighted in Chapter 4.[35]

Now I wish to point out a possible difficulty for this approach on another dimension. It has to do with the fact that content, on this approach, is not exhausted by relations to intentional objects. Rather, concepts that are linked in the same way with the same extra-mental object differ in content according to this approach if they are involved in different internal mental causal chains (e.g., chains of reasoning).[36] So, long-armed functional role theories are supposed to account for there being co-referential concepts with different contents. However, if content is standard-object aboutness, as argued above, if it is exhausted by its transcending nature, then the internal mental causal chains or segments thereof cannot differentiate contents, since they can determine neither intentional objects nor properties intentional objects are represented as possessing. If content involves any aspect that is not reference itself, then such an aspect too must be concerned with outward directedness—with properties objects are represented as possessing. Modes of presentation that are explicated in this way can differentiate co-referential concepts, but internal mental causal chains cannot.[37] They cannot differentiate contents for precisely the same reason that they cannot determine intentional objects or reference: they cannot reach the extra-mental world. The following brief discussion of short-armed functional role theories shows this.

According to short-armed functional role theories of content, the causal chains that figure in constituting content do not reach extra-mental objects but stop somewhere within the boundaries of the individual (e.g., at the nerve ends). Consequently, proponents of such theories do not take functional roles to determine reference. Examples of identical computer programs that can simulate utterly different activities (see, e.g., Fodor 1978; Rey 1980) are in fact examples of systems with identical functional roles but different intentional objects.[38] Moreover, short-armed functional roles do not determine even purport-to-refer,

---

[35] Most functional role accounts concern mental content, but some (e.g., Sellars 1963) concern linguistic meaning. The objections presented here apply to functional role accounts of both kinds.

[36] Harman (1987, p. 73) rejects the idea that there is a natural border between inner and outer, but this rejection is compatible with the idea that there are causal chains (or at least segments thereof) that are clearly inner and ones that are clearly external.

[37] Harman is of course aware that internal segments of those causal chains do not determine any relations to the represented realm. He assigns this task exclusively to the external links of the chains.

[38] For more on the inability of functional role theories to account for directedness to the external world, see BonJour (1998), McGinn (1982), Horowitz (1992), and Papineau (2006).

22 INTENTIONALITY DECONSTRUCTED

for nothing in relations among purely internal features can direct them outside, toward the extra-mental. This is also shown by examples of the kind just mentioned, for these examples concern *type*-different intentional objects rather than ones that happen to instantiate the same properties. That is, these examples are compatible with there being *different requirements* for being intentional objects. In general, short-term functional roles cannot determine any transcending aspect of content, and if, as argued, content is nothing but standard-object aboutness, then they cannot determine any aspect of content period.

Indeed, proponents of short-armed functional role theories of content usually take these theories to be only a part of a full account of content. In order to account for the essential transcending aspect of content, they endorse two-factor accounts that include, in addition to the functional component, a referential component, which is standardly explicated in terms of tracking relations (see, e.g., Block 1986). Again, whether reference can be thus secured is an issue to be dealt with in Chapter 4. Here let me dwell on the functional role component. If the view that content is nothing but standard-object aboutness is correct, then it seems that the (short-armed) functional role component in question cannot account for any aspect of content, and the idea of two-factor accounts should be rejected. However, the notion of narrow content might seem to help proponents of such accounts to rebuff this objection. In fact, it is narrow content and not (standard) content that is said to be constituted by functional role on such accounts (see, e.g., Loar 1981; Block 1986). Let's examine this notion, whose importance goes beyond the issue of functional role theories of content.

Narrow content is standardly characterized as content that is determined by individualistic properties of the individual who possesses it. Thus characterized, it is controversial whether narrow content is (at least in some cases) full-blown intentional content: that is, whether entities that possess it may refer to, or represent, extra-mental entities, and—in the terminology suggested here—involve intentional transcendence. Semantic internalists believe that individualistic properties can secure reference. Perhaps they can appeal to weakly relational properties in order to explain how this is possible. But what they cannot appeal to are short-armed functional roles, which, as noted, do not determine reference. Indeed, as noted, proponents of short-armed functional role accounts do not take such functional roles to determine referential content. If any notion of individualistically determined content can play a role in such accounts, it must be a notion of a non-referential aspect of content, such that does not, in itself, involve intentional transcendence. Such is the notion of narrow content that was advanced by philosophers who maintain that semantic externalism is true—that is, that individualistic features of individuals fail to determine full-blown referential content—yet that such features do determine some semantic or semantic-like non-referential feature. This feature is supposed to cooperate with contextual features to determine full-blown referential content. Sometimes the expression "narrow content" is used to refer to these semantic or semantic-like individualistic and solipsistic features, which are supposed to be functions from context to wide/referential/truth-conditional content (see Fodor (1987), and also Kaplan (1989), Perry (1977), and White (1982), who do not use the expression "narrow content").[39] The relevant contextual features may be either certain physical-environmental features (e.g., the microstructure of some object) or socio-linguistic ones (e.g., the way a term is used by some speakers).[40]

Narrow content thus understood is not an aspect of content in the sense of being ascribed by content ascriptions, since it is non-referential while this characterization of an aspect of content presupposes that content ascriptions are referential. Yet in another sense, narrow content thus understood is an aspect of content, for it is supposed to be something that participates in constituting (wide) intentional content.[41] However, we shall now see that this notion of non-referential narrow content, too, cannot render short-armed functional role accounts capable of accounting for any aspect of content. If narrow content is merely characterized as a function from contexts to wide intentional contents, then it does not differ in semantic status from the relevant contextual features (which might be bare physical facts): they are equal contributions to wide content, just that one is the organismic contribution while the other is the environmental contribution. Call it "semantic" or not,[42] we can see that the organismic contribution to content calls for a more substantive characterization. Consider: what determines the relevant context, for example, that in the case of "water"-thoughts it is the microstructure of some samples of liquid (if we stick to Putnam's (1975a) Twin Earth story)? Clearly, what makes H_2O the feature that determines the content in question is reality—it is the fact that this is the microstructure of those samples of liquid on Earth. But the question is why it is microstructures that matter in the first place. This question is an instance of a general question: namely, what determines the space of possible facts the actual among which is that feature that completes the determination of content? Nothing other than narrow content itself can play the role of this determination, and indeed the space of possible contextual features typically varies from one narrow content to another.

---

[39] In later work Fodor gave up narrow content (Fodor 1994).

[40] The idea that narrow content is constituted by short-armed functional role (see, e.g., Loar 1981; Block 1986) does not compete with the idea that it is a function from contexts to wide contents, since the former characterizes the way narrow content is determined, whereas the latter is concerned with the definition of "narrow content." Defining "narrow content" in terms of a function from contexts to wide contents does not settle the question of whether it is determined by functional role, by the way things appear to the subject, or in any other way.

[41] Narrow content thus understood differs from content as purporting-to-refer, in that such narrow content needs the contextual supplementation even in order to purport to refer.

[42] Block, a proponent of narrow content, claims that whether a theory of narrow content is properly called "semantic" is a question of ordinary language philosophy applied to technical terms like "semantics" (Block 1986, p. 626), and Fodor admits that his theory of (narrow) content is really "a 'no-content' account of narrow content" (Fodor 1987, p. 53).

24 INTENTIONALITY DECONSTRUCTED

Narrow content should operate like an open sentence, whose own nature constrains the possible ways in which it can be completed.

However, if this is what narrow content is supposed to be, then narrow content cannot but be given in terms of items in the represented realm: for example, in terms of microstructures. (It is not the specific microstructure, that, as said, is determined by reality; it is the space of possible microstructures, in contrast to the space of other properties of the stuff in question, that matters for the content of the thoughts in question.)[43] That is, to be even semantic-like, in the sense of being able to cooperate with contextual features so that full-blown referential intentionality is achieved, narrow content itself should refer to (or denote, if you like) extra-mental features. In other words, narrow content too transcends the mind to extra-mental reality. Thus, the supposed narrow content isn't really narrow. This conclusion in fact means that there is no (non-referential) narrow content.[44]

This conclusion has various implications regarding the utility of the notion of so-called narrow content for the issue of intentionality. Here I will only mention one: in having this transcending nature, so-called narrow content is not constituted by short-armed functional role. Short-armed functional role cannot determine even such a semantic-like aspect of content, since it does not reach extra-mental features.[45,46]

An approach to content that is similar to the functional role approach (and is sometimes taken to be a version of it) is normative inferentialism. According to this approach, it is not a mental state's actual causal-psychological patterns that determine its content, but its "legitimate," "worthy," or "licensed" inferential patterns. This idea might appear to be a non-starter, since (unless we are dealing with formal inferences between logico-syntactic meaningless signs, which is not

---

[43] According to Kriegel, "the shared narrow content of Oscar's and Twin Oscar's water concepts could be readily construed in terms of a relation to the property of being watery stuff" (Kriegel 2008, p. 311) However, it is the microstructures of the watery stuffs on Earth and on Twin Earth that are responsible for the fact that these concepts refer, respectively, to samples of H_2O and to samples of XYZ, so even on the assumption that "watery stuff" is construed in phenomenological terms, reference to extra-mental items such as microstructures is unavoidable.

[44] For other views according to which narrow content isn't so narrow, see Recanati (1994) and Jackson (2003). For an argument to the effect that narrow content is impossible, see Yli-Vakkuri and Hawthorne (2018).

[45] I briefly presented above the main consideration in favor of the functional role approach to content, according to which such an approach best explains the correlations between our content ascriptions to people's mental states and these states' causal-psychological powers. The foregoing discussion may be taken to undermine this consideration: if the standard-object aboutness view is true, then such an approach must be false, and, a fortiori, cannot be an adequate explanation of these correlations. It emerges from the discussion of the argument from the predictive and explanatory success of content ascriptions in Chapter 6 that such correlations need not even pressure us to accept contents. For further difficulties with functional role theories of content, see Horowitz (1992).

[46] Some philosophers (e.g., Loar 1988; Woodfield 1982) seem to understand the term "content" as simply denoting psychological functional roles, and as having nothing to do with intentionality, reference, or truth conditions. Their notion of content is thus unrelated to content ascriptions, and is not the notion employed here.

the case) the worthy or legitimate inferential relations of any token seem to be dependent upon its content. However, according to normative inferentialists, this isn't true, since there are norms of inference that are prior to content and so they can determine it or an aspect thereof. A prominent defender of this view is Brandom (1994, 2000). Like other normative inferentialists, Brandom does not make room for a referential dimension. For him, the grammar of "refers" misleads philosophers to think that this term stands for a relation, and consequently to search for theories that account for the nature of this odd relation (see, e.g., Brandom 1994, p. 323). According to my characterization, Brandom is an intentional anti-realist, who leaves out the constitutive aspect of content. Normative inferentialism of whatever variety also raises hard questions. For example, it isn't clear whence the relevant norms of inference can come (see Rosen 1997).[47]

But let's ignore this difficulty. I wish to make a brief remark about a possible normative inferentialist view that, unlike Brandom's approach, does aim to account for the referential dimension of content. Since on such a view content encompasses a dimension beyond the referential one, then, precisely like the standard ("naturalistic") functional role approach, it is incompatible with the view that there is nothing in content other than standard-object aboutness. Such a normative inferentialist view, too, can be subject to a distinction between a long-armed version and a short-armed version that differ with respect to whether the norms in question are object-involving or not. And, as with the two parallel versions of standard functional role semantics, on neither version is content exhausted by relations to extra-mental items. As to the referential dimension itself, we shall see in Chapter 4 that any possible normativist account of this dimension is subject to the same difficulties to which reductive-naturalistic accounts are subject.

1.6 The Plan for the Remainder of the Book

Chapter 2 discusses those studies in experimental philosophy that purport to establish the thesis that there is cultural diversity about questions such as "To whom does the name 'Gödel' really refer?" (as in Kripke's Gödel–Schmidt thought-experiment). This discussion serves to elucidate the role of theoretical considerations versus that of judgments over cases (the "method of cases") in theorizing about intentionality and reference. It is argued that no theoretical considerations can settle questions of reference determination, and that there can be no

---

[47] According to Brandom, meaning, but not its referential dimension, is constituted by social practices of giving and asking for reasons. For other normative inferentialists, see, for example, Peregrin (2008) and Travis (2000). For other normativist approaches to meaning, see, for example, Boghossian (2003, 2008), Gibbard (2012), and Kripke (1982).

expertise in judgments of reference. A tentative argument against intentional realism is then suggested—one that shifts the burden of proof in the debate—and the ground is laid for intentional anti-realism in general and the practice-dependence view of the truth conditions of content ascriptions in particular.

Chapter 3 argues against one of the prominent current approaches to intentionality, the phenomenal intentionality approach. I present it as an instance of a more general strategy that holds that intentionality is determined by a property that is intrinsic to the mind (an instance that takes the relevant property to be phenomenal), and argue against this general strategy as well. After presenting the theories of phenomenal intentionality on which I focus as those that suggest non-circular responses to the question of intentionality, I criticize the main arguments in their favor. Special attention is given to the argument from introspection. Indeed, it seems that the main reason for the belief of most people who give the issue any thought—philosophers and non-philosophers alike—that mental states of various kinds are intentional, is that we simply know this from the inside. I argue, first, that due to the transcending nature of intentionality, introspection cannot inform us of it, and second, that pure first-person judgments about intentionality are vacuous. That is, one's self-ascription of content depends, for its very meaning, on one's adopting a third-person point of view. For either of these reasons, arguments from introspection for both the phenomenal intentionality thesis and the thesis that phenomenality resolves content indeterminacy fail. In this context, a conceptual model for first-person knowledge of content is presented. According to this model, in cases of self-ascription of content one acts as a double agent: one introspects one's mental state and relates it to content from the third-person perspective. It is the second (third-personal and "unprivileged") stage that brings (ascribed) intentionality into the picture. Arguments are then presented against conceptual reductions of intentionality to phenomenality, on the one hand, and synthetic-empirical reductions, on the other. We shall see that if primitive intrinsic intentionality is not a viable option (since, as I argued above, primitive intentionality isn't), then shifting the burden of intentionality to another intrinsic property does not advance us one bit.

Chapter 4 criticizes the very idea of a naturalistic reduction of intentionality, which can be characterized as the idea of an extrinsic reduction of intentionality. This is the second prominent approach to this phenomenon. After presenting the rationale underlying the reductive-naturalistic approach, I examine possible models for this approach. The first is the scientific model of reductions, as in the case of water–H_2O. I argue that this model is inapplicable to the case of intentionality, since in this case there is no analogue to the reduced macro property: we cannot identify an explanandum that can both be reduced to external relations and fit intentional realism.

Various options for what might serve as such an analogue—such as conceptual role, logico-syntactic properties, and the first-person appearance of intentionality—are rejected. Only ascriptions of intentionality constrain the identity of the naturalistic relation: that is, its obtaining is merely the condition under which intentionality is ascribed, and so such reductive accounts are not realist accounts. Second, I attend to the conceptualist model, according to which it is the concept of intentionality (or of reference, or of think-of, etc.) that determines some naturalistic relation as the intentional relation. I argue that this option leaves aboutness out. A related, but independent, argument against the very idea of naturalistic reductions of intentionality is then presented. According to this argument, the difficulty to single out the intentional relation among the many world–mind naturalistic relations is insurmountable.

Chapters 5 and 6 develop the tenets of my version of intentional anti-realism, pursue its implications, and handle objections. In Chapter 5, I first present the negative thesis, according to which there can be no intentional states and content ascriptions lack truth conditions. The chapter draws together the threads of an argument for this thesis. Its premises are: (a) the negation of intentional primitivism (from Chapter 1); (b) the rejection of "intrinsic reductions" of intentionality, as in phenomenal intentionality theories (from Chapter 3); (c) the rejection of "extrinsic reductions" (from Chapter 4), and (d) the claim that such reductions are the only possible reductions of intentionality. The latter three premises jointly entail that intentionality cannot be "something else," whereas the rejection of primitivism means that it must be "something else." This is one way in which the inherent tension in the concept of intentionality manifests itself.

The elements of the positive thesis are then developed and defended. Among them is the idea that content ascriptions have practice-dependent truth conditions, as well as the claim that mental states that are standardly considered intentional exist and have most of the properties that are standardly attributed to them, yet absent intentional properties and, thus, absent representational truth values. I develop a notion of thick logico-syntactic structure and argue that, due to having structures in this (thick) sense, mental states can be true in a coherentist, or coherentist-pragmatist, sense (or "adequate," or however else we choose to refer to the epistemic merit secured by coherence). Thus, truth (or, at any rate, an epistemic merit that correlates with our considered judgments of truth) does not presuppose content or meaning. However, content ascriptions cannot be true (or adequate) even in this sense; they lie outside the field of knowledge.

The suggested notion of thick logico-syntactic structure also underlies my rejoinder, in Chapter 6, to the argument from the explanatory and predictive success of content ascriptions to intentional realism (an argument that forms another prominent reason for the widely held conviction that intentional realism is true). I argue that content ascriptions are also ascriptions of logico-syntactic structures—they carry logico-syntactic messages—and their explanatory and predictive success is due to the fact that mental states have those structures. At the same time, following Egan's observation regarding the role of content ascriptions in cognitive science, an important role played by the semantic messages of content ascriptions is pointed out: ascribing contents to mental states (i.e., affixing intentional characteristics to them) allows for the explanation of types of explananda that are of interest to us in our interactions with our fellow subjects. Other roles played by content ascriptions are also pointed out.

Chapter 6 also addresses the cognitive suicide charge against intentional anti-realism (the third important reason in favor of intentional realism), and further develops the notion of thick logico-syntactic structure and the intentional anti-realist theory. Since intentional anti-realism is committed to dismissing the "claim that" and "believe that" talk, taken at face value, it is committed to denying that intentional anti-realists claim or believe *that* there can be no intentional states. However, this implication is argued to be a legitimate and unproblematic characteristic of radical and revisionist philosophy. Intentional anti-realism replaces the "claim that" and "believe that" talk, literally construed, with "quoted" talk; it legitimizes the "claim that" and "believe that" talk only when construed as rhetorical devices that capture patterns of thick logico-syntactic structures, which are shared by various sentences and belief-states (that may belong to different languages). The quoted sentence "There are no intentional states" is true in the coherentist sense (or, at any rate, has that epistemic merit that is secured by coherence). The "fact that" talk, too, is relegated to the status of mere rhetorical device, and, relatedly, intentional anti-realism is shown to entail the rejection of the idea of segments of extra-mental and extra-linguistic reality as truth makers for belief-states or sentences, but without entailing idealism.

The chapter ends with another argument against intentional realism. Since intentional properties have been shown to be dispensable for all possibly relevant purposes, and no sound arguments support the claim that they are ever instantiated, the application of Ockham's razor leads to the conclusion that no such properties are ever instantiated. Furthermore, conjoining this argument with the argument from Chapter 2 (which is supposed to shift the burden of proof in the debate over intentional realism) yields a powerful argument against the possible existence of intentionality: that is, in favor of intentional anti-realism.

2

How to Settle Issues of Intentionality, and a Tentative Argument for Intentional Anti-Realism

2.1 Referential Diversity?

Whereas the direct concerns of the following chapters will be the very existence and constitution of intentionality, the direct concerns of the present chapter are some aspects of the epistemology of intentionality. In this chapter, I discuss, *inter alia*, studies in experimental philosophy purporting to establish cultural diversity in opinions about reference in specific cases. In so doing, I aim to elucidate the roles of theoretical considerations versus unsupported judgments or intuitions concerning such cases in theorizing about intentionality and reference. I will argue that no theoretical considerations can settle questions of reference determination, and that there can be no expertise in unsupported judgments or intuitions of reference. Based upon these conclusions, a tentative argument against the existence of intentionality is suggested, and the ground is laid for intentional anti-realism in general and the practice-dependence view of the truth conditions of content ascriptions in particular.

The discussion in this chapter revolves around the reference of names and considers a single case study, that of Kripke's Gödel–Schmidt example (Kripke 1980), which has attracted the attention of most writers on experimental philosophy of reference and intentionality (hereafter, "experimental philosophical semantics"). The example is as follows. Gödel is the person who proved the theorem of the incompleteness of arithmetic, and what most people know of him is simply that he is the person who proved this theorem. So, the only description that most people associate with the name "Gödel" is "the person who proved the incompleteness theorem." Now, Kripke asks his readers to imagine that, in fact, Gödel has not proven the theorem in question. Rather, unbeknownst to almost anybody, it was proven by Schmidt, a German mathematician, and upon Schmidt's (mysterious) death Gödel got hold of Schmidt's manuscript and claimed credit for the proof, which was thereafter attributed to him. Thus, the description in question is not true of Gödel, but rather of Schmidt. The descriptivist theory, then, is committed to the claim that, in such scenarios, when most people (those who associate with this name only the above-mentioned description) use the name "Gödel,"

Intentionality Deconstructed: An Anti-Realist Theory. Amir Horowitz, Oxford University Press.
© Amir Horowitz 2024. DOI: 10.1093/oso/9780198896432.003.0002

they refer by it to Schmidt, rather than to Gödel. However, claims Kripke, those uses of "Gödel" refer to Gödel. Hence, the descriptivist theory is false.

Kripke thus employs what is now known as "the method of cases" in arguing against the descriptivist theory of names (and, in turn, in arguing for his own theory or "picture").[1] If indeed those uses of "Gödel" refer to Gödel, rather than to Schmidt, then, trivially, the descriptivist theory of the reference of names in the version presented here is refuted. (Whether any alternative theory is thus supported is of course another matter. I will expand on this point later.) But what justifies Kripke's claim that the use of "Gödel" in such scenarios indeed refers to Gödel? Machery, Mallon, Nichols, and Stich (hereafter "MMNS,") (2004) challenge the idea that this claim is justified by "widely shared intuitions" (p. B3). Indeed, most philosophers endorsed the "intuition" that "Gödel" in that scenario refers to Gödel. In the experiment MMNS conducted, the Kripkean Gödel/ Schmidt story was presented to a group of Westerners and to a group of East Asians. The groups were also told about a person, John, who only believes about Gödel that he is the person who proved the incompleteness theorem. Afterward, the two groups were presented with the following question:

When John uses the name "Gödel," is he talking about:

(A) the person who really discovered the incompleteness of arithmetic,

or

(B) the person who got hold of the manuscript and claimed credit for the work?

MMNS report that most Westerners answered (B), whereas most East Asians answered (A). They conclude that East Asians, unlike Westerners, are in fact guided by descriptivist intuitions, since in their view when John uses the name "Gödel" he refers to the individual who satisfies the description "the person who proved the incompleteness of arithmetic," a description that he associates with the name "Gödel." Thus, MMNS maintain, the intuitions that were taken to support Kripke's argument are not universal. There is clear cultural semantic diversity (though there is also some intra-cultural variation). This fact raises questions about whose intuitions are to count: It is "*wildly* implausible that the semantic intuitions of the narrow cross-section of humanity who are Western academic philosophers are a more reliable indicator of the correct theory of reference...than the different semantic intuitions of other cultural or linguistic groups" (MMNS 2004, p. B9). The philosophers' methodology of the semantic task under consideration is put in jeopardy: constructing a theory of reference cannot be carried out from the armchair.

---

[1] For a comprehensive defense of the method of cases (and armchair philosophy in general), see Strevens (2019). For a critical account of the method of cases as a general philosophical method, see Machery (2017).

HOW TO SETTLE ISSUES OF INTENTIONALITY   31

Whether MMNS's conclusion, to the effect that there is cultural diversity in judgments concerning reference, indeed follows from the results of the experiment is a matter of some dispute. Indeed, various critiques have been mounted against this move. Some critics (e.g., Ludwig 2007; Devitt 2011) argue that Kripke was (or at any rate, that it is) right to defer to philosophers' intuitions. Others (e.g., Deutsch 2009) argue that the experiment does not undermine Kripke's argument because Kripke was not concerned with intuitions about the reference of names, or at least that the appeal to intuitions played a minor role in his case against descriptivism and in favor of the causal-historical picture (e.g., Ichikawa, Ishani, and Weatherson 2012). Some critics argue that the participants cannot be trusted to distill semantic intuitions from other views on the matter (e.g., Martí (2009) argues that the question posed to the participants evoked replies that are concerned with metalinguistic rather than with linguistic judgments), while still others (e.g., Deutsch 2009) argue that the experiment does not show a difference in the relevant semantic judgments: for example, because (at least, it cannot be ruled out that) the participants were concerned with speaker's reference rather than with semantic reference (see Stich and Machery (2012) for a reply to this charge).

I will not deal with those critiques that pertain to interpretations of Kripke, since I am concerned with how the topic should be viewed. I will also not address those critiques that pertain to the reliability of the experiments that were in fact conducted, for I am concerned with the possibility of cultural semantic diversity, not with its actuality. Even if, for some reason concerning the specific experiments in question, the cultural diversity in the participants' replies in these experiments does not indicate the presence of cultural diversity in semantic intuitions, experiments targeting the relevant semantic intuitions may be conducted. Indeed, advocates of experimental philosophical semantics themselves accept that their experiments need not be the last word on the matter and admit that more experiments (and more subtle ones) are required. Some have already conducted new experiments in response to critiques (see, e.g., Machery, Olivola, and De Blank 2009).[2] There is no a priori reason to rule out the possibility that those semantic intuitions turn out to be culturally divergent. That is, cultural semantic diversity is possible.

Now I wish to make a few remarks about what the diversity purportedly discovered by experimental philosophical semantics is and what it is not. These remarks will be relevant to the practice-dependence view of the truth values of content ascriptions, to be developed in Chapters 5 and 6. Some writers about experimental philosophical semantics write as though the lesson from such diversity is that the different cultures use names differently: Westerners use names causally whereas East Asians use names descriptively. Thus, Martí (2009) argues that, to examine the possibility of cultural semantic diversity, MMNS should not

---

[2] For more recent experimental research that is argued to confirm MMNS's conclusion, see Beebe and Undercoffer (2016).

have asked the participants in their experiment the ("metalinguistic") question about the reference of "Gödel." Rather, they should have asked them ("linguistic") questions such as "Should Gödel have claimed credit for the incompleteness theorem?" Their answers to such a question would show whether they are using the name "Gödel" descriptively or not (see also Martí 2020). Machery, Olivola, and De Blank (2009), who reply to Martí's criticism, also adopt this terminology in taking the issue to come down to which theory speakers' *use* of names conforms to.

However, the idea of such conformity between the use of names by speakers and a theory of reference is untenable. Consider the view that the fact that, for example, people associate a description that is uniquely true of Gödel in situations in which we refer to Gödel by the name "Gödel" strengthens the descriptivist theory. This view is false, since it is not given that we refer to Gödel in such situations; whether we do or not is precisely the issue. The question is whether we refer to Gödel in such situations *given our use of the name*: that is, given the circumstances in which we use it (circumstances that are depicted by the Kripkean story). There is no such thing as using a name descriptively, or, for that matter, causally. People simply use names in various circumstances, and the circumstances in which they use names do not settle the issue of what determines the reference of names, or in other words, which theory regarding the reference determination of names is true. Descriptivists do not claim that some actual use of names attests to the truth of their theory, and that had people used names in some different way, their theory would have been refuted. They claim, rather, that had people used names in some different way, the reference of their use would have been different, because the object satisfying the description associated with the name would have been different.

Relatedly, the diversity purportedly discovered by MMNS's experiment is diversity in practices of ascriptions of names. Whatever inferences are allowed from claims about ascriptions of reference to claims about reference, discovering that people have different judgments about the reference of a name does not entail that these people's uses of the name differ in reference. The experiment may expose reference *according to* those different cultural groups—that is, how they *ascribe* reference—and not what the reference of names is in their uses of names. The participants express their judgments about the reference of a name in certain situations, judgments that do not specifically concern the reference of their own uses of this name, and thus they do not indicate diversity in reference. MMNS's finding is that according to most Westerners, for example, the references of uses *by all*—Westerners and East Asians alike—are determined as depicted by the causal theory of names.[3]

---

[3] It wouldn't matter if the participants were asked about the reference of their own use in the scenarios in question, for the scenarios contain no data that distinguish themselves from others. Relatedly, they do not have any epistemic authority regarding the reference of their own uses, since no relevant facts are hidden (the scenarios also include the relevant information about what goes on in the speaker's mind).

I will not rely on MMNS's conclusion to the effect that there actually is cultural diversity in judgments concerning reference. I do accept it, though, and think that it can motivate acceptance of intentional anti-realism. For I find it hard to accept that Western culture, say, is by and large correct in its judgment of reference—that its practice of content ascription matches truth—whereas East Asian culture is by and large wrong on the matter, and its practice of content ascription fails to match truth, or vice versa. And if there is such cultural diversity yet it is not the case that the practice of one culture matches truth while that of the other doesn't, then there is no truth of the matter. And this last claim—if generalized both horizontally (to hold for expressions of all kinds) and vertically (to hold for mental content as well)—is intentional anti-realism. I by no means take this line of thought to constitute an effective argument for intentional anti-realism, but only to motivate the view. For I do not provide any argument for the claim that it is implausible that the practice of content ascription of one culture matches truth while that of the other doesn't, and, similarly, I do not establish but merely accept MMNS's conclusion. Besides providing some initial motivation for intentional anti-realism, that line of thought may play a role in softening reluctance toward it. To many people, philosophers and non-philosophers alike, intentional irrealism or anti-realism appears to be an utterly crazy and silly view. However, in my experience, once it is realized that it amounts to the claim that there is no right or wrong in cases of semantic diversity of the sort in question, reluctance toward this view is significantly decreased, and sometimes even turns into endorsement.

2.2 Do Philosophers Intuit Reference?

Some authors concerned with experimental philosophical semantics (e.g., Devitt 2011; Fischer, Engelhardt, and Herbelot 2015; Sosa 2007) rely on their accounts of the nature of intuitions. I am not going to delve into this matter, but only to stipulate how I use "intuitions" in this book. For my purposes, intuitions are judgments (or beliefs) that are held by one in spite of one not being able to justify them. The rationale for employing this notion of intuitions will become evident later.[4]

---

[4] Three remarks concerning intuitions. First, "intuition" in this sense does not refer to justified judgements that one would have held even if one had withdrawn their justification. There may be further complications along this dimension (e.g., cases in which one forgets the justification one used to have for a judgment though remembers that one had such a justification), but dealing with them is not important for the present concerns.

Second, since there seem to be cases where people find something intuitive although they don't believe it, some philosophers endorse the view that intuitions are inclinations to believe (see Earlenbaugh and Molyneux 2009). Nimtz (2012) suggests a disjunctive doxastic account of intuitions according to which intuitions are either beliefs or inclinations to believe. This issue also need not concern us here.

Third, intuitions in the sense used here may be said to be epistemically primitive, but they need not be psychologically primitive or unexplainable. One aim of experimental philosophy is to uncover the psychological mechanisms that underlie epistemically primitive judgments, and possibly relevant cross-cultural psychological differences.

34   INTENTIONALITY DECONSTRUCTED

This stipulation brings me to Kirk Ludwig's (2007) criticism of MMNS's case in favor of experimental semantics and against reliance on the philosopher's armchair intuitions. Ludwig advocates deference to philosophers. This is because in the cases with which we are concerned (e.g., the Gödel/Schmidt one) "a quick judgment is not called for, but rather a considered reflective judgment in which the basis for a correct answer is revealed" (p. 148). And, he continues:

> [The semantics of proper names] is a domain of considerable complexity when our ordinary vocabulary is not especially precise. We should instead [of conducting surveys of untrained people] expect that the relevant experts in the field of philosophical semantics will be better placed to give answers which focus on the right features of the cases and what they are supposed to be responding to....
>
> What is called for is the development of a discipline in which general expertise in the conduct of thought experiments is inculcated and in which expertise in different fields of conceptual inquiry is developed and refined. There is such a discipline. It is called philosophy. Philosophers are best suited by training and expertise to conduct thought experiments in their areas of expertise and to sort out the methodological and conceptual issues that arise in trying to get clear about the complex structure of concepts with which we confront the world.
>
> (Ludwig 2007, pp. 150–151)

What underlies Ludwig's preference for the judgments of philosophers is the thought that they are good at seeing conceptual connections, drawing inferences concerning the relevant issues, etc. If those judgments of philosophers are to be trusted, according to this line of thought, it is in virtue of the reasoning that philosophers employ and that underlies those judgments—philosophers are supposed to be good at such reasoning. They are supposed to be good at dealing with *theoretical considerations* that are relevant for resolving the issues in question. I do not wish to downplay these virtues of philosophers. I wish to point out, first, that Ludwig does not in fact speak of semantic intuitions in my sense. He speaks of semantic judgments that are supported by theoretical considerations; that are arrived at via reasoning and justification. The point I wish to raise is not verbal. The point is that whether Ludwig's deference to philosophers and his rejection of experimental semantics are justified boils down to the question of the role of reasoning and theoretical considerations in figuring out the reference of expressions and in constructing a theory of reference. The question is whether reasoning and theoretical considerations—such that do not rely on unsupported judgments or intuitions—suffice to settle issues of reference. According to Ludwig, the issue is whether the public is more competent in the relevant argumentation: that is, whether the common wisdom is better than the wisdom of experts. Had this been the issue, then Ludwig would have had the upper hand, for generally those who are trained in some area are better at dealing with it than those who aren't. But the issue is different. It is, if you like, whether wisdom is enough, or unsupported intuitive judgments are needed to settle such questions.[5]

Ludwig believes that philosophers are more competent to consider issues pertaining to semantics and, therefore, we should defer to their judgments on the question of reference. But this does not settle this question unless it is also accepted that considerations of the kind with which philosophers engage—and that do not involve raw (i.e., unsupported) intuitions—suffice to settle issues of reference. This question is not simply a methodological question. It is a question that touches upon the essence of reference determination and theories of reference. But instead of addressing this question regarding the role of reasoning and theoretical considerations in figuring out reference, Ludwig's treatment presupposes an answer to it. Moreover, it is the wrong answer. I will point out the additional premise on whose truth Ludwig's case for deference to philosophers on issues of reference and against experimental semantics depends, and argue that it is false.[6]

Before turning to this issue, I will address the view that we should even defer to the raw intuitions of philosophers.[7] The reason for this privileged attitude toward philosophers (and perhaps linguists as well)—which underlies the "expertise defense" against the challenge that experimental philosophy poses to armchair philosophy—might be that their training and experience make them more sensitive to semantic facts.[8] Exactly as physicians' intuitions—that is, their unsupported judgments—are alleged to be more reliable than laypersons' intuitions on medical matters (e.g., various medical diagnoses), the intuitions of philosophers of language are more reliable than those of the laypersons on semantic matters. Or as Hales puts an analogous point concerning scientists: "Scientists have and rely on physical intuitions, intuitions that are trained, educated, and informed and yet are good indicators of truth for these very reasons. In the same way, the modal intuitions of professional philosophers are much more reliable than those of either inexperienced students or the 'folk'" (Hales 2006, p. 171).

However, leaving aside the general issue of philosophers' expertise in concept application (and regardless of whether scientists' or physicians' *raw intuitions* should be trusted), I wonder what kind of training and experience might make

---

[5] MMNS discuss the idea that we should appeal to reflective intuitions—namely, intuitions that are informed by a cautious examination of the philosophical significance of the probes—in constructing a theory of reference and dismiss it on the grounds that such intuitions may be reinforced intuitions.

[6] The requirement that theoretical considerations suffice to settle issues of reference does not mean that such considerations are supposed to embody valid arguments with no premises, or from self-verifying premises, etc. They have to embody arguments that are acceptable by our regular standards for evaluating arguments.

[7] It might be that this is also Ludwig's view: namely, that he also believes that the philosophers' conceptual proficiency makes them better intuiters.

[8] The expression "expertise defense" standardly refers, in this context, to the appeal to the alleged superiority of philosophers' intuitions rather than to their more general expertise which includes also their argumentative proficiency.

36 INTENTIONALITY DECONSTRUCTED

philosophers more apt to have the right intuitions in Gödel/Schmidt cases, or about reference in general. Let's assume that philosophers do indeed have extensive practice in finding out reference in various cases. If their practice involves the employment of theoretical considerations (where the expression "theoretical considerations" is used in a broad sense that includes argumentation, conceptual analysis, and the like), it is unclear why it is supposed to make them any better in finding out that which, *ex hypothesi*, cannot be settled by theoretical considerations.[9] Or suppose that the philosophical practice in question also involves the philosophers' employment of raw intuitions. In order to acquire competence in this enterprise—in order to improve their performance—they have to operate some external test that would verify or falsify these intuitions. But in this realm, that is assumed to be beyond theoretical considerations, no such test—no feedback mechanism—is at their disposal. The idea that they have some reliable access to semantic facts that is independent of their theoretical considerations and intuitions makes no sense.

Michael Devitt, who argues for the superiority of experts' semantic intuitions over those of ordinary competent speakers, takes intuitions to be "empirical theory-laden central-processor responses to phenomena, differing from many other such responses only in being fairly immediate and unreflective, based on little if any conscious reasoning" (Devitt 2006a, p. 103). The experts' intuitions are more reliable according to Devitt since their underlying empirical theories are better than the laypersons' theories. But what could the relevant theories that underlie semantic intuitions be? The natural option is theories of reference determination. But if we adhere to this option, then what we get is that theories of reference determination are not supported in virtue of conformity to semantic intuitions; rather, the intuitions pop up because we (more precisely—some of us) already hold the theories. In such a picture, it seems that the experts do not need the intuitions to serve as data for arriving at the right theory—they already have the right theory—so discovering their intuitions becomes irrelevant to the task of constructing a theory of reference. (The idea that the popping up of the intuitions makes philosophers *conscious* of a theory which they previously held *unconsciously*, but which nonetheless their philosophical expertise attests to being the right theory, is baseless, to say the least.) Furthermore, the cases under consideration are supposed to play a role in exposing the right theory of reference among competing philosophical theories. So, in those cases, at least some philosophical theories do not get it right. Should we defer to the judgments of those philosophers whose judgments of reference in the past proved true? According to what test? Should we make a philosophical referendum? Thus, the idea that we

---

[9] Of course, we need not compare their performance with that of people who do not understand what reference is or what they are asked to do in the experiments in question.

HOW TO SETTLE ISSUES OF INTENTIONALITY   37

can trust the philosophers' intuitions because they are probably underlain by the right theories breaks down.[10]

One might think that various empirical theories, such as linguistic or psychological theories, can underlie intuitions concerning reference. However, insofar as such theories are not also concerned with the determination of reference, I cannot see how they can underlie such intuitions. Alternatively, one might think that intuitions of reference can be based upon epistemic or metaphysical theories (e.g., essentialism). But if intuitions of reference—that is, *judgments* of reference—can be based upon such theories, then we should assess the philosophers' intuitions in terms of the theoretical considerations that are supposed to back them. That is, we find ourselves in the realm of theoretical considerations, to be dealt with in the next section. It does not matter to the present issue whether or not what we call "intuitions" are in fact—even only sometimes—underlain by theories of some kinds, for, if they are justifiable by appeal to theoretical considerations, we should consult those considerations, and if they are not, then the underlying theories do not lend them any support. This seems to characterize claims regarding theories of whatever kind that are supposed to underlie the intuitions in question. In fact, there is something strange in the idea of deference to experts as it figures in the present discussion. It is one thing to advocate for laypersons to defer to experts, and quite another to advocate for experts to consult with experts (experts in the same field, including themselves), not by attending to their arguments and evidence, but by simply relying on their intuitions, and such deference is precisely what the present suggestion advocates. It does not advocate for philosophers to exercise their philosophical skills, but rather for them simply to accept their colleagues' or their own intuitions. If the thought is that no theoretical considerations can back judgments of reference, then why defer to those whose intuitions are supposed to be underlain by theories?

It might be objected that I paint the situation with too broad a brush. According to this objection, I take intuitions to be completely independent of any reasoning, whereas this is empirically implausible. Specifically, in the case of philosophical

---

[10] For a critique along different lines of Devitt's claim that we should defer to experts' linguistic intuitions, see Stich and Machery (2012). See also Machery (2012, 2015). Devitt advocates deference to linguists' intuitions regarding syntax as well)see, e.g., Devitt 2006a, 2006b, 2010(. Gross and Culbertson criticize Devitt on this issue (see Culbertson and Gross 2009; Gross and Culbertson 2011; see also Maynes and Gross 2013). For various critiques of the expertise defense in general—not specifically the one that concerns reference—see Machery (2017), Alexander and Weinberg (2007), and Weinberg et al. (2010). Some of the critiques brought by Weinberg, Gonnerman, Buckner, and Alexander concern issues that figure in my critiques—in particular, the issues of feedback mechanisms and of underlying theories. But these critiques differ from mine, which aim, specifically, at the alleged expertise concerning reference, and engage with specific characteristics of semantics. Also, the former critiques aim to show that philosophers' intuitions about hypothetical cases vary with irrelevant factors as do laypersons' intuitions, whereas the thesis of MMNS, on which I focus, does not rely on this claim. Horvath (2012) argues against the case made by Weinberg, Gonnerman, Buckner, and Alexander in favor of this claim. In this context, see also Grundmann (2012).

38 INTENTIONALITY DECONSTRUCTED

intuitions, plausibly, they are the product of complex forms of reasoning that structure the philosophers' thinking, which provides them with reliable intuitions.[11] However, what is important for my argument is not that the intuitions in question are independent of any reasoning on the part of the people having them, but rather that these people cannot justify them. That is to say that, for example, one cannot justify one's adhering to the intuition that "Gödel" refers to Gödel over the intuition that "Gödel" refers to Schmidt. The point is that, if one is able to justify one's adhering to such an intuition, we should assess one's justification and need not rely on any assumed expertise. And if one's underlying theories and proficiency are not enough to justify one's intuitive choice on the matter—if there is a justificatory gap between one's underlying theories and proficiency and one's choice—then we are unjustified to rely on one's intuitive choice.[12]

I think it is fair to conclude that deference to the raw semantic intuitions of philosophers as a way to discover how reference is determined is unjustified. Let's now go back to theoretical considerations regarding reference determination and address the question of whether such considerations can settle issues of reference.

2.3 Can Theoretical Considerations Settle Issues of Reference Determination?

I wish to argue that reason and theoretical considerations do not completely settle issues of reference determination. I will do so via a discussion of Deutsch's (2009) critique of experimental semantics (which is related to Ludwig's critique). According to Deutsch, Kripke does not rely on intuitions in claiming that "Gödel" refers to Gödel.[13] Rather, he focuses on *the fact* that "Gödel" refers to Gödel (see, e.g., Deutsch 2009, pp. 447–449). If this is true, then, a fortiori, Kripke does not rely on the supposed universality of his semantic intuitions. Of course, Deutsch does not think that Kripke and (some) other philosophers have some direct contact with semantic facts. Rather, he takes Kripke to bring considerations in favor of his claim that "Gödel" refers to Gödel and similar other claims. Indeed, Deutsch mentions a few considerations that Kripke brings in support of this claim.

---

[11] I am grateful to Arnon Cahen for pressing me to address this and other issues in this section.

[12] One might also object to my argument by suggesting that the intuitions in question may be fully justified by one at an unconscious level. But then, the first horn of the dilemma strikes again: if one's endorsing some intuitive judgment is justifiable by appealing to whatever theory one has acquired (even though one applies it in the cases at hand only unconsciously), then philosophers should be able to reconstruct one's processes and assess the justification they embody. (Recall that the justification in question need not be embodied by valid arguments with no premises, or from self-verifying premises, etc. It has to be acceptable by our regular standards for evaluating justifications. The dilemma applies to justification understood in this way.)

[13] For a similar claim, see Ichikawa, Ishani, and Weatherson (2012). For the claim that philosophers in general do not rely on their intuitions as evidence, see Cappelen (2012), Deutsch (2010), and Williamson (2004, 2005, 2007). For replies, see Devitt (2015) and Alexander (2012a, 2012b).

HOW TO SETTLE ISSUES OF INTENTIONALITY   39

I am not concerned with the question of whether Kripke, or any other philosopher who deals with the issue of reference determination, appeals to intuitions. The question with which I am interested, in the present context, is whether intuitions may or should play a role—and if so, what role—in theorizing about reference. Deutsch's interest, too, is not merely exegetical. Rather, he is interested in supporting the substantive claim that intuitions are irrelevant to theorizing about reference. As he says: "Facts such as the fact that competent speakers intuit that the island is the referent of 'Madagascar' are data for a psychological theory, one that does not have any clear bearing on a theory of reference" (p. 449).

I accept that drawing conceptual connections, making inferences, and other reflective activities should play a role in constructing a theory of reference determination.[14] But to exclude intuitions from any role in such theory construction, what has to be shown is that such activities can single out reference in each and every case, leaving no indeterminacies, and without involving raw semantic intuitions. Deutsch hasn't shown this, and I will argue that it is false. As we shall now see, theoretical considerations are limited in two respects. First, they may, perhaps, serve to rule out certain candidates for reference determination, but they cannot single out the right kind of reference determination. Second, even their ruling out candidates for reference determination is not innocuous: it presupposes a background of a practice of reference ascription (of some level of generality).

In order to appreciate the limited role of theoretical considerations, let us look at Kripke's three arguments in favor of the claim that "Gödel" refers to Gödel on which Deutsch relies.[15] Here is how Deutsch (2009, pp. 451–452) presents these arguments:

(a) Kripke points out that the imaginary Gödel-case has real life analogues. All that many of us "know" about Peano is that he was the discoverer of certain axioms concerning the natural numbers. But it turns out that Dedekind discovered those axioms. If descriptivism is true, many of us have been referring all along to Dedekind with our uses of "Peano." But we have not been referring to Dedekind with those uses. We have been referring instead to Peano, *mis*attributing to him the discovery of the axioms. This is not simply a further putative counterexample; it strengthens the claim that the Gödel-case is a counterexample by showing us that the way in which we *ought* to judge, with respect to the imaginary Gödel-case,

---

[14] Intentional anti-realism makes room for theories of reference in a sense to be discussed in Chapters 4 and 6.

[15] Deutsch does not mention in this context Kripke's modal arguments against descriptivism, and rightly so, since the debate over experimental philosophical semantics is concerned with reference determination in the actual world, and these arguments are irrelevant to this issue. As Kripke himself acknowledged, rigid designators can pick up their reference in the actual world by means of descriptions.

40 INTENTIONALITY DECONSTRUCTED

should line up with the way in which we do in fact, and correctly, judge about the real-life Peano case. (See Kripke, 1980, pp. 84–85.)

(b) Kripke argues that the view that "Gödel" refers to Schmidt—the prediction made by descriptivism concerning the Gödel-case—suggests a more general view to the effect that *one can never be mistaken* in uttering a sentence of the form "*n* is the *F*," when "the *F*" denotes, and is a definite description one associates with "*n*," a proper name. But one *can* be mistaken in uttering "Peano is the discoverer of the axioms," even if one associates "the discoverer of the axioms" with "Peano." The falsity of this general view is evidence that Kripke is right in claiming that "Gödel" does not refer to Schmidt, in the Gödel-case. (See Kripke, 1980, pp. 85n, 87.)

(c) Kripke argues for an alternative account of the way in which "Gödel" refers (the causal-historical account) which explains, Kripke thinks, why "Gödel" refers to Gödel in the Gödel-case. The existence of a satisfying general theory of reference that predicts that "Gödel" refers to Gödel in the Gödel-case counts in favor of the view that "Gödel" refers to Gödel in the case. (See Kripke, 1980, pp. 91–93.)

I do not think that these arguments make Kripke's thesis of the reference determination of names resilient to conflicting intuitions (and thus to cultural semantic diversity). As to (a), I doubt whether it can be taken to stand on its own. This argument mentions the idea of misattribution that is the focus of (b) and which I will address below. If we leave this idea out, it seems that this argument has no non-rhetorical force beyond that of the Gödel/Schmidt case itself. One who does not take it as evident that "Gödel" refers to Gödel in Kripke's counterfactual scenario would not take it as evident that "Peano" refers to Peano in the actual world. The actuality of the latter example—precisely as the presumed actuality of the ascriptions of reference made with respect to this actual case—makes no difference. Relatedly, if the Gödel case—taken on its own—depends on an appeal to intuition, the Peano case cannot discharge it from this dependence, for the latter case similarly depends on intuition.

Let me jump to (c). I grant that the existence of a satisfying general theory of reference that predicts that "Gödel" refers to Gödel in that counterfactual scenario counts in favor of the view that "Gödel" refers to Gödel in that case, but whether or not the causal-historical view is satisfying depends to a significant extent on whether this and other predictions that it makes are true. So, this view cannot be taken to settle the issue of the reference of "Gödel." And as before, if the Gödel–Schmidt case—taken on its own—depends on an appeal to intuition, the appeal to the causal-historical view cannot discharge it from this dependence.

This brings us to argument (b). It appears stronger than the previous ones. However, it is basically a negative argument. That is, to the extent that it is successful, it is effective against the descriptivist view of names, or, more precisely, against its baldest version. Perhaps the argument exposes a problem for this theory (or for this version), but the importance of this fact notwithstanding, the argument falls far short of constituting a strong reason in favor of any specific theory of reference.[16] For example, it does not favor any version of the causal-historical view over any other, and it does not even favor any such version over other versions of descriptivism, such as the cluster theory (although perhaps it can be modified so as to rule out the cluster theory as well). Thus, the theoretical consideration in question is limited in force.

But there is another respect, and an especially important one, in which the argument under consideration is limited in force. This argument presupposes some semantic intuition. It takes it for granted that the proper way to describe the fact that is unknown to the speaker in the Gödel–Schmidt scenario is along the lines of (1) "[It turned out that] Gödel did not prove the incompleteness theorem." It is this assumption that is incompatible with descriptivism. But although it seems natural to characterize the situation by employing such a sentence, it isn't necessary. We could instead say, for example, (2) "[It turned out that] the person we took to prove the incompleteness theorem did not in fact prove it." The fact that (2) is a proper way to describe the situation shows that descriptivism is not committed to denying the possibility of the error in question—it is only in conflict with a certain way of describing the relevant error. Of course, this still does not discharge descriptivism from the difficulty raised by the argument under consideration, for descriptivism conflicts with the assumption that (1) is a proper way to describe the situation regardless of whether there are other such ways. (1) appears to be a natural way to describe the situation under consideration. (It is (2) that might seem cumbersome and less natural, though it might not look that way upon recalling that the context in which it is supposed to be avowed is one in which *the only thing* hitherto believed about that person is that he has proven the incompleteness theorem.) I do not wish to suggest that (1) is not a proper way to describe the situation, but that whether it is or it isn't depends on our practice of describing such situations—it depends upon a choice that isn't necessary. For why assume that that person who (so it turned out) hasn't proven the theorem should be referred to by the name "Gödel"? Thus, our taking (1) to be the proper way to describe the situation presupposes the very intuition under consideration: namely, that "Gödel" refers to Gödel. If it isn't taken for granted that "Gödel" refers to Gödel, we cannot take it for granted that (1) is indeed a proper way to describe the error in question.

We have seen that prominent theoretical considerations—insofar as they are taken to rely on no intuitions concerning reference—do not settle issues of reference determination. But a stronger point can be made. It appears that any relevant consideration would presuppose a certain framework of reference ascription as mentioned above. If we don't know the right theory of reference, and we don't

---

[16] MMNS (2013) make a similar point. The fact that the theoretical consideration in question works only negatively in this sense is anything but surprising—see later.

42   INTENTIONALITY DECONSTRUCTED

know how the concept of reference is ever actually applied—that is, we don't know what the practice of reference ascription is and which objects it connects to representations in various cases—then we cannot know what the object of any representation is. We can think of two possible ("a priori") ways to secure such knowledge. The first is that we probe into the representation itself. This way is doomed to fail, because the idea that the intentional function of a representation is encoded in the representation itself, or in the system of representations to which it belongs, makes no sense.[17] The reason for this is that what is encoded in an entity (be it an individual object or state or a system to which such an object or state belongs) requires interpretation. That is, it requires the encoding of an intentional function that interprets it, which would itself require the encoding of an intentional function that interprets it, and so on.[18] The second possible ("a priori") way to secure knowledge of reference is to reflect upon the concept of reference. This way is also doomed to fail, since no such information is contained in the concept of reference. The concept of reference, or intentionality, which is in fact the concept of aboutness, has nothing to do with any specific relation.[19] It is neutral regarding the identity of the intentional function—for example, whether it is some causal function or some descriptive function—and does not prefer any specific relation over any other.

Thus, although theoretical considerations may discover constraints on reference, they fall short of yielding intentional objects and (relatedly) theories of reference determination. So, the philosophers' competence with such considerations is no competence in resolving issues of reference.

2.4 A Lesson for Experimental Philosophical Semantics?

In fact, we have seen that the case against experimental semantics that is based on the (even if implicit) assumption that theoretical considerations can settle issues

---

[17] Intentional functions, recall, are those functions that take us from intentional states to their intentional objects. It might be thought that semantic internalism is committed to the view that the intentional function is internally encoded. But first, this isn't so. Semantic internalism is committed to the view that the arguments of the intentional function are all internal. Consider descriptivism—a paradigm case of internalism. Its proponents claim that names are connected to their bearers by means of a descriptive function, not that this function is encoded in the mental representations that are associated with names. Second, and more importantly, my argument against the claim in question is general and does not presuppose semantic externalism. (Intentional primitivists reject the notion of an intentional function, but I argued against their view in Chapter 1.)

[18] One cannot object to this reasoning by claiming that what is required is not interpretation but rather the obtaining of a connection (e.g., a causal one) between the representation and what it represents, for the current issue is not that of reference but that of knowledge of reference. Relatedly, it is not enough for the present purpose to assume that intentional objects are encoded in their representations in the sense that we can elicit them from their representations *given the intentional function*.

[19] Recall that intentionality is simply (standard-object) aboutness, nothing more. In Chapter 4, I will argue that the conceptual identification of intentionality or reference with any specific relation leaves aboutness out.

of reference, thus leaving no room for appeals to semantic intuitions and for surveys studying them, fails, for this assumption is false. But, further, rejecting the claim that theoretical considerations can completely settle issues of reference also appears to contribute to a positive case in favor of experimental philosophical semantics. For, if indeed (1) theoretical considerations cannot settle issues of reference, (2) giving preference to raw intuitions *of experts* is unjustified, and (3) the universality assumption regarding semantic raw intuitions is undermined, then (4) armchair philosophy of language is in trouble. I argued for the truth of (1) and (2). Given their truth, conducting semantic surveys for finding out whether (3) is true plays an important role in considering the status of armchair philosophical semantics. This is an important role of experimental philosophy. I believe that those semantics surveys indeed undermine the universality assumption, as noted, and thus that (given (2) and (3)) they also undermine armchair philosophical theorizing about reference.

The claim that surveys of the kind under consideration play this role is, of course, different from the claim that such surveys can be taken to settle issues of reference. However, it might be thought that experimental philosophy also sets an alternative way for theorizing about reference. One may reason thus: If theoretical considerations do not suffice to decide on the truth of ascriptions of reference and theories of reference, then the only viable alternative is to appeal to raw semantic intuitions regarding the "predictions" of the relevant theories in various cases. And if there is no advantage to appealing to experts' raw intuitions, and the raw intuitions of all (or most) groups of competent speakers are on a par in their epistemic status, it seems that we should survey folk raw intuitions. Had there been theoretical considerations that completely settle questions of reference, then (as far as those settled cases are concerned) experimental philosophical semantics—as a methodology for uncovering reference—would have lost its sting and conducting surveys for disclosing semantic intuitions would have been, at most, a negligible substitute for the real thing. But according to the reasoning just presented, the inability of theoretical considerations to settle questions of reference seems to open the door for significant experimental philosophical semantics.

It is not my goal to assess the evidential power of intuitions of the kind under consideration, but let me briefly comment on this issue, without attempting to reach conclusivity. We should view such reasoning with suspicion. Insofar as it refers to reference conceived realistically—that is, to reference that is a real, and not merely ascribed, property of its bearer—it commits itself to an idea that cannot be taken for granted at this stage of the discussion: namely, the idea that theorizing about reference conceived realistically is indeed possible.[20] Why assume that folk

---

[20] Theorizing about reference conceived as non-real but merely ascribed property is certainly possible, for it involves an enquiry of the practice of ascriptions of reference. See section 2.5 as well as Chapters 4 and 6.

44 INTENTIONALITY DECONSTRUCTED

intuitions have evidential value (beyond that of experts' intuitions), and, given that theoretical considerations cannot settle issues of reference determination, that theorizing about reference conceived realistically is still a plausible project?[21] As Knobe and Nichols remark:

> In a typical experimental philosophy paper, the evidence being gathered is about the percentages of people who hold various sorts of intuitions, but the theories under discussion are not about people's intuitions but about substantive philo-sophical questions in epistemology, metaphysics, or ethics. It may appear, at least on first glance, that there must be some sleight of hand involved here. How on earth could information about the statistical distribution of intuitions ever give us reason to accept or reject a particular philosophical view?
>
> (Knobe and Nichols 2008, p. 6)

We may call this "the puzzle of experimental philosophy." It certainly applies to experimental philosophical semantics. Recall Deutsch's claim that data concerning speakers' intuitions about reference are merely data for a psychological theory.[22]

It might thus be thought that experimental philosophical semantics has the tragic fate of bringing its own death; that once it has undermined the universality of semantic intuitions, no role is left for it in theorizing about reference. We certainly cannot accept it as a general truth that the existence of (significant) universality in semantic intuitions would be indicative of their truth, but non-universal intuitions do not possess stronger evidential value. Should the majority rule in cases of diversity? Should the intuitions of some group of people count more? Still, some philosophers take "folk" judgments that are expressed in answers to semantic surveys as evidence for the truth of a substantial account of reference (see, e.g., Nichols, Pinillos, and Mallon 2016). Other philosophers approach the issue from a different direction. Thus, Knobe and Nichols' own response to the puzzle they raise is that "First we use the experimental results to develop a theory about the underlying psychological processes that generate people's intuitions; then we use our theory about the psychological processes to determine whether or not those intuitions are warranted" (Knobe and Nichols 2008, p. 8). Such an endeavor goes significantly beyond the systematization of the intuitions reported in surveys. It involves the postulation of intuition generating mechanisms, a pos-tulation which can suggest which intuitions (if any) should be trusted, in cases in which universality is confirmed and in cases in which it is undermined.[23]

---

[21] Recall that there is nothing against which we can test the reliability of intuitions in cases that cannot be settled by theoretical considerations.

[22] Fischer, Engelhardt, and Herbelot (2015) characterize this challenge to experimental philosophy as the challenge of avoiding a naturalistic fallacy. See also Fischer and Collins' (2015) discussion of the issue.

[23] For a similar approach see Fischer, Engelhardt, and Herbelot (2015).

HOW TO SETTLE ISSUES OF INTENTIONALITY   45

Plausibly, the feasibility of this approach to experimental philosophy varies from one domain to another. I believe (though, again, establishing this is not among my goals here) that we have reason to be skeptical about its feasibility when reference is concerned. This is so, because we should be skeptical that an allegedly objective semantic fact, which is supposed to make true a semantic ascription such as that "Gödel" refers to Gödel, participates in any psychological causal mechanism (and differs in causal power from the allegedly objective fact that, e.g., "Gödel" refers to Schmidt). On the other hand, experimental philosophical semantics is feasible and significant if reference is conceived in some irrealist or anti-realist way: that is, if conforming (or failing to conform) to practices of semantic judgments is all there is to the epistemic merit of a content ascription.[24] I argued that had there been theoretical considerations that completely settle issues of reference, then experimental philosophical semantics, as a methodology for uncovering reference, would have lost its sting. In other words, experimental philosophical semantics that seeks to uncover reference is underlain by the view that theoretical considerations cannot settle issues of reference determination. It is only on the assumption that this view is correct, if at all, that raw semantic intuitions can enter the scene—to fill the vacuum. I will now argue that the view that raw semantic intuitions can play such a role invites an anti-realist view of reference. That is, I will suggest a transcendental argument from the possibility of experimental philosophical semantics—from that view that underlies experimental philosophical semantics—to a version of intentional anti-realism. On the assumption that theoretical considerations do not settle questions such as whether "Gödel" refers to Gödel or to Schmidt, I will argue, there is no truth of the matter.

2.5 An Argument for Intentional Anti-Realism

The argument is as follows. In the absence of decisive considerations on such questions, there is no test for the truth of the intuitions in question, other than that of coherence with the practice of reference ascription.[25] So if semantic facts are supposed to lie out there, independent of practice, then, *ex hypothesi*, they make no difference to our knowledge: that is, they are unknowable. Such an epistemic predicament sounds troublesome, and some may consider it a sufficient reason to rule against the obtaining of such facts. But let's strengthen the case. Such alleged semantic facts also make no difference to theoretical considerations,

---

[24] As we shall see in Chapter 5, content ascriptions on such a view can be true (or adequate) in a non-absolute sense, and specifically, they can be practice-dependently true (or practice-dependently adequate).

[25] Note that the present claim concerns the *test* for the truth of intuitions. The claim that there is no practice-independent *criterion* for their truth will be now shown to follow.

46 INTENTIONALITY DECONSTRUCTED

for, recall, theoretical considerations do not suffice to show which semantic facts obtain. Further, such alleged facts make no difference to (first-level) linguistic use, for, as noted, theories of reference need not differ in prediction with respect to such use. What about second-order linguistic use: that is, ascriptions of reference? Trivially, different semantic facts—such as "Gödel" referring to Gödel and "Gödel" referring to Schmidt—would, if they obtain, be correctly ascribed by means of different ascriptions, but speakers would not use a certain ascription because it reflects a semantic fact. Rather, they would use it because they (rightly or wrongly) *believe* (or intuit, if you like) that it reflects a semantic fact. Nor do such semantic facts have explanatory power with respect to any other kinds of behavior. For example, my belief about the identity of the mathematician who proved the incompleteness theorem may explain why I went to attend Gödel's lecture (or why I rather stayed at home), but such an explanation is entirely indifferent to whether my use of "Gödel" refers to Gödel or to Schmidt. So, those supposed semantic facts (1) are unknowable, (2) make no difference to theoretical considerations, (3) make no difference to first-level linguistic use or to second-order linguistic use, (4) have no explanatory power. We can conclude that there is no reason to postulate the obtaining of such practice-independent semantic facts that are supposed to lie out there; moreover, no sense can be given to such postulation. Independently of a practice of content ascription, "Gödel" does not really refer either to Gödel or to Schmidt or to anything else. Independently of such a practice, it cannot. Since the Gödel–Schmidt case serves here as a mere example, this line of thought holds for any expression and any mental concept. The argument holds for "Gödel" thoughts precisely as it holds for "Gödel" utterances. That is, nothing can refer to anything, which is the thesis of intentional anti-realism.[26]

Consider a possible objection to this line of thought. One might draw an analogy between our raw semantic intuitions and our perceptions (or perceptual beliefs) to argue that we have as good a reason to believe that our raw semantic intuitions reflect independent semantic facts as we do for trusting that our perceptions (or perceptual beliefs) reflect independent facts. Shouldn't we assume, similarly, that our semantic intuitions indicate the obtaining of practice-independent semantic facts? I think not. The plausibility of the claim that our perceptions reflect independent facts depends on the plausibility of the claim that (perceived) facts produce perceptions by virtue of some causal mechanisms. For the analogy to work, then, it should be plausible that the independent semantic fact that is supposed to make true a semantic intuition such as that "Gödel" refers to Gödel, produces this intuition by virtue of some causal mechanisms. Further, this fact

---

[26] Jackman (2009) connects experimental philosophical semantics and cultural semantic diversity with the view that semantic intuitions play a constitutive (or "constructive") role with respect to reference. Cohnitz (2015) and Cohnitz and Haukioja (2015) argue for a similar view. There is affinity between the views of these philosophers and my own (though I avoid the terminology of "constituting reference," which may sound realistic), but neither suggests the argumentative move that I suggest here.

should be different in causal powers from the independent semantic fact that, for example, "Gödel" refers to Schmidt. But ascribing such causal features to supposedly independent semantic facts makes no sense. Noticing the causal ineffectiveness of such supposed facts should highlight the force of the argument against them.[27]

This transcendental argument is important for the issue of experimental philosophical semantics, since it shows that the significance of this project, as one that aims to answer the traditional philosophical question of reference (or the question it turns out to be), depends on the truth of intentional anti-realism, which is anything but a trivial thesis. The view that underlies experimental philosophical semantic thus conceived—namely, that no theoretical considerations can settle issues of reference and that raw semantic intuitions are indispensable for settling questions of reference determination—leads to the rejection of semantic facts as independent of any practice of reference ascription. This practice-dependence view of the truth of content ascriptions, and intentional anti-realism in general, will be defended and developed in Chapters 5 and 6. Now, note that this view gives experimental philosophical semantics pride of place, for according to it, the way to know the truth values of content ascriptions, in the sense in which they may be said to be true, must involve acquaintance with the practice (or practices) of content ascription.[28] On this intentional anti-realist approach, the question of reference becomes, to a considerable degree, a psychological-anthropological question. The project of experimental philosophical semantics is essential to answering the traditional philosophical question of reference—or, perhaps better put, the question it turns out to be. The puzzle of experimental philosophy is thus resolved for experimental philosophical semantics.[29]

Our main concern is with the anti-realist approach itself. Recall that the view that underlies experimental philosophical semantics and that was shown to lead to the rejection of semantic facts that are supposed to lie out there, independent of any practice—namely, the view that no theoretical considerations can settle issues of reference—was also argued to be true (on grounds that are independent

---

[27] It might be thought that the relevant analogy here is with moral knowledge—which is supposed to be a priori—rather than with perceptual knowledge. Thus, if a moral realist can present an effective argument for the possibility of moral knowledge (knowledge of moral facts or of whatever entities that are supposed to make moral beliefs true) in the absence of a causal mechanism that connects moral beliefs with the presumed moral facts, then the absence of a causal mechanism that connects semantic intuitions with the presumed semantic facts does not undermine the view that our semantic intuitions attest to there being (practice-independent) semantic facts. However, the analogy breaks down. For the moral realists' arguments for the possibility of moral knowledge (see, e.g., Enoch 2010, 2011) are not supposed to establish the view that moral beliefs may be true—this is the task of direct arguments for moral realism—and our specific issue is that of providing reasons for the claim that content ascriptions may be true. Of course, things would have been different had there been effective arguments for intentional realism, but I argue throughout the book against any argument that I know of in favor of this thesis.

[28] This is true insofar as the assumed practice is the actual one. See Chapter 5.

[29] I expand on this issue in Horowitz (2015a).

48 INTENTIONALITY DECONSTRUCTED

of experimental philosophical semantics). Thus, if the transcendental argument presented above is effective, the rejection of such semantic facts is established. And since this view regarding the insufficiency of theoretical considerations for settling issues of reference was argued to be true on general grounds, it seems to apply to expressions of all kinds, and to mental states of all kinds (e.g., it applies to "Gödel"-involving thoughts precisely as it applies to "Gödel"-involving utterances of sentences). It might seem, then, that the argument establishes a thoroughgoing intentional anti-realism.

Still, for several reasons, the strength of this argument is limited. First, it might be that the argument cannot be unrestrictedly generalized, because issues of reference can be settled in some cases by means other than theoretical considerations (or intuitive judgments). Specifically, in the case of some kinds of mental states, it might be that issues of reference can be settled by directly observing them: that is, by introspecting them. Some philosophers who accept the phenomenal intentionality thesis argue for this view. I argue against it in Chapter 3. Second, it is of the nature of such arguments—arguments that rule against differences which make no difference—that reasons in favor of the thesis that they attempt to undermine not only add evidential support for that thesis (support which may be weighed against the evidential support lent by them), but also undermine the arguments themselves. Thus, if plausible reasons are provided in favor of intentional realism, the argument above should be rejected. However, that nature of such arguments may also work in their own favor. Indeed, in Chapters 5 and 6 I criticize the central reasons suggested in favor of intentional realism, and thus not only remove obstacles to intentional anti-realism, but also supplement the present argument in favor of intentional anti-realism in a way that turns it into a powerful argument (showing, we may say, that intentional realists cannot carry the burden of proof that the original argument shifts upon them).[30]

---

[30] The claim that supposedly practice-independent semantic facts lack explanatory power with respect to behavior may raise issues that require clarification. I provide this further clarification in Chapter 6, in discussing the argument from the predictive and explanatory success of content ascriptions.

3

Against Phenomenal Intentionality as Intrinsic Reductive Intentionality

3.1 Preliminaries for Phenomenal Intentionality

I argued, in Chapter 1, that intentionality cannot be primitive. In other words, I argued that "If aboutness is real, it must be really something else" (as Fodor put it), and in still other words, that intentionality—if real—is reducible. What can intentionality be reduced to? There are three main approaches to this issue in the philosophical literature: the reductive-naturalistic approach, the phenomenal intentionality approach, and the normativist approach. We can also divide the possible reductive approaches along another dimension: some are intrinsic reductions and some are extrinsic reductions. In reductions of the first kind, the intentionality of a mental state is reduced to an intrinsic property of this intentional state: that is, to a property the state possesses in itself, independently of the instantiation of any property by any other entity. In reductions of the second kind, the intentionality of a mental state is reduced to an extrinsic (i.e., non-intrinsic) property of the intentional state. Phenomenal intentionality reductions fall into the first category (though there may be an extrinsic variation of such reductions as well—see later in this chapter), while naturalistic reductions fall into the second.[1]

In the present chapter, I argue against intrinsic reductions of intentionality at large, but the main focus will be on phenomenal intentionality reductions.[2] I attempt to show that intentionality cannot be reduced to, or grounded in, phenomenal consciousness. In fact, I argue against the idea that phenomenal consciousness plays a role—even a partial one—in constituting intentionality: for example, that it secures content determinacy. ("Reduce," "ground," and "constituted by" are used here more or less interchangeably, but in some contexts their

---

[1] Normativist reductions of the kind that is relevant to our issue are extrinsic reductions, and I will address them in the next chapter.

Note that short-armed functional role reductions, according to which properties of other mental states are determiners of the content of a mental state, are extrinsic reductions in this sense. We may say that they are *extrinsic intra-mental reductions*. But for convenience, and since (as argued in Chapter 1), such reductions leave out the essence of intentionality, I will hereafter assign the expression "extrinsic reduction" to refer to the *extra-mental* reductions that will be discussed in Chapter 4.

[2] I do not discuss in this chapter primitivist (non-reductive) theories of intrinsic intentionality, since I argued in Chapter 1 against any primitivist approach to intentionality.

Intentionality Deconstructed: An Anti-Realist Theory. Amir Horowitz, Oxford University Press.
© Amir Horowitz 2024. DOI: 10.1093/oso/9780198896432.003.0003

50 INTENTIONALITY DECONSTRUCTED

different nuances will be in play.) I will both criticize arguments for the thesis of phenomenal intentionality (with an emphasis on the argument from introspection) and suggest arguments against it. I will also generalize my case against the thesis of phenomenal intentionality, showing this case to undermine the very idea of (non-primitive) intrinsic intentionality.

There are various views regarding the connections between phenomenal consciousness and intentionality. On the one hand, there are theories—usually referred to as "representationalist"—that attempt to reduce phenomenal consciousness to intentionality. For (pure) representationalists, the phenomenal character of a mental state is determined by its representational content.[3] On the other hand, there are views that reduce intentionality to, or ground it in, phenomenal consciousness. My concern here is with such views. There are some views according to which the intentional determines the phenomenal and is also determined by it, and usually (though not always) such views are not considered reductive. I will discuss both views that advocate only unidirectional dependence—of the intentional on the phenomenal—and views that advocate symmetrical dependence. We shall see that these different kinds of views differ in their significance.

The conscious states that are supposed to determine intentionality are phenomenally conscious states, those that instantiate a what-it's-like element. Since other forms of consciousness—various forms of cognitive consciousness such as access consciousness—presuppose intentionality, intentionality cannot be reduced to any of them, and phenomenal consciousness is the only candidate.[4] The thesis according to which intentionality is grounded in phenomenal consciousness is usually called "the phenomenal intentionality thesis" (or "PIT"), and I shall use this expression in this sense. Some proponents of theses that are thus referred to have in mind different ideas, and sometimes a different understanding of "intentionality." More has to be said and will be said (in sections 3.2 and 3.3) about the meaning of this thesis.[5]

---

[3] For pure representationalism, see Bourget (2010) and Thau (2002). Most representationalists are impure representationalists: for them, phenomenal character is constituted by representational content *plus* some (functional) feature (see, e.g., Tye 1995; Dretske 1995; Jackson 2004). For impure non-reductive representationalism, see Chalmers (2004). Different from both are higher-order thought (or higher-order representation) theories of phenomenal consciousness (see Rosenthal 1986, 1993, 2004, 2005; Lycan 1996; Gennaro 1996; Carruthers 1996, 2000, 2005). Such theories are sometimes characterized as attempts to reduce phenomenal consciousness to "second-order intentionality."

[4] Note that, for this very reason, phenomenal intentionalists cannot argue that intentionality is reducible to phenomenal consciousness while phenomenal consciousness is reducible (even partly) to intentional cognitive elements. The view that intentionality is reducible to phenomenal consciousness while phenomenal consciousness is reducible to functional relations among mental states, regardless of these states' intentionality, is not subject to the same difficulty, but it is subject to another one: that is, to the inability of functional role theories to account for intentionality (see Chapters 1 and 4).

On the distinction between phenomenal consciousness and cognitive consciousness see Block (1995).

[5] For various versions of the phenomenal intentionality view, see Chalmers (2004, 2006, 2010), Farkas (2008a, 2008b, 2013), Georgalis (2006), Horgan and Graham (2012), Horgan, Tienson, and Graham (2004), Horgan and Tienson (2002), Kriegel (2007, 2011, 2016), Loar (1987, 1995, 2003), Masrour (2013), McGinn (1991), Mendelovici (2018), Mendelovici and Bourget (2020), Mendola

What motivates views that ground intentionality in consciousness? One motivation that underlies such views concerns the idea of intrinsic intentionality. The view of phenomenal intentionality (as understood by most of its proponents) is the prevalent version of this idea. This view is, trivially, a reductive view,[6] but at the same time, on the assumption (which is accepted by most proponents of this view) that phenomenal consciousness is an intrinsic property of mental states, this view is committed to the idea that intentionality is an intrinsic property of mental states. That is, this view takes various mental states to have intentionality in themselves, independently of the instantiation of any property by any *other* entity (and so, trivially, regardless of interpretation and of any stance one adopts toward them). The mind is intentional, on such a view, since the mind is conscious; and it is intrinsically intentional, since it is intrinsically conscious.[7] Thus, endorsing this view appears to be a plausible choice for those who are attracted by the supposed intrinsicality of mental intentionality—in contrast to linguistic intentionality, for example—and are not satisfied with intentional primitivism.

It is typical of views that ground intentionality in consciousness in one way or another that they take intentionality to be deeply related to the first-person point of view. This seems to be part of their appeal. A prominent reason for the certainty that appears to characterize our epistemic attitude toward our having intentional properties concerns the fact that intentionality *seems* to be a first-person characteristic, one that is directly accessible from the first-person perspective. The importance of the idea of first-person intentionality and of its manifestation as phenomenal intentionality works also in the opposite direction: once we are convinced in its falsity, a central motivation for intentional realism loses its sting. If it is not the case that intentionality is that close to us (as I will indeed argue), then it is not so preposterous to maintain that it is a chimera; the issue becomes one of theoretical consideration rather than of direct evidence.

The idea of phenomenal intentionality as intrinsic intentionality is also related to the idea that the conscious mind is the source of all intentionality. According to the latter idea, the intentionality of everything other than the conscious mind is grounded in the intentionality of the conscious mind. On this approach, the intentionality of the conscious mind is original, whereas the intentionality of all

---

(2008), Montague (2009, 2016), Pautz (2008, 2013, 2021), Pitt (2004, 2009); Searle (1989, 1992), Siewert (1998), Smithies (2013a, 2013b), Speaks (2015), Strawson (2010), and Woodward (2019).

[6] Though the expression "phenomenal intentionality" is used to apply to views such as Pautz's (2013, 2021), who takes the intentional relation of sensory experiences to be the irreducible source of all determinate intentionality.

[7] On one level of analysis, proponents of the thesis that reduces intentionality to consciousness need not endorse the view that consciousness is an intrinsic property of the mind—they can endorse phenomenal externalism (which is usually, though not always, presented as an intrinsicist view). In fact, most of them do endorse the intrinsicist view. On another level of analysis, phenomenal externalism is not an option for proponents of the phenomenal intentionality thesis (as we shall see in section 3.3), and for this reason it makes sense to focus on phenomenal intentionality as intrinsic intentionality.

52 INTENTIONALITY DECONSTRUCTED

other entities—if real and not merely ascribed—is derived: it is derived from the intentionality of the conscious mind. An intentional non-conscious entity (e.g., the utterance of a sentence) inherits, or derives, its content from a conscious entity with the same content. Intrinsic intentionality is necessarily original, as noted in Chapter 1, yet the notion of original intentionality has importance of its own in the context of phenomenal intentionality, for a prominent motivation for the introduction of the notion of phenomenal intentionality is precisely to identify the source of all (real) intentionality.

The idea of a source of intentionality is important for the combination of the following two reasons. First, unless there is original intentionality there is no intentionality at all,[8] and second, various cases that appear to be cases of intentionality also appear to be cases that lack original intentionality. Language is the prominent example. It appears that utterances of sentences, for example, could have different meanings from those they have, and this implies that their meanings are not intrinsic to them. But further, it seems that what lies behind the possible variation of the utterances' meanings is the utterances' relations to mental intentional states. So, those meanings appear to be derived ones, and thus, in order for them to be real (rather than merely ascribed) the source from which they derive (the ultimate source, at any rate, even if not the immediate one) must have original intentionality.

The intentionality of this supposed ultimate source—the mind—indeed appears to be original. For one thing, intentional attitudes appear not to be subject to that variability and dependence to which language is subject. As Searle put it,

> [T]here is no way the agent can have a belief or a desire without it having its conditions of satisfaction...that the belief has those conditions of satisfaction is not something imposed on the belief by its being *used* in one way rather than another, for the belief is not in that sense *used* at all. A belief is intrinsically a representation...it simply consists in an Intentional content and a psychological mode.   (Searle 1983, p. 22)

If indeed beliefs are intrinsically intentional, then their intentionality, as noted, is original. However, the assumption that beliefs are not used (which is not self-evident) does not mean that they have intrinsic intentionality, and thus does not entail that they have original intentionality. It might be that they have their contents in virtue of bearing some naturalistic relations to environmental items, or that they do not have real contents at all (but merely ascribed ones). We shall later

---

[8] Dennett (1987b, 1990) argues, along such lines, that indeed there is no real intentionality, though he employs different terminology (e.g., he uses the expression "intrinsic intentionality" in the way I use "original intentionality," or in a way close to it).

see that the appearance in question is indeed misleading, and that the very idea of intrinsic intentionality is flawed.

This is not to say that mental states, including phenomenal ones, cannot be the source of intentionality. If some reductive-naturalistic account for the intentionality of the mental is true, then mental states may have original intentionality, and, arguably, be the sources of all intentionality.[9] So, undermining the idea of intrinsic mental intentionality, on which mental states possess their intentionality by virtue of their mental nature (be this nature phenomenal or other), does not necessarily undermine the idea of the mind as the locus of original intentionality and the source of (all) intentionality.

Still, the role of the idea of intrinsic mental intentionality, and specifically, of the more plausible representative of this idea—phenomenal intentionality (that takes the relevant mental nature to be phenomenal nature)—in enabling the mind to be the ultimate source of intentionality, is unique. On this idea, it is the mental nature of (some) mental states that enables them to have original intentionality. On the other hand, it is essential to the reductive-naturalistic picture that the privileged semantic status of the mind (if it has such) is not anchored in its supposedly unique intrinsic nature, and the intentionality of language can be accounted for in principally the same way as the intentionality of the mind. Indeed, in such a picture the semantic priority of the mental is—if it exists—"deeply contingent," and there are naturalistic approaches that account straightforwardly for the intentionality of language (e.g., Stampe 1977; Millikan 1984), and even assign it priority (e.g., Sellars 1963; Harman 1999). (See Chapter 4.)

* * *

Since this chapter is particularly long, let me present a road map of its following sections. In section 3.2 I initially present the thesis of phenomenal intentionality. In section 3.3 I further elaborate on the meaning of this thesis, emphasizing its concern with grounding intentionality in phenomenal character. This elaboration sheds light on the status of various accounts of intentionality in terms of phenomenality as reductions. In section 3.4 I present and criticize arguments for the thesis of phenomenal intentionality, with special emphasis on the argument from introspection. In section 3.5 I discuss the issue of conceptual connections between intentionality and consciousness. I first present and criticize the arguments of Searle and McGinn that attempt to establish connections between these phenomena, and then use my criticism as a step in an argument to the effect that there are no such connections, and so the notion of a conceptual intentionality-to-phenomenality reduction should be rejected. In section 3.6 I argue that the very idea of synthetic intentionality-to-phenomenality reduction should be rejected. Thus, I present a case against the very idea of the phenomenal intentionality

---

[9] In fact, I think that the idea of content derivation is flawed. See Horowitz (2021).

54 INTENTIONALITY DECONSTRUCTED

thesis. In section 3.7 I show that the arguments of the previous sections actually target the ideas of intrinsic conceptual reductions and of intrinsic synthetic reductions, respectively, and so we should reject the very idea that intentionality is reducible to any intrinsic mental property, not only to phenomenal consciousness. In section 3.8 I discuss the suggestion that consciousness secures content determinacy and show that it should be rejected for the same reasons that undermine the idea of phenomenal intentionality. In section 3.9 I explain what has been shown and what has not been shown in this chapter regarding phenomenal intentionality.

3.2 The Phenomenal Intentionality Thesis

According to the thesis of phenomenal intentionality that will be our focus:

> Conscious intentional states are intrinsically, *by their very [phenomenal] nature*, directed toward whatever they are directed toward.
> (Horgan and Tienson 2002, p. 530)

The basic idea of this thesis is that conscious mental states of various kinds determine, or constitute, or ground, intentionality; more specifically, it is the conscious phenomenal character of these states that constitutes their intentional profile. Thus, Horgan and Tienson defend the thesis that

> There is a kind of intentionality, pervasive in human mental life, that is constitutively determined by phenomenology alone.   (p. 520)

This kind of intentionality is pervasive, according to Horgan and Tienson. It is instantiated not only by those mental states that are standardly referred to as "experiences," but also by, for example, propositional attitudes, which, Horgan and Tienson argue, also have phenomenal characters, ones which are inseparable from their intentional contents.[10] In what follows I will ignore the issue of how pervasive this kind of intentionality—"phenomenal intentionality"—is, and use "the phenomenal intentionality thesis," or "PIT," to refer to the thesis that

There is a kind of intentionality that is constitutively determined by phenomenology alone.

---

[10] The idea that propositional attitudes have characteristic phenomenology and that it plays a role in determining their content has received much attention recently—see, for example, the contributions to Bayne and Montague (2011). I do not address this idea specifically, since my case against the phenomenal intentionality thesis is intended to apply to mental states of all kinds. For a critique of the idea that cognitive phenomenology plays a role in constituting intentionality see, for example, Pautz (2013, 2021). For a general overview of the debate over cognitive phenomenology, see Sacchi and Voltolini (2017).

According to this thesis, the relevant phenomenal states have intentional contents in themselves—regardless of any external facts, regardless of interpretation, regardless of any stance one adopts toward them. They have their intentional contents intrinsically. The intentionality of those mental states is an intrinsic property of the mind, according to PIT, since it is grounded in another mental property that is an intrinsic property of the mind: namely, phenomenal character. This thesis—and in particular what the constitution in question requires—will be further explicated as we go along. For now, it is worth emphasizing that the phenomenal intentionality thesis as presented here yields an answer to the question of intentionality: that is, to the question in virtue of what mental states of certain kinds possess their intentionality. Its answer is that it is in virtue of their phenomenal characters. It is theories of phenomenal intentionality that purport to provide answers to the question of intentionality, and only such theories of phenomenal intentionality, that are our focus here. The success of such theories would amount to establishing the existence of phenomenally constituted intentionality. Note that establishing *that* intentionality is constituted by phenomenal character need not involve explaining *how* its phenomenal character enables a mental state to be directed upon its intentional object. Answering this hard question is one way of answering the question of intentionality. I will refer to this issue later in this chapter.

3.3 Phenomenal Intentionality as Grounding Intentionality

I will now provide further clarification of the nature of the question with which we are concerned in this chapter and show that it is not addressed by various theories that connect intentionality with phenomenality. Let's start with a distinction drawn by Uriah Kriegel. Kriegel (2011) characterized the thesis of phenomenal intentionality as the thesis that conscious experiences have intentional properties *in virtue of their phenomenal characters*, and distinguishes two senses of that locution. One is the doctrinal sense, in which the intentional property of an intentional state is grounded in its phenomenal character. The other is the neutral sense, in which the intentional property of an intentional state merely counterfactually depends on its phenomenal character, so that, had the experience not had its phenomenal character, then it would not have had this intentional property. Kriegel commits himself to the thesis of phenomenal intentionality in the neutral, weaker, sense. He states that "my concern in this book is not to argue for the primacy of the experiential over the intentional, merely for the primacy of the experiential-intentional over the non-experiential intentional" (p. 45). Thus, in Kriegel's picture, although phenomenal experiences are the source of intentionality, intentionality is not grounded in phenomenal character. Indeed, Kriegel suggests another account for the constitution of the intentionality of experience—a

56 INTENTIONALITY DECONSTRUCTED

reductive-naturalistic account that does not mention the phenomenal characters of experiences (although intentionality counterfactually depends on them in his picture).[11]

My general interest, recall, is with theories that ground intentionality in something else, and thus answer the question of intentionality. And the concern of the present chapter is with such theories where the something-else is phenomenal consciousness—theories the success of which would amount to establishing the existence of phenomenally constituted intentionality. This concern dictates the theories of phenomenal intentionality that are my focus here, and the theories that are not. Only theories according to which phenomenal states have intentional properties in virtue of their phenomenal characters in Kriegel's doctrinal sense fit this characterization; theories that are satisfied with phenomenal–intentional counterfactual dependence, or supervenience, do not. Kriegel's own theory of intentionality falls into the latter category. According to it, phenomenal states have intentional properties in virtue of their phenomenal characters in the neutral sense (we may refer to this aspect of Kriegel's theory as its "phenomenalist aspect"), and they have them in virtue of some naturalistic non-phenomenal properties in the doctrinal sense of "in virtue" (this is the "non-phenomenalist aspect"). Such a theory provides a response to the question of intentionality, but this response does not concern phenomenal character. An account that consists in the phenomenalist aspect of Kriegel's twofold account (i.e., one that leaves out the naturalistic non-phenomenalist aspect)—even if successful—would leave the question of intentionality unanswered, for it would leave a gap between the non-intentional and the intentional. Such an account does not show what it is about phenomenal characters that makes states that possess them intentional. An account that consists in the non-phenomenalist aspect (i.e., that leaves out the phenomenalist aspect)—if successful—would answer the question, leaving no gap between the non-intentional and the intentional, and so it is the non-phenomenalist aspect that does the work. Bridging the gap—reducing the intentional to the non-intentional—is what makes an account an answer to the question of intentionality. If we wish to examine the soundness of accounts that provide such answers by appealing to phenomenal character, we have to consider only such "doctrinal" accounts of phenomenal intentionality, to which I reserve the name "the phenomenal intentionality thesis," or "PIT." The issue goes far beyond terminology. It concerns the very basis of intentionality and might have implications concerning its very existence.

Theories that hold mere dependence of the intentional on the phenomenal are not alone, among theories that connect intentionality with phenomenality, in failing to deliver the goods in question. So do theories that take intentionality and

---

[11] Kriegel (2011) also suggests an adverbialist account of intentionality, but he assigns higher probability to the truth of the reductive-naturalistic account.

phenomenal consciousness to be mutually dependent. Whether or not we refer to such theories as "reductive," they do not ground intentionality in phenomenal character in the relevant sense of "grounding": namely, that in which the claim that intentionality is grounded in some phenomenon answers the question of intentionality. Consider pure (phenomenal) representationalism, the view that phenomenal character is exhaustively determined by representational content. Since on such a view the phenomenal characters of experiences are inherently intentional, this view might seem to support PIT. Yet, this is misleading. It is not only that pure representationalism does not support PIT (in the sense under consideration), but further, the two views are incompatible. For if phenomenal characters are inherently intentional, then they can only be said to constitute intentionality *as being themselves constituted by intentionality*. (Of course, the intentionality in the *explanans* is the same as the intentionality in the *explanandum*.) This holds true also for impure representationalism, on which the intentionality of experience is only part of what constitutes its phenomenality, for this view too is committed to the idea that phenomenality is inherently intentional. The view that intentionality is grounded in phenomenality is incompatible with the view that phenomenality is grounded in intentionality. Grounding is essentially asymmetrical, for alleged mutual grounding of two phenomena would leave the two phenomena in the air, away from the ground. Relatedly, if it is committed to either version of representationalism, the phenomenal intentionality thesis can only provide a *virtus dormitiva* explanation of intentionality.

Referring to Angela Mendelovici's approach to phenomenal intentionality may shed further light on the issue. Mendelovici (2018) shows that even a theory that identifies consciousness with intentionality may be said to be a theory of one of these phenomena in terms of the other and not vice versa. She advocates the view that intentionality arises from phenomenal consciousness in the sense that it is nothing over and above it. Further, on her view (which she calls "strong identity PIT*"), intentionality arises from phenomenal consciousness (not by, for example, being grounded in it, but) *by being identical to it*—intentionality and phenomenal consciousness are one and the same thing. Mendelovici admits that there is no ground to consider strong identity PIT* as, in itself, a theory of intentionality in terms of consciousness rather than a theory of consciousness in terms of intentionality. However, she argues that there is ground to thus consider the conjunction of strong PIT* and an additional assumption. This additional assumption is that the phenomenon of intentionality/phenomenal consciousness "has more of the characteristics we might have previously attributed to phenomenal consciousness than the characteristics we might have previously attributed to intentionality" (p. 111). It is thus "more like what we generally take phenomenal consciousness to be like than what we generally take intentionality to be like" (p. 112), and this view may be said to "fit" the intentional unto the phenomenal. Mendelovici indeed argues for this assumption. For her, intentionality/phenomenal

58   INTENTIONALITY DECONSTRUCTED

consciousness is closer to (pre-theoretical) phenomenal consciousness than to (pre-theoretical) intentionality due to the following four characteristics: being scarce, being internalist, being non-relational, and being resistant to naturalization. Thus, there is a sense in which her theory is a theory of intentionality in terms of phenomenal consciousness—the symmetry that characterizes the relation between intentionality and phenomenal consciousness on this identity theory notwithstanding.[12]

I think that Mendelovici highlights an interesting sense in which consciousness may be prior to intentionality even if the two are identical, and—assuming that her claim as to the primacy of phenomenal consciousness is true—she thus motivates taking her (extended) theory as a theory of intentionality in terms of consciousness. I do not dwell on the question whether this claim is true, for the notion of intentionality that figures in it—and which is the notion that is the focus of Mendelovici's project of phenomenal intentionality—is not my focus here. In particular, Mendelovici's notion of intentionality does not, in itself, concern reference and truth conditions.[13] And anyway, theories that advocate symmetric dependence between consciousness and intentionality cannot provide an adequate reply to the question of intentionality even if they give priority to consciousness in the above-mentioned sense. To see this, consider the question of what makes an experience (originally) intentional. If Mendelovici's theory is taken to provide an answer to this question, its answer cannot be anything but that it is the phenomenal character of an experience that makes it intentional. (It is certainly not the four characteristics mentioned above.) But then we must understand this theory as also committed to the view that it is an experience's intentionality that makes it phenomenal. So, according to this theory, phenomenal character makes experience intentional being itself intentional. On such an approach, you cannot get intentionality by injecting (to use Kriegel's terminology) something other than intentionality into the world. If you inject phenomenal character into the world, you get intentionality merely because it is not something else. This (primitivist) approach to intentionality specifies what makes something intentional only circularly: that is, by appealing to the intentional.[14]

---

[12] For other theories that take phenomenal character and intentionality to be mutually dependent, see Chalmers (2004) and Pautz (2008).

[13] It is "The feature that in paradigm cases we sometimes both (i) notice introspectively in ourselves and (ii) are tempted to describe using representational terms, such as 'about,' 'of,' 'represent,' 'present,' or 'saying something'" (Mendelovici 2018, p. 6). Note that Mendelovici does not define intentionality *as* aboutness. Sacchi argues (on grounds different from those I suggest) that this feature cannot be "identified with intentionality, notwithstanding the fact that we tend to describe it using terms like 'of' or 'about'" (Sacchi 2022, p. 690).

[14] Mendelovici does not regard her view of intentionality as primitivist; she takes it to be a reductivist view. The reason for this is that on her view intentionality "arises from"—that is, it is nothing over and above—something else. Beyond the terminological issue of the meaning of "primitivism" and "reductivism," there is a substantial issue here. The important point for me is that theories on which you only get intentionality by injecting intentionality into the world do not answer the question

All theories on which consciousness and intentionality are symmetrically dependent on each other fail to tell us non-circularly what must be injected into the world to get intentionality. We can see that the claim I made about phenomenal intentionality and representationalism remains intact: a theory of phenomenal intentionality that does give a substantive answer to the question of intentionality—a theory according to which phenomenal character constitutes intentional content—is incompatible with representationalism, which presupposes intentionality. A fortiori, representationalism does not support such a theory.

Similarly, the thesis of phenomenal externalism, according to which external objects play a role in constituting phenomenal character (see, e.g., Byrne and Tye 2006; Dretske 1995, 1996; Hill 2009; Lycan 2001; Tye 2000), is incompatible with PIT. On a version of phenomenal externalism that is a conjunction of representationalism and semantic externalism (or at any rate on one that is committed to the view that the external object that is constitutive of phenomenal character is an intentional object of the experience), phenomenal character can only constitute intentionality as being constituted by intentionality. Hence, this version conflicts with the idea of phenomenal intentionality as grounding intentionality. On a version of phenomenal externalism that does not involve representationalism, the externalist nature it attributes to phenomenal characters is irrelevant to intentionality and so to the phenomenal intentionality thesis.

Note that the reasoning presented above does not target all intentionality-phenomenality identity theories. It undermines the explanatory power of those identity theories that do not, in themselves (independently of other assumptions), assign priority to any of the properties to be identified, such as the conjunction of (phenomenal) representationalism and PIT. This point can be realized by considering the analogy that Mendelovici draws between her theory of intentionality and the mind–brain identity theory. The latter theory, "which states that every mental state is identical to some brain state, is compatible with the claim that every brain state happens to be identical to some mental state" (Mendelovici 2018, p. 111), and the theory that combines both claims is "a theory of mental states in terms of brain states rather than a theory of brain states in terms of mental states...for mental/brain states are, at bottom, more like what we previously thought brain states are like than the other way around" (p. 111). It might be argued that this analogy also undermines my claim that a theory that advocates phenomenal–intentional identity does not answer the question of intentionality, However, there is a significant difference between the two theories, for the mind–brain identity theory, as standardly conceived, states, non-circularly, what makes something mental: namely, the possession of some physical properties. Thus, it gives priority to the physical over the mental, and in this crucial respect is not analogous to

---

of intentionality and do not explain the occurrence of this phenomenon. (The argument from Chapter 1 against the primitivist approach to intentionality applies also to such theories.)

60 INTENTIONALITY DECONSTRUCTED

Mendelovici's thesis of phenomenal intentionality. The mind–brain theory that is analogous to Mendelovici's thesis would be one that does not give priority to the physical over the mental. It would not be satisfied with stating that what makes something mental (or have its specific mental nature) is its physical nature, but rather would add that what makes something physical (or neural, or have a specific neural character) is its mental character. Such a theory specifies what makes something mental only circularly: that is, by appealing to the mental. On such an approach, you cannot get mentality by injecting something other than mentality into the world; if you inject the relevant physical structure into the world, you get mentality merely because it is not something else—because it involves mentality. It is such theories—theories that are committed to a bidirectional dependence—that lack explanatory power according to the reasoning presented above.

As we have seen, according to the phenomenal intentionality thesis that is our focus, phenomenal character constitutes (or grounds) intentionality; it is what makes various mental states intentional. I take this idea of the constitution of intentionality as not allowing phenomenal character to constitute intentionality whilst phenomenal character *is itself intentional*, and I am going to address this idea as thus understood. This choice is not arbitrary. It is based on the notion that those theories according to which phenomenal character is supposed to constitute intentionality being itself intentional do not non-circularly answer the question of intentionality; thus, they fail to tell us what makes something intentional—what must be put into an entity to make it intentional—and to establish the existence of intentionality by establishing the existence of phenomenally constituted intentionality.[15] Relatedly, if taken to provide explanations for the phenomenon of intentionality, the explanations in question would be *virtus dormitiva* explanations.

3.4 Arguments for the Phenomenal Intentionality Thesis

3.4.1 The Accuracy Conditions Argument

Why should we believe the thesis of phenomenal intentionality? Let's start with Charles Siewert's argument for this thesis. According to Siewert (1998, pp. 188ff.),

---

[15] Of course, theories according to which intentional properties are primitive properties of experiences also do not suggest answers to the question of intentionality. For a primitivist form of PIT, see Woodward (2019). Pautz, who charges the phenomenal intentionality approach with "just saying" that conscious experience explains intentionality and leaving it at that, suggests a multistage theory of intentionality, the first stage of which takes the intentional relation of sensory experiences—"the *conscious-of* relation"—to be an irreducible relation (see Pautz 2013, 2021). He thus "leaves it at that," precisely like full-blown phenomenal intentionality theorists. The other stages of Pautz's theory employ the interpretivist (or "best system theory") approach of David Lewis and his "naturalness" principle. I take interpretivism to be subject to indeterminacy and thus to be an anti-realist approach to intentionality (see, e.g., Dennett 1978b). I further believe that Lewisian naturalness is problematic (see Chapter 4).

AGAINST PHENOMENAL INTENTIONALITY AS INTRINSIC REDUCTION   61

conscious experiences are often assessable as accurate or inaccurate in virtue of their phenomenal characters—their phenomenal characters endow them with accuracy conditions. Since having accuracy conditions is having an intentional property, some conscious experiences have intentional properties in virtue of their phenomenal characters: that is, the thesis of phenomenal intentionality is true.

The crucial step in this argument is the premise that conscious experiences are often assessable for accuracy in virtue of their phenomenal characters. I think that Siewert is only entitled to this premise if it is taken to mean that, as a matter of fact, we often take conscious experiences to be assessable for accuracy in virtue of their phenomenal characters, or, in other words, that we assign them accuracy conditions in virtue of their phenomenal characters. However, this is certainly not enough to yield the conclusion that conscious experiences have intentional properties in virtue of their phenomenal characters; it only yields the conclusion that we assign them intentional properties in virtue of their phenomenal characters. And the difference between these two conclusions is of utmost importance. It is the difference between the thesis of phenomenal intentionality—which, due to its commitment to experiences' having real contents in virtue of their phenomenal characters, may be dubbed "phenomenal intentional realism"—and the thesis we may dub "phenomenal intentional ascriptivism," which is committed to our ascribing intentional contents to phenomenal states in virtue of their phenomenal properties, but is not committed to the reality of those ascribed contents. Establishing the latter thesis may be a worthwhile project, but not in the context of asking whether content ascriptions are ever true or can be true.[16] We shall see in sections 3.4.2, 3.4.3, and 3.5.2 that yet other arguments for the thesis of phenomenal intentionality fail to support a thesis stronger than phenomenal intentional ascriptivism.

3.4.2 The Empirical Adequacy Argument

It is common practice in theorizing about intentionality and reference to defend theories by appealing to their "empirical adequacy" and to the empirical inadequacy of their rivals. (Reliance on these is an instance of the method of cases.) Some proponents of phenomenal intentionality also appeal to considerations of empirical adequacy in supporting their views, though none of them, to the best of my knowledge, takes such considerations, in themselves, to provide conclusive

---

[16] For another criticism of Siewert's argument, see Gertler (2001). For a response, see Siewert (2004). Mendelovici (2018, p. 92, n. 14) doubts Siewert's claim that intentional states give rise to accuracy conditions all by themselves, and suggests a revised version of Siewert's argument. I will address this argument upon criticizing the argument from introspection in section 3.4.3.

62 INTENTIONALITY DECONSTRUCTED

evidence in support of any version of this thesis. At any rate, showing the empirical adequacy of the phenomenal intentionality thesis—that is, that its "predictions" match our practice of content ascriptions—falls short of establishing it. Empirical adequacy in this sense is a necessary condition for the truth of the phenomenal intentionality thesis but not a sufficient one. Mendelovici and Bourget (2020) and Mendelovici (2018) argue for the phenomenal intentionality thesis on the grounds of its empirical adequacy (which they take to consist in matching content ascriptions there are good empirical reasons to accept) and the empirical inadequacy of its main competitors, but they show awareness of the fact that empirical adequacy is not enough to support this thesis. Its success, they admit, depends on phenomenal consciousness' having the power to give rise to intentionality (Mendelovici and Bourget 2020, p. 20, n. 20). The empirical adequacy of the thesis in question can only support phenomenal intentional ascriptivism.[17] A central goal of the present chapter is to show that phenomenal consciousness does not have the power to give rise to intentionality, and so that phenomenal intentional realism is false. In a context that calls intentional realism in general and phenomenal intentional realism in particular into question, a move from phenomenal intentional ascriptivism to phenomenal intentional realism is not allowed.[18]

3.4.3 The Argument from Introspection

Perhaps the main reason for the widely held belief that mental states of various kinds are intentional—that is, for intentional realism—is that we simply know this from the inside. Horgan and Tienson's argument for the phenomenal intentionality thesis is along these lines. They support this thesis by appealing to introspection. Introspection reveals, they maintain, that when seeing red things, the red that we see is seen as a property of objects, objects that are seen as located in a three-dimensional space, rather than as an introspectable property of one's own experiential state. Introspection shows that "the what-it's-like of experiencing red is already intentional, because it involves red as the intentional object of one's experience" (Horgan and Tienson 2002, p. 521). It is built into the phenomenology of the experience that it is experience *of*—it is an experience of something

---

[17] Mendelovici and Bourget's notion of intentionality (which does not concern reference and truth conditions) as well as their version of the phenomenal intentionality thesis are different from those that are the focus of this book, but their claim that the success of the empirical adequacy consideration to defend the phenomenal intentionality thesis depends on phenomenal consciousness' having the power to give rise to intentionality straightforwardly applies to the version discussed here.

[18] There are several other arguments for phenomenal intentionality that (implicitly) assume intentional realism, and so are irrelevant to a work that calls this assumption into question. Such are arguments according to which PIT is the best explanation of internalism, or of narrow content (see Loar 2003; Horgan, Tienson, and Graham 2004; Farkas 2008a), and Kriegel's (2007) argument to the effect that PIT best explains the phenomenon of intentional inexistence.

that is external to the mind. The upshot of this argument is that experiences intrinsically have intentional contents that are inseparable from their phenomenal characters and so are constitutively determined by them.[19]

Horgan and Tienson write that their case for the thesis of phenomenal intentionality "is just a matter of introspectively attending to the phenomenal character of one's own experience" (p. 526), but their argumentation is not entirely clear. Sometimes they seem to support the move from the claim (which they take to be introspectively established) that a kind of intentionality is inseparable from phenomenal character to the claim that this kind of intentionality is constitutively determined by phenomenal character by leaning on other considerations: for example, that any phenomenal duplicates "share a pervasive kind of mental intentionality" (p. 526). But sometimes it seems that the claim about phenomenal duplicates is itself supported by introspection, or that the case for phenomenal intentionality does not require it. Either way, their case depends on the above-mentioned claim regarding introspection, and my criticism of it targets this claim.[20] Another option is to view the claim that any pair of phenomenal duplicates share intentionality as supported by semantic intuitions. But whatever the merits of reliance on intuitions regarding semantic matters are in general, in the present context it is clearly illegitimate. When we are concerned with the question of whether phenomenal characters endow some entities with (real) intentionality, independent of third-person interpretation, rather than merely underlying the ascription of intentionality, intuition-based judgments miss the mark.

For Horgan and Tienson's argument to be effective, it must be true both that introspection attests to the claim that experience is, in and of itself, intentional—that it is inherently intentional—and that the evidence of introspection on this matter should be trusted. I accept the first of these points: that is, I accept Horgan and Tienson's claim as a claim about our phenomenology of experiences. I agree that this phenomenology is indeed intentionalistic, or, in other words, that (in the normal course of things) our experiences seem to us to be inherently intentional. Introspecting mental states such as experiences *appears* to reveal intentional

---

[19] The employment in this argument of the idea that introspection of experience reveals mind-independent properties (i.e., that experience is transparent) is reminiscent of Harman's argument against mental paint and in favor of the representational theory of phenomenal consciousness (Harman 1990). For criticism of Horgan and Tienson's argument that is based in part on the relation between their argument and Harman's, see Bordini (2017). On the other hand, Loar (2003) argues that the transparency of experience that figures in Harman's argument is compatible with the view of phenomenal intentionality, and according to Kriegel, "the transparency of experience—the fact that phenomenology appears, from the first-person perspective, to be inherently intentional—is surely evidence for the existence of phenomenally constituted intentionality" (Kriegel 2007: 321). In his later work (Kriegel 2011), Kriegel is skeptical regarding the ability of introspection to provide evidence for taking experiences to be *intrinsically* intentional.

[20] Bordini (2017) takes Horgan and Tienson to suggest two arguments for the thesis of phenomenal intentionality: the argument from introspection alone, and the argument from phenomenal duplicates, which also relies on introspection. Bordini criticizes both arguments.

64 INTENTIONALITY DECONSTRUCTED

objects. This claim needs some refinement, which will be provided below, but for now let's accept it as is. This claim does not settle the issue, for the issue is not how experience appears to be, but how it is. Can this appearance be trusted? Is introspection a reliable guide on the matter? I wish to argue that it isn't, and that its verdict by no means supports the thesis that, owing to its phenomenal character, experience is intrinsically intentional. The point I wish to make is not that this verdict is fallible, but rather the stronger point that it is simply irrelevant to the truth of the matter.[21]

Trust in the verdict of introspection concerning content seems natural, and Horgan and Tienson are not alone in cherishing this verdict. Searle, for example, argues that Quine's argument for the indeterminacy of reference (Quine 1960) and Davidson's argument for the inscrutability of reference (Davidson 1979) constitute *reductio ad absurdum* of the linguistic theories on which they rely, respectively (namely, Quine's linguistic behaviorism and Davidson's conception of meaning as public). This is because "we know from our own case that we do mean by 'rabbit' something different from 'rabbit stage' or 'undetached rabbit part'," and, similarly, "we do know in our own use of language that we are referring to Wilt, for example, and not to Wilt's shadow...I know what I mean" (Searle 1987, pp. 139–141).

Searle does not explain why he takes the first-person perspective to be a reliable indicator, let alone to provide certainty, with respect to our meanings and contents. Horgan and Graham (who take themselves to be supplementing Searle's critique of Quine and Davidson) deal briefly with this issue: "Are there features of one's mental life whose presence is so obvious as to be beyond doubt? Indeed there are: viz., *phenomenal* features....Phenomenal character is distinctively *self-presenting* to the experiencing subject" (Horgan and Graham 2012, p. 33). According to Horgan and Graham's reasoning, since phenomenal intentionality is fully constituted by phenomenal consciousness, and the latter is self-presenting, phenomenal intentionality too is self-presenting, and the first-person perspective's testimony regarding them can be trusted. But this reasoning is not effective. Saying that some feature is self-presenting seems to convey the idea that if this feature exists, then it is presented to the subject. But it is not this characteristic that is required for establishing the existence of phenomenal intentionality through introspection, but rather its mirror image. That is, this introspection-based justification of PIT should be based on the idea that if phenomenal characters appear to the subject, then they exist. Let's grant the truth of this idea. Why should we believe that it implies the truth of an analogous idea that pertains to

---

[21] Pautz (2013) argues that introspective reports about intentionality are fallible. He also argues that the claim that content determinacy is introspectively obvious must be false since there are philosophers who do not accept it. I do not think that this argument is convincing, since philosophers are notorious for denying the obvious. (This book is likely to be taken to exemplify this phenomenon.) Pautz (2021) suggests other objections to the phenomenal intentionalist's reliance on introspection.

intentionality, when we are not entitled to assume that these two mental features are connected with each other? Even if we accept both the self-presenting nature of phenomenal consciousness and the principle that anything that is constituted by a characteristic that is self-presenting is itself self-presenting, we cannot infer that intentionality is self-presenting unless we assume that phenomenal character constitutes intentionality, which of course we are not entitled to. So, we cannot rely on the self-presenting nature of intentionality to infer that experiences that appear to be intrinsically intentional are indeed intrinsically intentional (and not even that they are intentional *simpliciter*).

We might think that introspective judgments concerning intentionality should be trusted, on the grounds that, as far as the mental is concerned, there is no appearance/reality gap and what seems to be the case is the case. There is, of course, a long philosophical tradition that adheres to this "appearance is reality" principle concerning the mind.[22] But whether or not this epistemic principle holds for various mental characteristics, or for some mental dimension, I will now argue that it does not hold true for intentionality: introspection by itself cannot reveal intentional contents or inform us that there are such.[23] The basic idea of this argument is that the notion of intentional content is not a notion of what's in there, in your head. It is rather a notion of how what's in your head is connected to items that are (typically) in the extra-mental world—a connection that is thus (typically) beyond the reach of introspection. Recall that intentionality is transcendence: it is one entity's transcending itself to another; and what transcends an entity cannot be noticed upon observing that entity. Thus, introspecting a mental state—looking at it, as it were—cannot reveal that it is (intrinsically) intentional.

This claim certainly needs to be defended. For one thing, why can't intentionality, as transcendence, be introspected, if the supposed intentional transcendence does not necessarily involve any external entity or happening, as suggested by intentional inexistence? In other words, why can't intentionality-as-purporting be introspected? Phenomenal intentionalists may agree that introspection cannot reveal the intentional objects of experiences, but insist that it can reveal intentional contents. They may agree that it cannot reveal the truth of content ascriptions construed transparently and what makes them true, but insist that introspection can reveal the truth of opaque content ascriptions and what make them true. In other words, introspection can reveal contents in the sense of purporting to refer, or purporting to represent. This is what Brian Loar, who argues for phenomenal intentionality, says:

---

[22] For a recent presentation and defense of this principle, see Whiting (2016).
[23] We should not confuse appearance of intentionality with appearance of intentional objects. The former appearance testifies to the latter if it is reliable, but the reliability of the former is what is at stake here.

66 INTENTIONALITY DECONSTRUCTED

> We cannot phenomenologically separate the pure visual experience from its *purporting* to pick out objects and their properties....In some sense, ordinary visual experience comes phenomenologically interpreted....*Phenomenal intentionality* is a phenomenologically accessible feature of virtually all perceptual experience and of perceptually based concepts, e.g. visual demonstrative concepts....This is a non-relational phenomenal feature....When I say that directedness is "phenomenal" I mean merely that I can identify it in experience. I apparently can tell that hallucinatory experiences have a "purporting to refer" property that is also present when visual experiences pick out real objects in the normal way.   (Loar 2003, pp. 238–240)

Thus, it is intentionality-as-purport-to-represent that is taken by Loar to be determined by phenomenality, and it is supposed to be a non-relational—certainly not environmental-involving—feature of experiences. So, phenomenal intentionality thus understood seems to be accessible to introspection, and we seem to have good reason to trust introspection's affirmation of its existence.

However, we shall see that even intentionality-as-purport is not accessible to introspection, which therefore cannot be considered an indicator of such an alleged phenomenon. This is so since even intentionality-as-purport is transcendence. The idea of intentionality-as-purport is significant, since the possibility of failure to represent—the possibility of intentional objects that do not exist—is essential to intentionality, but it is of course also of the essence of intentionality—as purport—that the purport may succeed. Contentful attitudes need not be satisfied, but (leaving aside the idea of contents of the impossible, if there is a sense to it) they may—they are necessarily satisfiable (typically by extra-mental entities); depending on the world's cooperation, contents *may* match it. The possibility of such a match, this satisfiability, this directedness toward, is intentional transcendence. The supposedly intentional-as-purporting mind transcends itself to the possible.

It might be thought that since intentionality-as-purport is only a relational property in the weak sense (namely, a relation one of whose relata need not exist), then it is an intrinsic property of minds.[24] On this model, an intentional state is intrinsically such that *if* some object (perhaps characterized in terms of some properties) exists (or would exist, or would have existed), then it is (or would be, or would have been) this state's intentional object. However, whether intentionality-as-purport is intrinsic or not, the transcendence of the mind to the

---

[24] As far as dispositional properties are concerned, they characterize materials only given the causal laws of the world. But there seem to be relational properties in the weak sense that are intrinsic in an absolute sense: for example, an object that is 10 cm long is, intrinsically, shorter than any possible object that is 12 cm long. The argument now being suggested against the introspectability of intentionality-as-purport does not assume that the notion of intentionality-as-purport is not that of an intrinsic property of its possessors.

extra-mental does not disappear here—it just takes a slightly different form. We can realize this by focusing on the question of intentionality. Instead of asking what it is that makes the mind represent objects external to itself, we should ask what it is that makes the mind such *that those conditional sentences* are true of it; what it is that makes it such that *had there been* an object with such properties— that is, such *non-mental* properties—*it would have* represented it.

We thus get a sense of intentionality-as-purport as object-related, as directedness outward, as transcendence. Importantly, in being transcending in this sense, intentionality-as-purport is beyond the reach of introspection. Introspection by itself cannot access the fact of representing, which transcends the state it observes. To realize this, note, first, that our ability to reveal by introspection that some state is intentional depends on introspection's ability to reveal a specific intentional property, specific intentionality-as-purport. Second, to know by observation that a state is such that it would represent an object with such and such properties (that may also be relational ones), one needs to read off those properties from the things observed: that is, from the state held to be intentional. It is here that the transcendence of intentionality forcefully comes into play. How can introspection read off properties of (actual or would-be) intentional objects of mental states? Such reading off requires that those properties inhere in the supposedly intentional states (how else could we access them by observing these states?), but this makes no sense.[25] Saying that those states are representations of objects and that we can read off represented properties from their representations would be mere rhetoric, for the point is precisely that, due to the transcending nature of representationality, we cannot read off properties of supposed represented objects from supposed representations. And this point also holds for intentionality-as-purport: the identity of a supposed intentional object is independent of its existence (pardon existentialists), and, so, reading off its properties from the mental state requires that they inhere there.

Horgan and Tienson's point may be taken to be precisely that we do read off represented properties from experiences—that this is simply a fact (and arguably, this is also shown by Harman's argument regarding the transparency of experience). However, the consideration brought above aims to show that there cannot be such a fact, and so these philosophers only show that it *seems* to us that we read off represented properties from experiences.

Those who believe that we can read off, by means of introspection alone, the supposed representational characters of mental states—their supposed directedness toward objects—might appeal to an analogy with arrows, which point toward objects, or with drawings of objects. Consider arrows. It might be argued

---

[25] It might be that phenomenal externalism gives sense to the notion that represented properties inhere in the states representing them, but, as noted, this view is not an option for phenomenal intentionalists.

68   INTENTIONALITY DECONSTRUCTED

that the directedness of arrows toward objects (in virtue of relational properties of the objects) can be noticed while observing the arrows themselves, and that the same holds for the arrow-like directedness of the intentionality of the mental. However, the arrow example can be of no help to phenomenal intentionalists, since an arrow in itself does not represent and does not purport to represent anything. If it represents or purports to represent at all, it is only relative to a convention, to an interpretation, etc. So, observing an arrow in abstraction from convention or interpretation—at any rate, observing it in itself—cannot reveal purport to represent.[26] The example of drawings may appear more relevant, since it may be thought that by observing a drawing we observe what it represents. However, this is true in the sense that we observe properties that are shared by the represented object and the drawing: that is, we observe properties that indeed inhere in the drawing. (It might be that upon observing the drawing we form in our mind the same image that we typically form upon observing the object itself—one that is different from the image of the drawing—but then we do not observe the object by merely observing the drawing.) Thus, the notion that we introspectively know that the phenomenal mind has (intrinsic) intentionality-as-purport cannot profit from the arrow example and the drawing example, which do not dissolve the mystery of how we can discover supposed represented properties by introspecting supposed representations.

Handling an objection to the suggested reasoning against the introspectability of intentionality will clarify and further support it. According to this objection, this reasoning presupposes that the (immediate) object of introspection is a "quoted" non-intentional mental level that is the bearer of intentionality (e.g., the mental sentence "Grass is green"), and, thus, that to know anything about one's intentional content one must go beyond introspection and "disquote," as it were, its (immediate) object (e.g., moving to the content *that* Grass is green). However, this presupposition is unwarranted. As McDowell (1992) argues, no mental level that is not intentional—"a flat psychological surface," to use William James's (1909/1975) apt expression—is given to us in introspection. Rather, in introspecting our intentional states we are immediately aware of them as intentional.

This objection is similar to Horgan and Tienson's claim that introspection of experiences reveals them to be intrinsically intentional (and, thus, also similar to Harman's case against mental paint) and my reaction to this objection is similar to my reaction to this claim. The objection's premise that in introspecting our intentional states we are immediately aware of them as intentional is a claim about the phenomenology of experience. With some qualifications (to be made later), I agree that, in the normal course of things, the (immediate) object of introspection in cases of apparent intentionality does not *seem* flat; it seems intentional.

---

[26] The automaticity that is in play in interpreting arrows is in no conflict with this—see the discussion of McDowell's objection later in this section.

To use Loar's above-cited words, "experience comes *phenomenologically* interpreted" (my emphasis). But if what I argue about intentionality and the jurisdiction of introspection is right, then the verdict of introspection regarding intentionality should be confined to this seeming and it is illegitimate to take it to attest to the real nature of the mental state. This is not an issue that is settled by phenomenology, so my reasoning does not presuppose that the (immediate) object of introspection— what is given to us in this process—is a "quoted" non-intentional mental level that is the bearer of intentionality. Rather, the issue is an epistemic-justificatory one. Insofar as the objection in question is taken to go beyond phenomenology and to suggest that no flat, non-intentional, mental level *exists* in the case of experience, and thus that experiences are intrinsically intentional, it is unwarranted, for it is not in the power of introspection to establish this. That our immediate awareness of experiences as intentional does not indicate that they are intrinsically intentional is also shown by the case of language. In the normal course of things, we are immediately aware of words and sentences as meaningful—it is not that we are first aware of them as flat entities and then become aware of their meanings. Yet, their meanings (if they have meanings) are most plausibly not intrinsic to them. At any rate, our awareness of them does not indicate that their meanings are intrinsic to them ("aware as" is used here in a non-factive sense), and certainly, one who holds that experiences are the source of intentionality wouldn't take linguistic entities to have meanings intrinsically.[27] It is not only that the claim that experiences or other mental states are different in this regard still awaits justification. Rather, in accordance with what I have argued, no such justification can be solely rooted in the first-person perspective.[28]

Let me recap the case against the phenomenal intentionalist's reliance on introspection. The mere satisfiability of intentional states (in contrast to actual satisfaction) makes them world-involving, for had it not, their actual satisfaction (e.g., truth) would be impossible. An intentional state is such that *if there is, or were, or had been*, such and such an object, then *the state represents it, or would represent it, or would have represented it*, respectively. The very purport to represent (whether successful or not) already embodies intentional transcendence, and since transcending intentional properties cannot be read off from mental states,

---

[27] Perhaps arrows are similar to utterances of sentences in that the psychological process of "reading" them has become immediate and automatic. This has no bearing on the point that the arrow's directedness is not in the arrow itself but is rather imposed upon it, even if we are not aware of this fact. This point does not concern psychology.

[28] The issue of the epistemic authority of introspection with respect to intentionality should also be distinguished from the issue of the content determination of second-order beliefs. Tyler Burge (1988) argues that the contents of our second-order beliefs are determined by the very same external factors that (as Burge believes) determine the contents of our first-order beliefs, which are their intentional objects. Thus, the fact that the contents of our (first-order) beliefs are externally determined does not prevent us from having (second-order) beliefs about our (first-order) beliefs. Yet this observation does not affect the claim that we are not justified to take one's introspection-based second-order beliefs concerning the (alleged) intentionality of one's mental states to be true.

intentionality—even unsatisfied intentionality-as-purport—lies beyond the jurisdiction of introspection.

That's for intentionality and intentionality-as-purport. A close relative to intentionality-as-purport that might be thought to be within the epistemic jurisdiction of introspection is narrow intentionality. Various proponents of phenomenal intentionality (Farkas 2008a, 2008b; Horgan and Tienson 2002; Georgalis 2006; Horgan, Tienson, and Graham 2004; Kriegel 2007, 2011) take it to be narrow intentionality. However, in Chapter 1 we saw that so-called narrow content isn't really narrow, and this has implications regarding its accessibility to introspection. Narrow intentionality, or (as it is usually referred to) narrow content, is standardly characterized as content that is determined by individualistic properties of the individual who possesses it. On this understanding, narrow content may be full-blown referential content, so that entities that possess it may involve intentional transcendence. Appealing to narrow content, thus understood, cannot help phenomenal intentionalists rebuff the claim that introspection cannot provide evidence for intrinsic phenomenal intentionality, since the intentionality that may be thought to be within the epistemic jurisdiction of introspection should be non-referential; indeed, it should not be even potentially referring—purport-to-refer—as we saw.

What about narrow content as a function from context to wide/referential/truth-conditional content? Proponents of phenomenal intentionality would certainly not take introspection to detect such functions (i.e., to detect anything *as* such a function). If introspection can detect narrow content—and what is at stake is whether it detects anything *as* content or content-like, in some respect (rather than as a flat psychological surface)—then narrow content must have another semantically relevant aspect. In fact, narrow content must have a more substantive characterization for semantic reasons, unrelated to the issues of introspectability and phenomenal intentionality. As we saw in Chapter 1, what determines the relevant context that is supposed to cooperate with narrow content to form referential content (in other words, what determines the space of possible facts the actual among which is that feature that completes the determination of content) can be nothing other than narrow content itself. Narrow content should operate like an open sentence, whose own nature constrains the possible ways in which it can be completed.

But, as I argued, if indeed this is what narrow content is supposed to be, then narrow content cannot but be given in terms of extra-mental features. (In the Twin Earth scenario, for example, it must be given in terms of microstructures.) That is, to be even semantic-like, in the sense of being able to cooperate with contextual features so that full-blown referential intentionality is achieved, narrow content itself should refer to (or denote, if you like) extra-mental features. In other words, narrow content too transcends the mind to extra-mental reality. As said, supposed narrow intentionality isn't so narrow, which means that in fact

AGAINST PHENOMENAL INTENTIONALITY AS INTRINSIC REDUCTION   71

there is no (non-referential) narrow content. What is important in the present context is that in being transcending, in this sense, the supposed narrow content cannot but lie beyond the epistemic jurisdiction of introspection. The appeal to narrow content, precisely like the appeal to intentionality-as-purport, cannot save the phenomenal intentionalists' reliance on introspection.

In sum, we have seen that intentionality lies beyond the epistemic jurisdiction of introspection.[29] It is impossible to argue that intentionality is intrinsic to experience and is constitutively determined by phenomenal character by relying on the verdict of introspection.[30,31] Note that on my analysis, introspection does not provide even prima facie support for phenomenal intentionality—it is simply irrelevant to it. Mendelovici suggests revising Siewert's argument from accuracy conditions that was discussed above as follows: "When you are in certain phenomenal states, it seems to you that you are assessable for accuracy. The best explanation for this apparent assessability for accuracy is that because of being in your phenomenal state, you are representing. If that's right, then at least some phenomenal states give rise to intentional states, and there is phenomenal intentionality" (Mendelovici 2018, p. 92, n. 14). If my critique of the reliance on introspection to reveal phenomenal intentionality is on the right track, it underlies this reasoning as well.[32] For according to this critique, introspection is inapt for revealing intentionality, and the assumption that phenomenal states represent does not explain the seeming of phenomenal intentionality. Even if they do represent, the essential transcending aspect of intentionality (and this, recall, is the issue) can have no bearing on this seeming and cannot explain it.[33]

---

[29] For a different attack on the idea that we have first-person knowledge of intentionality, see Gopnik (1993).

[30] Pitt (2004) argues for the phenomenal intentionality thesis with respect to thoughts on the grounds that we are normally able to introspectively identify each of our occurrent conscious thoughts as having the content it does, and this ability presupposes that each occurrent conscious thought has a phenomenology that is constitutive of its content. If what I have argued in this section is correct, we should reject the premise of Pitt's argument that we can introspectively identify each of our occurrent conscious thoughts as having their content. It only seems to us that we identify contents.

[31] It might be thought that my argument to this effect presupposes a specific model of introspection: namely, the self-monitoring or self-scanning model. But my argument neither employs nor presupposes any claim about introspection that Horgan and Tienson's introspection-based argument (or any other introspection-based argument for the same conclusion known to me) does not employ or presuppose. More importantly, it isn't accurate to say that my argument presupposes any such model of introspection, since the argument does not presuppose anything about the mechanism responsible for introspective judgments concerning intentionality. It may be said to presuppose that such judgments are only responsive to internal elements, but this presupposition seems to be justified insofar as we are interested in phenomenally constituted intentionality.

[32] Since Mendelovici is concerned with intentionality in a different sense than that with which this book is concerned, one that does not essentially involve reference and truth conditions, it might be that this critique is irrelevant to it. My point concerns intentionality in a sense that does essentially involve reference and truth conditions.

[33] Georgalis bases his approach to intentionality on the notion of minimal content that "represents the subject of the intentional state as the subject conceives it" (Georgalis 2006, p. 7). It is accessed from and only from the first-person perspective, and when we deliberately form an intentional state such as an image to be of some particular individual, we cannot err in identifying whom our intentional state

72 INTENTIONALITY DECONSTRUCTED

This limitation of introspection also prevents introspection from settling questions of content determinacy. If, for all we know from the third-person perspective, there is indeterminacy concerning content, meaning, or reference, the first-person perspective cannot resolve it. Searle's claims that "we know from our own case that we do mean by 'rabbit' something different from 'rabbit stage' or 'undetached rabbit part'," and that "we do know in our own use of language that we are referring to Wilt, for example, and not to Wilt's shadow...I know what I mean" (Searle 1987, pp. 139–141) are unwarranted. We do not know these things from our own case, even if it seems to us that we do. The claim that I know by introspection that by "rabbit" I mean rabbit involves an illegitimate leap from the realm of representations to the realm of the represented objects. I will later discuss the very idea that consciousness secures content determinacy.

I conceded the first premise of Horgan and Tienson's argument from introspection—namely, the claim that the verdict of introspection is that sensory experience is intentional—but took issues with the second (implicit) premise: namely, the claim that we should trust this verdict. Let me clarify some points concerning the concession. As David Papineau (in personal communication) pointed out to me, my claim that the phenomenology of experience is intention-alistic cannot be such as to imply anything about the nature of this experience, since, on my view, experience does not involve even purport-to-represent. So, if we are merely inclined to believe that experience is intrinsically intentional, Papineau asked, what about opponents of phenomenal intentionality: are they inclined to believe that experience is intrinsically intentional even though they do not in fact believe this? I have three alternative responses to this question. The first, put roughly, is that we are inclined to believe—on the basis of introspection—that some experiences are intentional, but opponents of phenomenal intentionality (though sharing this inclination) do not in fact come to believe this. The second response, put roughly, is that opponents of phenomenal intentionality do come to believe this, but discard this belief upon reflection. A third response (similar in spirit to the first), put roughly, is that we come to have a perception-like state with a mind-to-world direction of fit, rather than a belief, to the effect that our experience is intentional. This perception-like state ("seeming" may be an apt name for it)

---

is of. "[T]he possibility of error in these circumstances does not make any sense, not because I have some special mental powers or because I am cognizant of a special kind of entity. That an image is of the particular individual in question is a *constitutive* element of the very act of forming the image. It could not be *that act* if it were not *of that individual*" (p. 5). If what I argue here is correct, then what is conceived or identified from the first-person perspective can neither be intentional content nor, in itself, indicate the existence of intentional content. It is *the seeming* of intentional content that can be thus conceived and identified. Also, the fact that the object is constitutive of the act does not entail that we cannot err about the identity of the object; it only entails that such an error would be an error about the identity of the intentional state, and it takes another argument to show that error of this latter kind is impossible.

AGAINST PHENOMENAL INTENTIONALITY AS INTRINSIC REDUCTION   73

suggests to us a belief with the content that the experience is intentional, a suggestion that is rejected by opponents of phenomenal intentionality.[34]

I am not sure which of these responses I prefer. The thought that top-down
influence is ineffective with regard to such fundamental matters, as well as my
own experience, pushes me toward the second. However, all need refinement
(that can help get rid of the "roughly" in their formulations). As a first approxi-
mation, we can say that the beliefs in question are not beliefs that the relevant
experiences are intentional (saying that would be over-intellectualization), but
rather, they are beliefs that the relevant experiences involve some extra-mental
objects (whether actual or merely possible). But this statement is still misleading,
since it refers to the beliefs in question in terms of (second-order) content, while
referring to them in terms of content is merely a rhetorical device. I do not take
these mental states to have contents. On my view, they are mental responses of a
certain non-intentional sort elicited by our experiences (and this also holds true
for those perception-like states). We will be able to understand what this sort is
in Chapters 5 and 6, which explicate what remains of mental states stripped of
intentionality and what the nature of content ascriptions is in the framework of
intentional anti-realism.

3.4.4 Disquotation and the Sense of First-Person Content Ascriptions

Now I wish to suggest a more radical claim concerning the reliance on introspection for detecting intentionality. The claim is that content ascriptions that are
based upon introspection alone are not only unjustified and should not be relied
upon, but rather, they are vacuous. The argument of the previous sub-section
might be taken to raise the question of what happens when we make ascriptions
of contents from the first-person perspective (hereafter, "self-ascriptions of
content"), and the argument to be suggested in the present sub-section (though
independent of the previous one) and the ensuing discussion will also shed light
on this issue.

The argument for this claim exploits the idea of disquotation. Let's focus on
propositional attitudes. (I will shortly show that the argument applies to perceptual experiences as well.[35]) Suppose that upon introspecting one's thought "Grass
is green," one forms the belief that one is thinking that grass is green. So, one is
moving from the "quoted" "Grass is green" to the content *that* grass is green. One,
as it were, disquotes one's "Grass is green"-thought. We can take this move to be a

---

[34] See Papineau's (2021, ch. 3) and Raleigh's (2009) discussions of this issue.
[35] I believe that, at least generally, propositional attitudes involve our public languages (see Harman 1973; Devitt and Sterelny 1987, ch. 9), but the argument does not depend on this view.

74 INTENTIONALITY DECONSTRUCTED

move from object-language to meta-language, if we like. The important point is that (the typographic similarity notwithstanding) this move is not trivial. To make this move—that is, to make any non-vacuous ascription of content to my introspectable "quoted" representation; for the disquoted repetition of the intro-spectable "inscription" to have cognitive value—we must have independent semantic/referential access to the content in question (independent, that is, of one's first-person introspective access). Such a move must involve the application of the intentional function—the function that connects thoughts or concepts (in the psychological senses, rather than the semantic ones) with contents—which secures one's independent access to the content. In other words, one must also inhabit a third-person point of view. Only relative to an independent semantic/ referential access, which is secured via an intentional function (in other words, via a scheme of interpretation), will self-ascriptions of content be rescued from merely quoting a flat un-interpreted inscription, and thus from vacuity.[36] (I can adopt the point of view of another person, or of "society," but I need not: if, for example, naturalistic semantics of some variety is effective, it can endow me with the required referential access.)

The example of the thought "Grass is green" might create the impression that this argument presupposes that the direct objects of introspection are mental sen-tences. I do believe that the so-called propositional attitudes have sentence-like structures and argue for this claim in Chapter 6, but the present argument does not rely on it. Consider the possible objection that the argument does not apply to perceptual experiences, since it seems even more obvious that we are immediately aware of our perceptual experiences as intentional than that we are immediately aware of our propositional attitudes as intentional (or as object-involving in some sense). This difference in obviousness is irrelevant to the cogency of the argument, since this argument, like the argument of the previous sub-section, does not conflict with the view that in introspecting our intentional states we are immediately aware of them as intentional—that they appear to have specific contents. The argument allows that the processes that culminate in self-ascriptions of content are partly unconscious—that our seemings (as if) of intentionality are mediated (unconsciously) by our access to non-intentional features of mental states.[37] So the obviousness of the claim that we are immediately aware of our perceptual experiences as intentional (in a non-factive sense of "aware as") does not threaten the claim that first-person judgments of intentionality in cases of perceptual experiences must be susceptible to a move analogous to disquotation and to presuppose a distinction analogous to that between an object-language

[36] One cannot read this function off from one's thought, for representations do not encode infor-mation about their own intentional functions (see Chapter 2).

[37] And, so, in writing that we introspect "Grass is green," I do not mean that we introspect it *as* "quoted."

stage and a meta-language stage. If intentionality is standard-object aboutness, then the formation of content ascriptions in such cases must consist of "externalizing phenomenology": that is, of moving from reddish experiences to red objects, for example. This is so, even if we are first *aware* of reddish experiences not as reddish experiences but as experiences of red objects (as Harman and Horgan and Tienson argued).

Now if the argument that content ascriptions that are based upon introspection alone are vacuous applies to perceptual experiences, it certainly does not rely on the idea that the direct objects of introspection are mental sentences. It only relies on the idea that in forming content ascriptions via introspection there must be a transition from the flat non-intentional to the intentional, an idea that follows from the notion of an intentional function. (This does not mean that this process involves some awareness of the flat non-intentional stage. It may be that we are only aware—in a non-factive sense—of the supposedly intentional state as intentional.) Such transitions, it is argued, require a third-person perspective.

The fact that this argument avails itself of the notion of an intentional function might invite an objection that concerns, again, perceptual experiences. Consider the claim that to move from the introspectable "Grass is green" to the proposition or content *that* grass is green I have to apply the intentional function that connects concepts with contents. Proponents of phenomenal intentionality might argue that even if this claim is true of propositional attitudes (and some of them, like Horgan and Tienson, would deny this), it isn't true of perceptual experiences (when "percepts" replace "concepts"). It ignores the option that the intentionality of perceptual experiences is intrinsic to them, and so the notion of an intentional function should be rejected as far as they are concerned. To assume that this notion does apply to perceptual experiences (or perhaps to mental states in general) is to beg the question against the view that intentionality is an intrinsic property of experiences (or of other mental states as well).

However, no question begging is involved here, for the argument in question is not an argument against phenomenal intentionality (or intrinsic intentionality in general). It is an argument against an argument for phenomenal intentionality. So, to establish PIT by relying on introspection, PIT's proponents have to undermine the notion of an intentional function. Indeed, without defending this notion, my argument does not unconditionally establish the vacuity of purely first-person content ascriptions. But it does establish this when conjoined with the anti-primitivist argument from Chapter 1: any anti-primitivist view of intentionality is committed to the notion of an intentional function.

I hope to have shown that one's self-ascription of content depends, for having cognitive value, on one's having a third-person point of view. So pure introspective reports about intentional contents are vacuous. A fortiori, one cannot *know* about one's content without having a third-person point of view.

76   INTENTIONALITY DECONSTRUCTED

Thus, we see again that the argument from introspection for phenomenal intentionality has a false premise.

The present argument too has an immediate implication for the issue of indeterminacy. If there is epistemic third-person indeterminacy concerning the intentionality of a linguistic act or of a mental intentional state—that is, if we cannot know its determinate content (or even whether it has a determinate content) from the third-person perspective—then the dependence between the first-person perspective and the third-person perspective prevents the first-person perspective from supplementing the third-person one; it prevents it from securing knowledge of the supposedly determinate contents. The fact that "rabbit" in my thought appears to me to refer to rabbit rather than to undetached rabbit parts leaves intact the possibility that this concept does refer to undetached rabbit parts. Or to anything else. Or to nothing. A purely first-person based judgment that "rabbit" refers to a rabbit is vacuous. The first-person perspective needs the help of the third-person perspective, yet the former was supposed precisely to help the latter—the third-person perspective was assumed to involve this indeterminacy. So, if indeed there is semantic indeterminacy from the third-person perspective (and I believe there is—see Chapter 4), this indeterminacy is still with us when we appeal to the first-person perspective.

The claim that one cannot know about one's contents without having a third-person point of view might seem to be in tension with the familiar view that one is better situated than others to know what one is thinking. In fact, even the claim that intentionality is beyond the jurisdiction of introspection seems to be in tension with this view. But there is one sense of this familiar view in which it is in no tension with the claims advanced here. Here is a rough characterization of the structure of acquiring knowledge of content. Two components are involved in acquiring knowledge of content: knowledge of the representation, the bearer of content, and knowledge of the intentional (representing) function, which connects representations with their contents or intentional objects.[38] It is the latter component that is third-personally accessible (which does not mean that one cannot adopt it with respect to one's own contents). The former may be accessed either from within or from without, and plausibly, when it is accessed from within, the access is privileged to this or that extent. (At any rate, nothing written here is in conflict with this idea. I do not intend to provide here a model of this introspective stage.[39]) In such a case of self-ascription, one acts as a double agent: one introspects one's conscious state,

---

[38] In cases in which one's knowledge of content involves deference to another's knowledge of content, the suggested model is meant to apply to the knowledge of the subject deferred to rather than to the knowledge of the deferring subject.

[39] Among other things, I also do not mean to reject any sub-distinction in this process, such as the one between attention and classification.

AGAINST PHENOMENAL INTENTIONALITY AS INTRINSIC REDUCTION   77

and relates it to content from the third-person perspective—that is, ascribes content in accord with an intentional function.[40]

On this picture of self-ascription of content, first-person access has neither an indispensable nor a unique role in revealing intentionality, and considerations pertaining to first-person access have no bearing on the issue of intrinsic intentionality—the alleged advantage of the first person to detect intentionality vanishes. It is the second stage, which is third-personal, that brings intentionality into the picture. However, this two-stage picture of acquiring knowledge of content is merely a conceptual one—it is not committed to the notion that such knowledge is possible. This picture accommodates intentional anti-realism; it is just that, if intentional anti-realism is true, the result of this process isn't veridical and so isn't knowledge.

One may wonder whether the irrelevance of introspective evidence to intentionality—whether it is due to the vacuity pointed out or merely to the fact that intentional facts lie beyond the merely internal jurisdiction of introspection—means that intentional facts cannot be constituted by phenomenal character. As mentioned above, it is typical of views that ground intentionality in consciousness, in one way or the other, that they take intentionality to be deeply related to the first-person point of view. So, the epistemic dissociation between intentionality and that point of view means that a prominent motivation for the thesis of phenomenal intentionality loses its sting. But can we conclude, further, that this thesis is false? Had this thesis been defined in terms of the accessibility of intentionality from the first-person perspective, it would have been undermined by the above-mentioned considerations. The thesis of phenomenal intentionality is not defined in this epistemic way, but rather in terms of intentionality being constituted by or grounded in phenomenal character. This fact, however, does not settle the substantive issue of whether what isn't accessible from the first-person perspective can be determined by phenomenal character. Even if we assume that phenomenal character itself is essentially tied with the first-person perspective, we cannot automatically move to the view that phenomenal intentionality cannot but be thus tied.

I do not know whether we can rule out the possibility that phenomenal character (or any other intrinsic mental property) constitutes intentionality, yet, due to the nature of intentionality—that is, to its transcending nature—it escapes the gaze of introspection. In other words, I do not know whether we can rule out this

---

[40] As should be clear by now, this two-stage process need not be a conscious process, one in which we consciously move from representing our own representations as flat to representing them as intentional, or world-involving (and the "knowledge" of the representation and of the intentional function need not be conscious). This fact enables this model of self-knowledge of content to provide an explanation for the erroneous seeming of intrinsic intentionality: since this process isn't conscious, we do not notice the interpreting stage involved in self-ascriptions of contents, which stage is further blurred by its disquotational nature. Some philosophical reflection is needed to notice that this move isn't trivial.

78 INTENTIONALITY DECONSTRUCTED

possibility without showing directly that phenomenal character (and other intrinsic mental properties) cannot constitute intentionality. Thus, I am unsure whether the above noted dissociation undermines PIT, and so I leave it open that it doesn't: that however deep the limitations of introspection discussed above may be, it is still compatible with the metaphysics of intrinsic phenomenal intentionality. So, in the next sections I argue against the very possibility of intrinsic phenomenal intentionality, and also, more generally, against the very idea of intrinsic intentionality, without relying on this limitation of introspection. Thus, exposing this limitation moves the discussion from the arena of direct evidence to that of theoretical consideration.

3.5 Conceptual Connections between Consciousness and Intentionality

John Searle and Colin McGinn are not usually associated with the phenomenal intentionality camp, yet the idea of the intentionality–phenomenality connection is conspicuous in their writings. Both philosophers present arguments for what are in fact analytical/conceptual reductions of intentionality to phenomenality. By "analytical/conceptual reduction," or just "conceptual reduction," I simply refer to reductions that connect the concepts of the reduced phenomenon with the concepts of the reducing phenomenon. I will attempt to show that these arguments fail, and then to undermine the very idea of conceptual connections between phenomenal consciousness and intentionality.

3.5.1 Searle's Argument

Though Searle (1992) rejects the distinction between phenomenal consciousness and other forms of consciousness and does not mention phenomenality in presenting his argument on the matter, he argues for connections between intentionality and what is in fact phenomenal consciousness. I presented Searle's argument for these connections in Chapter 1 as a possible objection to the view that intentionality is exhausted by standard-object aboutness. I will now present this argument again, highlighting it as an argument in favor for PIT.

Searle argues that the link between intentionality and consciousness "lies in the notion of an aspectual shape" (Searle 1989, p. 52). According to him, every intentional state essentially has an aspectual shape under which its intentional object is represented. The desire for water, for example, is different from the desire for H_2O—even though there is no way to satisfy the one without satisfying the other—due to their difference in aspectual shape. The presence of aspectual shapes, according to Searle, implies (in a sense to be immediately qualified)

AGAINST PHENOMENAL INTENTIONALITY AS INTRINSIC REDUCTION 79

accessibility to consciousness. The aspectual shape must matter to the agent and exist from her point of view. Searle asks what facts about intentional states give them their particular aspectual shapes, and provides different replies for the cases of conscious and unconscious intentional states. In the conscious cases, it is the way the agent is conscious of the intentional object. On the other hand, unconscious intentional states have aspectual shapes as "possible contents of consciousness." Ultimately, then, it is consciousness that is responsible for the aspectual shape. Since, in the conscious cases, the way the agent is conscious of the intentional object is constitutive of the aspectual shape and essential to its identity, and the aspectual shape is constitutive of the intentional state and essential to its intentional identity, the way the agent is conscious of the intentional object, the way she experiences it, is constitutive of the intentionality of the state and essential to its intentional identity (Searle 1989; 1992, pp. 155–160).

According to Searle, then, intentionality must involve either phenomenality or what we may call "potential phenomenality." But it seems clear that Searle also takes consciousness to be a determiner of intentionality.[41] He seems to be committed to the idea that the aspectual shape is responsible for the intentionality of conscious intentional states. In other words, the ability of these states to represent objects in the world relies on their aspectual shapes, which are constituted by consciousness. For Searle, aspectual shape determines intentionality—it determines that a state refers to that object that satisfies the condition set by its aspectual shape—and is determined, in the conscious cases, by the way the agent is conscious of the intentional object.[42] Searle thus explains what it is about mental states that semantically connects them with objects in the world: it is their having phenomenal characters, which determine aspectual shapes, which are, in turn, satisfiable by the objects. He thus replies to both the question of intentionality (namely, the question of what constitutes intentionality) and the hard question of intentionality (namely, the question of how anything in the mind can represent anything outside the mind).

Searle's argument and position raise interpretational issues and philosophical difficulties. For example, it isn't clear how the potential to be conscious can explain actual intentionality, and, relatedly, whether it is legitimate to take unconscious

---

[41] This claim does not conflict with Searle's claim that a network of intentional states and background capacities participates in determining intentionality (see Searle 1983, ch. 5; 1992, ch. 8), for these are already required to constitute aspectual shapes in the first place: in the example, they contribute to constituting the evening-star aspectual shape, thus to making an object—that object that satisfies the condition of being the evening star—the intentional object of the intentional state whose aspectual shape it is.

[42] Of course, the aspectual shape does not by itself determine the identity of the object to which the intentional state refers—this also depends on what object in fact fulfils the required condition. By saying that the aspectual shape is supposed to be sufficient for intentionality, I mean that it endows the state whose aspectual shape it is with specific directedness, regardless of what object—if any—is in fact directed by it. Note also that Searle opposes views according to which a state's actual intentional object plays a part in constituting its content.

80   INTENTIONALITY DECONSTRUCTED

intentionality to be real, underived, intrinsic intentionality.[43] I will avoid both interpretational issues and the issue of unconscious intentionality and focus on the alleged consciousness–intentionality connection. I will now argue that relying on the notion of aspectual shape can serve to establish neither that consciousness determines intentionality nor that intentionality determines consciousness.

As I argued in Chapter 1, the temptation (that is perhaps stronger in the case of perceptual experiences) to identify the aspect under which an intentional object is represented by an intentional state with the way the agent is conscious of the intentional object should be resisted. That intentional states have aspectual shapes amounts to their representing their intentional objects as possessing properties.[44] Thus, Venus is sometimes represented as *being* the evening star, and sometimes as *being* the morning star; these are properties of Venus. Insofar as intentional aspectual shapes are characterized in terms of the properties the intentional objects are represented by them as possessing, they are not the ways the agent is conscious of the intentional object and do not involve such ways: these two sets are conceptually distinct and cannot be identified with one another on purely analytic grounds. There may be various constraints on the experiential ways in which minds can represent objects as possessing certain properties, and perhaps also on the properties that experiences of certain sorts can represent (assuming that experience can represent anything), but no conceptual link connects kinds of phenomenally conscious states with aspects of intentional states that are characterized in terms of properties of the states' intentional objects.[45,46]

It wouldn't have mattered had Searle defined "aspectual shape" differently (i.e., not in terms of properties of objects). The point is essential rather than terminological: if aspectual shapes are characterized in terms of worldly properties, Searle should show what connects them to kinds of experiences; if they are characterized in terms of kinds of experiences, he should show what connects them to properties objects are represented as possessing. He has done neither, and we saw that he can do neither, due to the conceptual gap between these two. What is especially important for us is that considerations concerning aspectual shapes cannot provide any reason to believe that phenomenality determines intentionality.

---

[43] For criticism of Searle's view that unconscious intentional phenomena are possible contents of consciousness, see, for example, Fodor and Lepore (1994) and Kriegel (2011).

[44] Recall that we should distinguish between the claim that intentional states represent objects *in virtue of* properties of the objects and the claim that intentional states represent objects *as* possessing properties. The properties in virtue of which objects are represented may but need not be the properties objects are represented as possessing.

[45] I criticized Searle's argument along these lines in Horowitz (1994). For a similar critique, see Van Gulick (1995).

[46] In arguing in favor of a representational view of consciousness, Alex Byrne (2001) employs the same idea that underlies Searle's argument and is subject to the same confusion.

3.5.2 McGinn's Argument

Colin McGinn connects phenomenality with intentionality in a way that is reminiscent of Searle's. According to McGinn, "perceptual experiences are Janus-faced: they point outward to the external world but they also present a subjective face to their subject; they are of something other than the subject and they are like something for the subject" (McGinn 1991, p. 29). This is an innocuous claim. But McGinn then goes on to make the ambitious claim that these two faces of experiences are mutually dependent: "what the experience is like is a function of what it is of, and what it is of is a function of what it is like" (p. 29). For McGinn, the intentionality of experience essentially involves a conscious, first-person, aspect. Consciousness, the inward-looking face, is essential to the content of experience, which is "shot through with subjectivity...what an experience is as of already contains a phenomenological fact—how the subject is struck in having the experience" (p. 34).

McGinn bases this view upon a claim about sense modalities. Sight and hearing, for example, represent different secondary qualities, and

> bats perceive different secondary qualities from us when they employ their echolocation sense; it is not that they perceive precisely the same qualities and embed them in a different (non-representational) medium. That is, there are subjective distinctions that are generated by—and are captured in terms of—distinctions of content. And if so, the link between content and phenomenology is anything but contingent.   (p. 36)

McGinn's claim that there is a non-contingent connection between consciousness and intentionality may be said to pertain to two related but different levels. One level is that of individuation: McGinn argues that subjective distinctions are captured in terms of distinctions of content. The other level is that of the essence of intentionality and phenomenality, respectively: McGinn argues that a state's being conscious is necessary for it to have intrinsic content, and that its being conscious is also sufficient to render the information it carries intrinsically intentional. Let me address these two issues in turn.

I think McGinn fails to show that subjective distinctions are captured in terms of distinctions of content, and thus that the consciousness–intentionality connection is "anything but contingent." Indeed, experiences of some phenomenal types are typically taken to represent environmental features of some types rather than of others. But even if we adopt the intentional realist perspective, and assume that experiences of some phenomenal types do typically represent environmental features of some types rather than of others, this does not show that the link between the phenomenal and the intentional is non-contingent. Why assume that sight and hearing represent qualities of different types because they differ in their

82   INTENTIONALITY DECONSTRUCTED

phenomenal character? It makes better sense to assume that if they represent qualities of different types, this is because their representational systems (which also include the relevant sense organs) are sensitive to different environmental qualities. At any rate, for McGinn's argument to work, it must rule out the logical possibility that, for example, visual experiences represent those kinds of qualities that are usually represented by auditory experiences.[47] (It must reject even such a logical possibility since it aims to establish a conceptual connection between content and consciousness.) McGinn does not attempt to carry out this task.

Let's turn to the second level: namely, to McGinn's claim that a state's being conscious is necessary for it to have intrinsic content—that is (in my terminology), real original content—and that a state's being conscious is sufficient for rendering information intrinsically intentional. McGinn acknowledges the existence of contents that are not conscious (e.g., contents of machines and sub-personal contents of processes in the nervous system), but he takes conscious contents to be unique. It is their having an inward-looking face that allows conscious states, and only them, to possess real original content.

Why should we believe that the inward-looking face distinguishes intrinsic from non-intrinsic content? It isn't clear. McGinn writes: "Remove the inward-looking face and you remove something integral—what the world *seems* like to the subject... what an experience is as of already contains a phenomenological fact—how the subject is struck in having the experience" (p. 34). But this last claim certainly requires justification, which seems to be absent. We may be helped by Kriegel, who elaborates on McGinn's claims:

> If the source of the asymmetry between conscious and unconscious content is indeed the inward-looking face of the former, then it may be reasonably concluded that conscious states are intrinsically intentional in virtue of their inward-looking face... the fact that it presents its content to the subject.... This makes sense: the reason an internal state that impersonally carries information about Atlanta is not directed at Atlanta "in and of itself"—that is, not directed at Atlanta independently of third-person interpretation—is that it does not present Atlanta *to* anyone. It just happens to entertain certain systematic relations with Atlanta. Unless someone notices—becomes aware of—these systematic relations, no real intentionality has taken place. In a way, the reason a conscious thought about Atlanta is inherently directed at Atlanta is that it *cannot* go unnoticed—it already *comes with* a subject's awareness of it, namely, the awareness constituted by the inward-looking face of conscious experience.
>
> (Kriegel 2003, pp. 289–290)[48]

---

[47] A similar point is raised by Bailey and Richards (2014).

[48] I think that in his book about phenomenal intentionality (Kriegel 2011), Kriegel does not adhere to this idea.

I do not identify here any reason to believe that if indeed a state's carrying information about Atlanta—due to systematic relations between them—is not enough to constitute a representation of Atlanta independently of some third-person interpretation, then the fact that this information is presented to anyone provides the missing link. This would have been true had "presented content" been intrinsically intentional, but to assume that it is, is to beg the question. It seems that a conscious content is just that—a content that is conscious. We still haven't seen a reason in favor of the idea that its being conscious contributes to its semantic identity, nor to its being real and original content.

Perhaps McGinn's point is that, as a matter of fact, we ascribe contents independently of third-person interpretation to conscious states and only to conscious states. I am not sure that this claim is true, but let's grant that it is. Such an appeal to the practice of content ascription implies nothing regarding the nature of content itself. Trivially, the appeal to the practice of third-person content ascription cannot be taken to show that conscious experiences have contents independently of such a practice. And as to first-person content ascriptions, I already argued that they are an illegitimate evidential source for intentionality.

Let me digress to make a brief clarification about phenomenal representationalism. According to McGinn, "The content of an experience simply does contribute to what it is like to have it, and indeed it is not at all clear that anything else does" (p. 35). On such a view, experiences' phenomenal characters are inherently (or, one may say, intrinsically) intentional. This appears to be the (pure) representationalist account of phenomenality. However, such an account does not appear to fit McGinn's approach to consciousness. The issue may be clarified if we distinguish between two sorts of views according to which intentionality determines phenomenality, one that takes the latter to be thin and another that takes the former to be thick. According to McGinn, intentionality is "shot through with subjectivity" and, thus, thick. So, we can characterize his version of (pure) representationalism as subjectivist. Searle seems to endorse such a view as well.[49] On the other hand, on standard (pure) representationalism, intentionality is laden with nothing but its semantic content, understood as pure aboutness, and phenomenality consists of nothing more, and is, then, thin. (Pure) representationalism may thus be said to embody a deflationist view of phenomenality, one that takes subjectivity out of consciousness or downplays it. Certainly, much more would need to be said on this issue if we were attempting to understand phenomenality, but this is not the focus here.

---

[49] Recall Searle's charging the reductive-naturalistic approach to intentionality with leaving out the subjective aspect of this phenomenon (Searle 1992, ch. 2).

3.5.3 Against Conceptual Reductions of Intentionality to Phenomenality

We saw that the similar considerations brought up by both Searle and McGinn in favor of the conceptual reducibility of intentionality to phenomenality fail to support this reducibility thesis. Of course, rejecting one family of considerations in favor of PIT by no means undermines PIT. But I will now use my criticism of these considerations as a step in an argument against PIT itself. We shall see that undermining the identification of the aspect under which an intentional object is represented by an intentional state with the way the intentional object appears to the subject, and thereby undermining the identification of what an experience is of with what it is like, does not merely undermine a specific family of arguments to that effect. Rather, it undermines the very idea that intentionality is conceptually linked to phenomenal consciousness.

If aspectual shapes and ways objects appear to subjects are conceptually distinct and cannot be identified on purely analytic grounds, then no analytic connection between consciousness and intentionality obtains. For the aspectual shape (or sense, or meaning—to put it in philosophically more familiar terms) is the conceptual bridge—it is the *only* possible conceptual bridge—between intentional states and their (actual or merely possible) intentional objects. Therefore, since the aspectual shape is not conceptually connected with the way things appear to the subject—in other words, with the what-it's-like aspect essential to phenomenal consciousness, or, in still other words, with how the subject is struck in having the experience (as McGinn puts it)—then nothing that determines intentionality is conceptually connected with this aspect. So, since, as we have seen, aspectual shapes and ways objects appear to subjects are indeed conceptually distinct and cannot be identified with each other on purely analytic grounds, then intentionality is not conceptually connected with phenomenal character. Thus, if there is an essential, intrinsic, connection between phenomenal consciousness and intentionality, such that the aboutness or of-ness of experience is intrinsically determined by its phenomenal character, this connection must be a substantive, synthetic one. Note that although this argument is expressed in terms of a specific notion—that of aspectual shape—it is a general argument against the conceptual reduction of intentionality to phenomenality, since, as noted, aspectual shape (or sense, or meaning) is the only possible conceptual bridge between intentional states and their objects. Once we realize both this point and the point made earlier, to the effect that there is a conceptual gap between aspectual shape (or sense, or meaning) and phenomenality, we see that no conceptual reduction of intentionality to phenomenality is possible.

We can use McGinn's approach to the phenomenality–intentionality connection to further support my general case against the possibility of such a conceptual connection. I wish to point out that it is rather the Janus-face metaphor, suggested by McGinn, that underlies the absence of a conceptual connection between consciousness and intentionality. For McGinn, recall, phenomenal consciousness is essentially inward-looking—that is, its essence is what experiences are like *for the subject*—whereas intentionality is essentially outward-looking: that is, its essence is pointing out *beyond the mental state that bears it*. So, although (on some level of analysis) mental states such as experiences may indeed be Janus-faced in the relevant respect—a phenomenal property and an intentional property may be instantiated by the same state—the concepts of these properties are completely independent of each other (we may say that the properties are conceptually distinct), and so a conceptual reduction of the one to the other is impossible. Now evidently, a property need not be inward-looking in order to be conceptually distinct from intentionality; a contrast is not required for properties to be conceptually distinct. It suffices that a property *lacks* an outward-looking facet, or, in other words, that it lacks externally looking "arrows." This means that for a phenomenality–intentionality conceptual connection to exist, the supposed reducing property cannot be a flat psychological surface (e.g., consciousness' mental paint), and, put positively, must itself involve intentionality (as it is according to representationalism). Specifically, the supposed reducing property must embody *the very same relationality* that intentionality is supposed to involve. So, on a view that attempts a conceptual reduction, intentionality is "grounded" in nothing but intentionality, for the inward-looking face can have the same relationality only if it has the same intentionality, and a fortiori only if it is already intentional. Such a "reduction" is unhelpful, as I argued above.

Phenomenal intentionalists may object to this line of reasoning in two (incompatible) ways. First, they may deny that intentionality essentially involves relationality. Indeed, various phenomenal intentionalists (e.g., Farkas 2008a, 2008b; Kriegel 2007, 2011, 2016; Mendelovici 2018; Pitt 2009) reject the relational conception of intentionality. This view erases that conceptual gap between intentionality and flat consciousness, but I argued (in Chapter 1) that intentionality essentially involves relationality in the weak sense, and the arguments presented above against intentionality-to-phenomenality conceptual reductions do not depend on intentionality essentially involving more than a weak relation. A commitment to aspectual shapes is not a commitment to actual reference to existing objects—it is compatible with the possibility of intentional inexistence. The same holds for the idea of the outward-looking face of intentionality, which concerns mere directedness, regardless of whether there exist objects toward which intentional states are directed. It is the mere potential to relate to objects that figures in these arguments.[50]

---

[50] As noted, phenomenal intentionalists usually take their accounts to be accounts of narrow content, and one might think that the reduction of narrow content to phenomenality (whether it is conceptual or synthetic) would be feasible, since narrow content is supposed to be non-relational.

86 INTENTIONALITY DECONSTRUCTED

The second way in which phenomenal intentionalists may object is to concede that intentionality is essentially relational, but to argue that phenomenal experience too is essentially relational (it is also "outward looking," we may say). Indeed, some proponents of PIT (see, e.g., Bourget 2019a, 2019b) endorse both a relational view of intentionality and a relational view of phenomenal properties. Bourget (2019a) even takes the relational view of phenomenal properties of perceptual experience to be analytically true. Since the relational view of intentionality is, if true, analytically true, the conjunction of these two views appears to overcome the difficulty I raised against the conceptual reduction of intentionality to phenomenality in the case of perceptual experience. However, in order to secure the conceptual connection between intentionality and phenomenality, more is required than for phenomenal properties of perceptual experiences to be specific relational properties. It is required that they embody the same relationality that characterizes the intentionality of the experiences in question. Yet this result faces that recurrent problem of making intentionality "grounded" in nothing but intentionality, for the inward-looking face can have the same relationality only if it is already intentional.[51]

3.6 Against Synthetic Reductions of Intentionality to Phenomenality

The claim that the supposed "reducing" property of intentionality must embody the very same relationality that intentionality is supposed to involve will now lead us to consider the idea that there is a synthetic connection between phenomenality and intentionality. According to this idea, the intentional relation is reducible to another relation, one that is not conceptually connected to it.[52]

However, as we saw, for the notion of narrow content to be a notion of content in a significant sense, it cannot but be the notion of a function from context to referential content, and such a notion presupposes denotation or whatever other reference-like relation to a space of possible facts and is thus relational (even if in the weak sense). So, it would be in the same predicament as wide content.

I think that the view that sensory experiences do not refer to particular objects but merely denote general properties (see Tye 2014) ascribes to sensory experiences such functions, but in any event the individualistic notion of content it is committed to is a relational one.

[51] This reply is reminiscent of my claim that PIT, as a theory of grounding intentionality, is incompatible with representationalism.

Due to the affinity between phenomenal relationalism and phenomenal externalism, the remark made in section 3.3 concerning phenomenal externalism and phenomenal intentionality is also relevant here. As noted, on a version of phenomenal externalism that is a conjunction of representationalism and semantic externalism, phenomenal character can only constitute intentionality as being constituted by intentionality, while on a version of phenomenal externalism that does not involve representationalism, the externalist nature it attributes to phenomenal character is irrelevant to intentionality and so to PIT.

[52] To be precise, the intentional relation is supposed to be reducible to what *appears to be* another (and conceptually distinct) relation. Such are reductions.

We saw that intentionality is relational, then, but (as the possibility of intentional inexistence shows) it is essentially weakly relational. If there are intentional states, then only occasionally (although, perhaps, frequently) they are relational in the strong sense. So, the issue of whether intentionality is reducible to something else is, first and foremost, the issue of the reducibility of its weakly relational nature. The weak intentional relation is supposed to be reducible to a weak relation that is not conceptually connected to it. What form should such a reduction take *when the reducing property is supposed to be phenomenal character?* In fact, phenomenal intentionalists who argue on non-conceptual grounds that the intentional is reducible to the phenomenal—those who endorse (in my terminology) synthetic intentionality-to-phenomenality reductionism—fail to provide an explanation of *how* a mental state's phenomenal nature allows it to be directed upon an extra-mental object.[53] Horgan and Tienson (2002) express awareness of this fact by admitting that they do not provide an answer to the hard question of phenomenal intentionality: namely, the question of "why should a mental state that is grounded in this physical or physical/functional state be *by its intrinsic phenomenal nature* directed in this precise manner?" (p. 530).

Some proponents of PIT suggest explanations that might seem to make progress toward answering this question. Thus, Katalin Farkas (2013) explains why we intuitively take experiences of some kinds (e.g., tactile ones) but not of others (e.g., pains) to relate us to mind-independent features, by appealing to certain elements of the structure of experience (e.g., match in temporal duration between the occurrence of the experiences and that of their putative external causes). It is these experiential elements that, according to Farkas, make some experiences "intentional." However, the sense of "intentional" in Farkas's discussion is phe-nomenological: that is, it concerns "what *appears* to be presented by an experience" (p. 99). Yet, as Papineau (2021, pp. 92–93) argues (and Farkas would agree), the contrast that Farkas draws is purely within the realm of experience, and those experiential elements do not reach out beyond themselves. Masrour (2013) makes a similar move: he suggest a Kantian account (in terms of schematic dynamical unity) for the "phenomenal objectivity" of experience: that is, for the fact that in having perceptual experiences we seem to encounter mind-independent items. Like Farkas's account, Masrour's account does not explain how the (alleged) directedness of experience is constituted by its phenomenality.[54]

---

[53] Non-conceptualist phenomenal intentionalists do not characterize the reduction in question as empirical, as synthetic, or as falling into any other category along these dimensions, and do not make the distinction between conceptual phenomenal intentionality reductions and synthetic-empirical ones. Non-conceptual reductions in general are usually characterized as empirical, but in the case of phenomenal intentionality characterizing them as synthetic seems to me to be more apt. (The expression "synthetic reductionism" is prevalent in discussions in meta-ethics.)

[54] Voltolini (2022) makes a similar point concerning Masrour's account as part of his general attack on PIT.

88   INTENTIONALITY DECONSTRUCTED

Though, trivially, explaining how phenomenality can secure intentionality would improve the dialectical position of PIT, a systematic failure to provide such explanations may not indicate its falsity, for arguably this is the fate of any synthetic a posteriori reduction. I am not sure that it is, but my argument against the reductions in question does not rely on this failure. Relatedly, my argument does not presuppose that the very existence of a conceptual gap implies a metaphysical gap. Rather, by eliminating the possibilities in logical space, I will argue that, due to their specific (weak) relational transcending nature, intentional properties cannot be grounded in phenomenal properties with which they are not conceptually connected.

Here goes. If the idea of a synthetic intentionality-to-phenomenality reduction makes sense, such reductions can be either direct or indirect. Direct synthetic intentionality-to-phenomenality reductions consist in a direct determination of the (weak) intentional relation by phenomenal character, with no mediation of another (weak) relation to which the (weak) intentional relation is reduced. Such direct reductions are non-starters. Consider, first, the idea that the phenomenal character of *a single* phenomenal state (or part or aspect thereof) constitutes intentionality or intentionality-as-purport in this way. The question is where the relationality (or weak relationality) of intentionality might come from (in the sense of what might constitute such relationality, rather than the causal sense of how a state that possesses a relational-intentional property might be produced). And, then, if we are not allowed to assume that phenomenality is constituted (even partly) by intentionality (an option that has been discussed here sufficiently to rule it out as irrelevant to our issue), no answer can be provided to this question, for no such external relation (even a weak external relation) is to be found in phenomenality that is not constituted by intentionality. The intentional relation cannot emerge *ex nihilo*: that is, *ex* the non-relational.[55]

Can intentionality be constituted by a combination of phenomenal elements? However such a notion of intentionality-to-phenomenality reduction is developed, it should be ruled out, since an intentional relation cannot emerge from a mere combination of elements that are not themselves intentional. This claim by no means presupposes that the intentional cannot be reduced to the non-intentional. It is compatible with the possibility of an extrinsic reduction. Its point is that the conjoining of non-intentional elements cannot do the trick. Think, for example, of conjoining linguistic elements, none of which even weakly represents anything, into a sentence. No such sentence (or any part thereof) would represent anything.[56]

---

[55] I am not presupposing here that the intentional relation is irreducible to a non-intentional relation. The next chapter deals with such reductions. This point will become clear immediately.

[56] In a related but different context, Papineau writes: "Entities get to be representational because of their relationship to things beyond themselves. So if we take a system of entities that are not yet so related, we cannot render them representational just by adding further such entities" (Papineau 2021, p. 107).

AGAINST PHENOMENAL INTENTIONALITY AS INTRINSIC REDUCTION   89

(The option that intentionality *causally emerges* from interactions among various phenomenal elements is irrelevant to the issue of how intentionality is constituted, for it allows us to account, at most, for the production of an event that is intentional, rather than for its possessing intentionality.)

There is, however, a related notion in logical space: namely, that intentionality is determined by dispositional properties of mental states that supervene on these states' phenomenal characters (dispositions that are of course rooted in the states' causal powers). Think, for example, of a mental state's disposition to initiate an action upon some object—an object that thereby becomes the intentional object of that mental states (and we may similarly think of a mental disposition to token some mental state upon encountering some object). Such an intentionality-to-phenomenality reduction is in fact the alternative to the direct one: it consists in phenomenal character determining a weak (non-intentional) relation, to which the weak intentional relation is reducible.[57] In contrast to the one-stage direct reductions, these intentionality-to-phenomenality reductions are two-stage reductions: the weak intentional relation—the intentional state's potentially being about object O—is reduced to another (non-intentional) weak relation that connects the intentional state with O when the right circumstances obtain (stage 1). In turn, a phenomenal property of the intentional state is responsible for its having this weak non-intentional relation (stage 2). If an indirect synthetic intentionality-to-phenomenality reduction is possible, it cannot but take this form.

Reductions of this form resemble extrinsic naturalistic reductions, but they are supposed to yield phenomenally constituted intentionality. Is it indeed the phenomenal character that determines intentionality in such cases? It is not, since it is possible for two phenomenally different states, or for a phenomenal state and non-phenomenal state, to share such weak relations or dispositions—dispositions for actual relations between the mental and the extra-mental. So as to reduce the outward-looking (weak) intentional relation, those (weak) non-intentional relations should themselves be "outward-looking": for example, dispositions to initiate actions upon intentional objects. Nothing about their inner nature is required, as long as it sustains the relevant extrinsic nature: they can be rooted in various intrinsic properties that are not necessarily phenomenal ones. (The Janus-faced character of experiences and the inward-looking/outward-looking chasm strike again.) If this is right, then it is not the phenomenal character that determines intentionality (as purport-to-refer) in such reductions. We may say that it is not the phenomenal state *qua* phenomenal state that determines intentionality. It is not that phenomenal states "are intrinsically, *by their very [phenomenal] nature,* directed toward whatever they are directed toward" (to use Horgan and Tienson's

---

[57] The current suggestion is concerned with dispositions to bear causal relations to objects rather than with actual causal relations because it must pertain to weak relations or weakly relational properties.

90 INTENTIONALITY DECONSTRUCTED

words cited above). The dependence between phenomenality and intentionality in such a case seems to fall short of yielding the "doctrinal in virtue" connection (in Kriegel's sense) that underlies grounding in the sense relevant to answering the question of intentionality. The reduction in question not only resembles an extrinsic naturalistic reduction, but in fact boils down to one.

This line of reasoning can be supported by considering an objection. It could be argued that there is one way (indeed, only one) in which the status of phenomenal character as the determiner of intentionality in this model is preserved. Think of the possibility that—according to the correct (reductive-naturalistic) theory of intentionality and the correct theory of phenomenal consciousness—a state that possesses those (weak) relational properties that are required for intentionality cannot but be phenomenal and cannot but have its specific phenomenal character.[58] The dispositional form of reduction mentioned here is compatible with such a possibility, which seems to block my argument that this reduction is not a reduction of intentionality to phenomenality (in the full-blown sense required for answering the question of intentionality): no non-phenomenal states can play the role that phenomenal states play, and it is phenomenal character (*qua* phenomenal character) that determines intentionality. However, this possibility too falls short of forming a reduction in the required sense. For on this possibility, that which constitutes intentionality also constitutes phenomenality, and so intentionality is not grounded in phenomenality. We may say that on this possibility, in order to get intentionality you have to inject phenomenality into the world, but this is true just because you inject phenomenality into the world by injecting intentionality. That is, on such an account intentionality is not in fact reduced to something else, and we do not get phenomenality-constituted intentionality.

Thus, all possible forms of synthetic intentionality-to-phenomenality reductions are doomed to fail. Since conceptual intentionality-to-phenomenality reductions have also been shown to fail, we can conclude that PIT is false. I hope to have reaffirmed the initial suspicion that the inward-looking cannot ground the outward-looking.

3.7 Against Intrinsic Reductions of Intentionality

The notion that intentionality is an intrinsic mental property can take either a primitivist form or a reductive form. In Chapter 1, I argued that intentionality cannot be primitive. For intentionality to nevertheless be an intrinsic mental property, it should be reducible to another mental property that is intrinsic to the mind. This is how PIT conceives of intentionality: being reducible to

---

[58] It seems to me that Kriegel's theory of intentionality (2011) and his theory of phenomenal consciousness (2009) coincide in such a way.

phenomenality, which is an intrinsic property of mental states (of at least some kinds), intentionality too is an intrinsic property of mental states (of at least some kinds). In the previous sections we saw that both analytic and synthetic intentionality-to-phenomenality reductions are doomed to fail, which means that we should reject the very idea that intentionality is reducible to phenomenal consciousness. Of course, establishing this is not establishing that intentionality is not reducible to any intrinsic mental property. We may ask, though, whether there are any alternative candidates to serve as such an intrinsic mental property. It seems there are none.[59] But I think the point is deeper.

Let's start with conceptual reductions. Recall my argument regarding the outward-looking nature of intentionality. As noted, since a contrast is not required for properties to be conceptually distinct, a property need not be inward-looking in order to be conceptually distinct from intentionality. It suffices that this property *lacks* an outward-looking face, or, in other words, that it lacks "externally looking arrows." Thus, the supposed reducing property cannot be a flat psychological surface, and, put positively, must itself be intentionality-involving (as it is according to representationalism), which is a self-defeating result. Since this reasoning does not make use of the notion of an inward-looking face or any other peculiar feature of phenomenal consciousness, it applies to the conceptual reduction of intentionality to any possible intrinsic property of mental states. So the problem with the conceptually based reduction of intentionality to phenomenality is an instance of the general problem with any conceptually based intrinsic reduction of intentionality.

The same holds for the considerations presented above against the synthetic intentionality-to-phenomenality reduction. As to direct reductions of this sort, precisely as we are not allowed to assume that phenomenality is constituted (even partly) by intentionality, we are not allowed to assume that any other mental property is thus constituted. And then we have no answer at our disposal as to where the relationality (or weak relationality) of intentionality might come from (and appealing to a combination of non-intentional mental elements would not help). As to indirect synthetic intentionality-to-phenomenality reductions, their impossibility is rooted in the fact that phenomenal character is an intrinsic property of mental states, coupled with the outward-looking face of intentionality. And thus, the point generalizes: Precisely as it is possible for two phenomenally different states, or a phenomenal state and non-phenomenal state, to share weak intentional relations (intentionality as purport-to-refer), it is possible for two mental states that differ in any intrinsic properties to share weak intentional properties. So no intrinsic mental nature determines intentionality (or intentionality as purport-to-refer). Thus, intentionality cannot be synthetically reducible to

---

[59] To repeat, since forms of cognitive consciousness presuppose intentionality, intentionality cannot be reduced to any of them.

92   INTENTIONALITY DECONSTRUCTED

any intrinsic mental property, precisely as it cannot be conceptually reducible to any such property. Shifting the burden of intentionality to another intrinsic mental property does not advance us one bit.

3.8 Indeterminacy Again

In section 3.4 I argued against the epistemic claim that semantic indeterminacy can be rejected by relying on introspection. A related claim, also made by some proponents of the phenomenal intentionality thesis, is that phenomenal consciousness provides semantic determinacy. Now we are in a position to see that this metaphysical claim is also false.

According to Horgan and Graham, who deal with the indeterminacy theses of Quine and Davidson, phenomenal consciousness constitutes content determinately.[60] At the same time, Horgan and Graham accept semantic externalism for various concepts, such as natural kind concepts. Galen Strawson deals with an indeterminacy problem that he dubs "the stopping problem": does a visual experience (or its accompanying thought) refer to the external object causing it, to the light waves it reflects, to some neural happenings in the subject's brain, etc? How does intentionality know where to stop? Strawson replies that what determines that the experience's intentional object is the external object is the experience's phenomenal character, by means of the conception (or "taking") it involves of what particular thing the experience is about (see Strawson 2010, appendix).

One question that arises both for Horgan and Graham and for Strawson is how the external link that connects the experience or thought to the object cooperates with the experience's phenomenal character to provide intentional determinacy. Horgan and Graham suggest that "The overall determinacy of thought...derives from the determinacy of phenomenal intentionality: externalistic intentionality is jointly dependent upon (i) phenomenally constituted, determinate, reference-eligibility conditions that govern externalistically reference-purporting thought constituents...and (ii) the presence of individuals or kinds, in a thinker's external environment, that satisfy those reference-eligibility conditions" (Horgan and Graham 2012, p. 338; see also Horgan, Tienson, and Graham 2004). This is not very clear, but I suppose the general idea is that phenomenal intentionality, that is narrow, determines satisfaction conditions that objects are referred to *as possessing*. The objects that are thus referred to are those objects in the subject's environment that bear the right external relations to the thoughts in question. So, an external relation determines the intentional object, and the phenomenal character

---

[60] Similar ideas are expressed in Horgan and Tienson (2002), Horgan, Tienson, and Graham (2004), and Loar (1987, 1995).

AGAINST PHENOMENAL INTENTIONALITY AS INTRINSIC REDUCTION   93

determines *as what* it is referred to: for example, *as a rabbit*, rather than as undetached rabbit parts.

On Strawson's view, it seems, external relations choose a short list of candidates (those different links of the chosen causal chain) for being the experience's intentional object, and the phenomenal character makes a further choice, selecting one of these candidates: namely, the external object that causes the experience. Yet how can the internal phenomenal character choose one of those candidates? Is it supposed to choose link number 2 of whatever causal chain leads to its occurrence? Perhaps the idea is that the experience's phenomenal character fixes *the type* of object or event that is represented by the experience (i.e., its being an external physical object rather than, say, neural activity), and the external link fixes *the specific* object of this type—it is that external object *that is causally linked to this very experience*. On this understanding, Strawson's handling of the indeterminacy challenge is similar to Horgan and Graham's.

Both solutions suffer from difficulties. Horgan and Graham's solution is partly based on semantic externalism, but seems to conflict with it, since, according to semantic externalism, narrow mental features fail to uniquely determine not only objects but also properties (or "conditions"). For example, narrow mental features cannot determine that for something to be under the extension of our "water"-thoughts it must be H_2O rather than XYZ.[61] Strawson's solution does not tell us what makes some (e.g., causal) world–mind relation rather than another relevant to the intentionality of mental states. Thus, it is ineffective against arguments according to which the short list of candidates, which the supposedly intentional object is a member of, is indeterminate. Among these arguments are Putnam's model-theoretic argument (Putnam 1980, 1981, 1988, 1989), according to which whether words refer to some items or to their permutations is indeterminate (within the framework of metaphysical realism), the argument to be suggested in Chapter 4, and perhaps Davidson's above-mentioned argument.

However, there is a deeper problem with both solutions. How, in principle, can experience deliver semantic determinacy? Neither Horgan and Graham nor Strawson provide an explanation for this. Perhaps Horgan and Graham view this question as an aspect of the hard question of intentionality, for which they do not pretend to know the answer. Strawson does raise the question. His reply is: "It just can. That's how it is. This is what we do. This is the power of the entirely natural phenomenon of conscious thought" (Strawson 2010, p. 353). Strawson confesses to hold "the *pff!* Thesis" that "when there's experience, *pff!*, there's intentionality" (p. 352).

---

[61] Farkas shows that phenomenal intentionalists can account for content in a purely internalistic way, but her argument assumes the correctness of the very idea that phenomenal character can constitute content. See Farkas (2008b); various parts of Farkas (2008a) are also relevant to the issue.

94 INTENTIONALITY DECONSTRUCTED

Notice the dialectic: intentionality of experience, Strawson accepts, is threatened by external indeterminacy (i.e., all external relations of an experience leave its intentionality indeterminate), and (Strawson confesses) we cannot *explain* intentional determinacy by the internal (by consciousness). But it must be the case that consciousness secures intentional determinacy, because it is a fact that experience has determinate content.

But why think it is a fact that experience has determinate content? Once we accept (1) that an appeal to the third-person perspective fails to establish determinacy and (2) that we don't have an explanation for how experience can deliver determinacy, then we have no reason to prefer the claim that there is intentional determinacy that is secured by phenomenality over the claim that intentionality is indeterminate (and hence unreal). Introspection, we saw, is no source of evidence for content. There seems to be no weaker reason (if not a stronger one) to move, rather, from the unexplainable to the non-factual. No explanation—no fact. That is, Strawson provides no reason to believe that consciousness cures external intentional indeterminacy. Neither do Horgan and Graham, who do not address the question.

Certainly, this would be different if there were strong reasons for believing in intentional realism, which is incompatible with intentional indeterminacy, which means that there is no fact of the matter regarding content. Assuming intentional realism and external intentional indeterminacy, we may reasonably conclude that phenomenality secures intentional determinacy and tolerate the unexplainable nature of this phenomenon. So, Horgan and Graham and Strawson's case depends on their providing strong reasons for intentional realism. The burden of proof is on them, and it is anything but easy. I believe that in this chapter and in Chapters 5 and 6, I undermine the prominent arguments for intentional realism.

But let us put to one side considerations of burden of proof. More importantly, if the arguments against PIT, presented above, are on the right track, it is no surprise that those philosophers who argue that consciousness is supposed to provide intentional determinacy do not explain how it could do so. One upshot of these arguments is that consciousness cannot do that. It can play no role in constituting content or any (semantic) aspect thereof.[62] It can neither constitute content from scratch, as it were, nor supplement external relations to secure determinate content. This is an upshot of those arguments, since what they in fact show is that consciousness can pick out no extra-mental element. So, if indeed external factors cannot ensure intentional determinacy, then we are bound to accept ubiquitous intentional indeterminacy—neither consciousness nor any other feature intrinsic to the mind can provide the cure.

---

[62] Since, as I argued, no intrinsic feature can play a role in grounding intentionality, Strawson's "taking" cannot do that as well.

3.9 What Has Been Shown and What Has Not Been Shown regarding the Intentionality of Phenomenal States

In this chapter, I have argued against the idea that conscious phenomenal properties play a role in constituting intentionality (or intentionality-as-purport, or narrow intentionality). I both criticized arguments in favor of this idea and argued against this idea itself. We saw that both possible options of reducing intentionality to phenomenality—the conceptual (analytic) and the synthetic—are flawed. Nor can phenomenal properties supplement external relations and secure determinate content.[63] I also explicated the idea of phenomenal intentionality as an instance of the idea of intrinsic intentionality, and generalized the arguments against the former, showing that no intrinsic mental property can ground intentionality. Intrinsic intentionality is intrinsic transcendence, or, as some philosophers of the phenomenological tradition referred to it, immanent transcendence. These characterizations allude to the tension inherent in this idea. The case suggested here against the idea of intrinsic intentionality can be said to make this tension explicit and show it to be irremediable.

It is worth emphasizing that the issue of this chapter has not been whether experiences are intentional. Rather, the issue has been whether they are intentional in virtue of their phenomenal character, or other intrinsic mental property (when this "in virtue" is understood in its strong, doctrinal, sense). I have argued that they aren't. I haven't argued that phenomenally conscious states are not intentional. For all I have argued, they may be intentional in virtue of their external relations, in the way suggested by some reductive-naturalistic theory. Similarly, nothing I have argued means or entails that the intentionality of experiences is not the source of all intentionality. As noted earlier, the reductive-naturalistic approach can make room for the idea that it is, though not in the same way as does the thesis of phenomenal intentionality. I argue against this approach in the next chapter.

---

[63] It is not one of this book's goals to scrutinize accounts of phenomenal consciousness, and so I do not discuss the ardent dispute concerning whether or not representational content exhaustively determines phenomenal character. Although (as I argued in section 3.3) PIT (in the strong sense in which it is understood here) is incompatible with representationalism, it might be that specific arguments against one of these views undermine the very connection between intentionality and phenomenality and so undermine the other view as well. Thus, anti-representationalist arguments to the effect that phenomenality does not essentially involve intentionality, such as Papineau's (2014, 2021) argument, are *ipso facto* arguments against the view that phenomenality determines intentionality. (Papineau indeed pursues this path and shows that his argument undermines the thesis of phenomenal intentionality.) It might be thought that if the arguments of this chapter against the phenomenality-intentionality connection are successful, they undermine not only phenomenal intentionality but also representationalism. I believe that the truth value of this conditional claim depends on whether the representationalist idea that "phenomenal character is *nothing but* representational character" is understood as "deflationist" or as "subjectivist," but the wider discussion that the issue deserves cannot be conducted in this framework.

4

Against Naturalistic Reductions
of Intentionality

4.1 The Idea of Intentional Naturalistic Reduction

In the previous chapter, I argued against both conceptual and synthetic reductions of intentionality to phenomenality, and, more generally, to any intrinsic mental property of supposedly intentional states.[1] In the case of synthetic reductions of intentionality to phenomenality (or to any other intrinsic mental property), the intentional relation is supposed to be reducible to another, conceptually distinct, relation, where the identity of this relation is determined by a phenomenal (or another intrinsic mental) property. My argument against such reductions targeted the determination of the relation in question by an intrinsic mental property but left intact the possible reducibility of the intentional relation to another (conceptually distinct) relation. Can there be an extrinsic reduction of intentionality, wherein the intentional relation is reduced to another relation that is not determined by any intrinsic mental property? In this chapter I argue against the idea of such a reduction.

The idea in question is that intentionality can be reduced to a naturalistic "tracking" relation. Invoking such a relation is supposed to account for the transcending nature of intentionality and can be viewed as a reply to Richard Rorty's claim (reported, e.g., in Putnam 1994, p. 285) that the mind is related to the world causally but not semantically. The reductive-naturalist may be taken to reply: the mind is related to the world causally *and therefore* (or *thus*) semantically. The essence of the reductive-naturalistic approach to intentionality is that one entity represents another simply by (or in the sense of) being related to the other entity by means of a naturalistic relation. The transcending nature of intentionality on this approach boils down to a relation of a familiar kind: intentionality transcends its bearer just as, say, the causal property of the kicking foot transcends the foot to the kicked ball. On this approach, the intentional relation is not *sui generis*. It is a relation of a kind well known to us, paradigmatically a causal relation of some kind, or a causal relation that obtains under some specified conditions, etc.

---

[1] Recall that in Chapter 1 I argued against theories that take intentionality to be reduced to interconnections among mental states: that is, short-armed functional role theories.

Intentionality Deconstructed: An Anti-Realist Theory. Amir Horowitz, Oxford University Press.
© Amir Horowitz 2024. DOI: 10.1093/oso/9780198896432.003.0004

The reductive-naturalistic approach may thus appear to dissolve the mystery of intentionality, which is the mystery of its transcending nature.[2]

Before turning to show that the reductive-naturalistic reply to the question of intentionality is inadequate, let me make a few clarificatory remarks. First, naturalistic approaches standardly have to face the challenge of characterizing "naturalistic." However, facing this challenge is not urgent for proponents of the naturalistic reduction of intentionality since this reduction simply aims to reduce the intentional to a *non-intentional* or *non-semantic* extrinsic element. Essential to the reductive-naturalistic approach to intentionality are the convictions that the entire world can be described non-semantically and that its complete non-semantic description implies its complete semantic description. Recall Fodor's words: "If aboutness is real, it must be really something else" (Fodor 1987, p. 97). Of course, many proponents of intentional reductionism are motivated by the desire to make room for intentionality in a purely physical world, and successful reduction of the intentional to the non-intentional would indeed amount to success in this task. But the above convictions have no necessary connection to the issue of physicalism.

What appears to make the characterization of "naturalistic" as non-intentional unsatisfactory in this context is the fact that the reductive-naturalistic research program is usually not taken to include the reduction of intentionality to normative elements. Such a reduction may be taken to ground one elusive phenomenon in another elusive phenomenon, unless, of course, the normative itself can be reduced to what is obviously naturalistic. But we shall see that reducing intentionality to any norm that cannot be reduced to what is obviously naturalistic is not even initially plausible, so including "non-normative" in the characterization of "naturalistic" in this context (which could be thought to require further elucidation) seems to lose importance.[3]

---

[2] The emergence of the phenomenal intentionality research program was, in part, a reaction to the reductive-naturalistic research program (see Kriegel 2013). My discussion reverses the chronological order for two reasons. First, the first argument to be presented against reductive naturalism relies on a claim argued for in my discussion of phenomenal intentionality: namely, that intentionality is beyond the reach of introspection. Second, the reductive-naturalistic idea is, in an important respect, a revisionist idea (see Chapter 5), and it makes sense to initially undermine a conservative embodiment of intentional realism.

[3] Some philosophers object to the reductive-naturalistic program on the grounds that, first, intentionality is essentially normative (in this or that sense), and second, normativity cannot be naturalized (see Kripke 1982). Adopting both claims makes the characterization of the naturalistic reduction of intentionality in terms of a reduction to the non-intentional insufficient. However, I think Jerry Fodor's following objection to the view that intentionality is irreducibly normative in any significant sense is decisive: "To apply a term to a thing in its extension *is* to apply it correctly; once you've said what it is that makes the tables the extension of 'table's, there is surely no *further* question about why it's *correct* to apply a 'table' to a table" (Fodor 1990, pp. 135–136). So I think that proponents of the naturalistic reduction of intentionality need not be bothered by its alleged normativity. I will later refer to the idea of accounting for the referential dimension of intentionality in normative terms.

My second clarificatory note also bears on the first one. The reduction that is the focus of this chapter aims to reduce intentionality to an external (extra-mental) naturalistic relation. Not all reductions of intentionality are relational, and not all relational reductions of intentionality employ external relations: that is, relations to the non-mental environment. Phenomenal intentionality reductions are typically (though not always) non-relational, whereas a short-armed functional role reduction, such as Block's (1986), is a relational but not extrinsic (in the sense of extra-mental) reduction. Examples of reductive theories in the sense under discussion are informational theories, optimal conditions theories, asymmetric dependence theories, long-armed conceptual role theories, and teleological theories. Such theories are sometimes referred to as "tracking theories."[4]

What is in fact important for my argument against intentional realism—after rejecting primitivism and intrinsic reductionism—is to rule out the possibility of reducing intentionality to external non-intentional relations. Since the arguments of this chapter aim (as they should) to rule out all possible reductions of this sort, it does not matter what the exact sense in which they are naturalistic is. The available theories (such as the ones just mentioned) are naturalistic in some roughly understood sense, having to do with their applying notions from the natural sciences (and for this reason I will hold on to the common terminology of "naturalistic theories" or "reductive naturalistic theories"). But none of their specific characteristics plays any essential role in the arguments to be suggested. My arguments aim to undermine the very idea of the intentional relation as an external non-intentional relation.

My third clarificatory note is that the extrinsic reductive-naturalistic approach need not restrict itself to accounting for the intentionality of the mental directly and to taking the intentionality of language, for example, to be merely derived. Rather, it is possible to suggest a naturalistic reduction that accounts straightforwardly for the intentionality of language. From the reductive-naturalistic perspective, the intentionality of the mind and that of language may be of the same kind, and the distinction between original (underived) and derived intentionality need not be deep. On Fodor's (1987) view, for example, psycho-semantics has priority over lingua-semantics only due to the fact that—or in the sense that—the relevant mind–world causal chains are shorter than the relevant language–world causal chains.[5] In the following discussion, I focus on the purported reduction of

---

[4] Such theories are offered by, *inter alia*, Artiga (2021), Dretske (1981, 1986, 1988, 1995), Fodor (1987, 1990), Garson and Papineau (2019), Harman (1982, 1987, 1999), Martínez (2013), Millikan (1984, 1989, 1993, 2004), Neander (2017), Papineau (1984, 1987, 2016, 2022), Piccinini (2020), Shea (2007, 2018), Schulte (2012), Stalnaker (1984), Stampe (1977), and Williams (2020), which also has an interpretivist aspect. For a critical review, see Loewer (2017).

[5] For reductive-naturalistic approaches that account straightforwardly (but in ways that are quite different from each other) for the intentionality of language, see Sellars (1963), Stampe (1977), Millikan (1984), and Harman (1999). Perhaps direct reference approaches can also be classified as falling under this category, but they may also be interpreted differently (see Kriegel 2011, p. 212).

the intentionality of the mental, but the discussion is supposed to apply (perhaps sometimes with adjustments) to the purported reduction of the intentionality of language (or of anything else) as well.

As Nicholas Shea observes, "[T]he recent history of attempts to naturalize representational content is a story of many ideas and no conclusive resolution. Every view faces problems as a full and unified theory of content. Nor is there consensus about which approach is more promising" (Shea 2013, p. 502).[6] The criticism to be suggested here does not concern any specific reductive-naturalistic theory or research program but rather aims to undermine the very idea of intentional naturalistic reductionism.

4.2 The Naturalistic Reduction of Intentionality as a Scientific Reduction

It might be instructive to compare the naturalistic reduction of intentionality with a scientific reduction, such as the infamous case of water–H_2O. What is reduced in this latter case is watery stuff. That is, stuff with watery properties is given and is reduced to something that underlies these properties. We couple two kinds of properties: macro properties (watery properties) and micro properties, and the micro properties are supposed to be able to figure in explanations of the macro properties. The general picture is that of some pre-theoretically given property (or properties) constituted by some underlying property. But there is no analogy in this respect between such a reduction and the supposed reduction of intentionality. There are no two properties (or sets of properties) in the case of intentionality, for there is no analogue to the macro (watery) properties. Let's refer to the naturalistic relation to which the intentional relation is supposed to be

---

A naturalistic approach that gives priority to the intentionality of the mind may be an account of content derivation, but it need not be. It is an account of content derivation if and only if the fact that the mental links in the causal chains that connect linguistic entities with the world are intentional plays an essential role in endowing those linguistic entities with intentionality. (That would be the case if, for example, linguistic intentionality is accounted for in the Gricean way, assuming that it is naturalizable.) If the intentionality of linguistic entities is anchored in the mere fact that they are causally connected with the world in a specific way, and the significance of the mental links simply consists in their being links in those chains, then the linguistic entities do not derive their intentionality from the mental links.

Somewhat paradoxically, on a version of intentional anti-realism that takes naturalistic relations to underlie content ascriptions (which is discussed in section 4.6) and assigns priority to mental intentionality over linguistic intentionality, the (merely ascribed) intentionality of the mental links is essential to the (merely ascribed) intentionality of the linguistic links. This is so because the priority in question is rooted in the fact that our practice of content ascriptions simply matches the contents ascribed to language to those ascribed to the mind. This is a matter of interpretive choice, whose rationale might be that our assertions usually indicate our thoughts (and therefore may be said to "express" them). See the discussion of mind–language relations in Chapter 5.

[6] Recently, Shea himself suggested a reductive-naturalistic theory of content (Shea 2018), but he confined his theory to contents of "sub-personal" (i.e., non-doxastic, non-conscious) mental states.

100   INTENTIONALITY DECONSTRUCTED

reduced and that is, thus, supposed to be analogous to the micro property as "R." "R" can stand for some causal relation that obtains under optimal conditions, for some evolutionary function, and so forth. The question I raise is what is the macro analogue that R is supposed to reduce: that is, what is the property that is supposed to be given to us pre-theoretically? I will argue that there is no such macro analogue. More precisely, there is no such property that can both be reduced to external relations—even to *weak* external relations—and fit intentional realism.

Let's start with the suggestion that it is those properties that we introspect in our experiences or other mental states as intentional that are reduced to R. In other words, the analogue to the macro properties in the case of intentionality is *what* we experience as intentionality (and not *how* it is experienced by us). Since we are dealing with the scientific, macro–micro, model of reduction, this suggestion seems natural: precisely as science reduces the macro properties that we experience (e.g., watery properties), naturalistic philosophy reduces the intentional properties that we experience. A reductive-naturalistic approach of this form is a realist approach with respect to intentionality if those properties are intentional properties. However, as argued in Chapter 3, intentional properties are beyond the reach of introspection. The first-person perspective simply cannot connect us to intentional properties.[7,8] So, intentionality cannot be reduced in this way. Alternatively, it might be suggested that R matches with the introspected mental states themselves—that is, with the bearers of intentionality—rather than with their intentional properties, but such a suggestion would be as implausible as the suggestion that, in the case in which we aim to reduce the intentionality of language, R matches with a word.

A related suggestion is that R is supposed to match *how* our supposed intentional mental states appear to us from the first-person perspective. This suggestion cannot help the reductive-naturalistic philosopher insofar as her view is a form of intentional realism, since the fact that our mental states appear to us to be a certain way is our having a certain attitude toward our mental states, or, in other words, our ascribing some properties to our mental states (rather than what our ascriptions ascribe). If the macro analogue that figures in the reductive-naturalistic picture is such an ascription and nothing more, then the naturalistic relation in question

---

[7] It might be argued that the introspection of intentionality plays exactly the same role in its reduction that is played by the experience of water in its reduction, and thus that there must be something wrong with this objection. However, there is no analogy in this respect. For whereas the introspection of intentionality does not indicate the existence of intentionality (as we saw), experiencing water does indicate the existence of watery properties, which identify the stuff to be reduced.

[8] Note that my case against this "first-person" conception of the naturalistic reduction of intentionality does not presuppose that experiences or other mental states do not have intentional properties. What this case requires is merely that the first-person perspective does not connect us to such properties. Neither does the whole argument against the naturalistic approach to intentionality that is developed on these pages presuppose that.

AGAINST NATURALISTIC REDUCTIONS OF INTENTIONALITY   101

is not an intentional relation; rather its obtaining is *merely* the condition under which intentionality is ascribed. A theory that specifies such a relation is a theory about that which underlies some content ascriptions (first-person ones), not about intentionality. If the macro analogue to which the reductive-naturalistic approach to intentionality appeals is this seeming, then this approach is a form of intentional anti-realism.[9]

Let's move to consider another candidate for being the macro analogue in the case of intentionality. One might think that intentionality can be identified (in the to-be-reduced level) by means of the logico-syntactic properties of our mental states. Now if such properties are supposed to be what R matches with, then it must be the case that they endow our intentional states with specific semantic interpretations—those properties should single R out and thus determine the semantic interpretations. Yet, clearly, logico-syntactic properties cannot do that: the constraints they put on semantic interpretations fall far short of yielding such unique interpretations, and they cannot determine specific outward-looking aspects of any set of mental states. Any combination of such properties is compatible with a multitude of semantic interpretations. If this does not seem obvious to you, you might consult Putnam's model-theoretic argument (Putnam 1980, 1981, 1988, 1989), according to which even the entirety of our "knowledge" (understood in non-semantic terms, hence the quotation marks) cannot uniquely determine truth conditions and is thus compatible with the existence of a multitude of models.[10] Evidently, such properties cannot single R out.

A related idea, due to David Papineau (see, e.g., Papineau 1993, p. 93; 2001), is that intentionality can be identified (in the to-be-reduced level) by means of the functional roles of our intentional states. This seems to be the rationale that underlies various reductive-naturalistic accounts. The following characterization of this idea is offered by Braddon-Mitchell and Jackson: "Belief that p is the theoretically interesting state that actually plays the folk functional roles distinctive of belief that p (from reflection on what we master when we master intentional vocabulary)" (Braddon-Mitchell and Jackson 1997, p. 481).[11] According to this idea, identifying this functional role is a matter of conceptual analysis; R (in my terminology) is that mind–world relation that is in fact had by intentional states,

---

[9] It might be claimed that the seeming in question is intentional, but as I claimed in Chapter 3, we need not take it to be intentional (we can take it to be a response of some non-intentional sort to experience). If my arguments for intentional anti-realism are effective, we should not. Chapter 6 sheds further light on this issue. (Note that such a claim does not target the present argument against intentional reductive naturalism, but rather the thesis of intentional anti-realism, which this argument does not presuppose.)

[10] I am referring to the first part of Putnam's argument, which is quite non-controversial. This consideration does not rely on the whole argument, which is in itself an anti-reductivist argument and is quite controversial.

[11] Braddon-Mitchell and Jackson, as well as Papineau, are concerned with teleological theories of content. Braddon-Mitchell and Jackson argue that such theories cannot conform to this model of reduction (as well as to other ones). Papineau (2001) responds to their critique.

102   INTENTIONALITY DECONSTRUCTED

and identifying it is an a posteriori matter. This idea is subject to a difficulty similar to the one that undermines the suggested logico-syntactic identification: it presupposes that the functional roles in question determine semantic interpretations, yet they do not. The distinction between short-armed functional roles and long-armed ones is relevant in this context. Short-armed functional roles are notorious for failing to uniquely determine reference and truth conditions—they are compatible with innumerable semantic characterizations—and so they do not single R out.[12]

As to long-armed functional roles, in order to single out intentionality, they must include R itself—the actual naturalistic intentional relation. That is, the functional role of the intentional state with the content that p must include the fact that this state bears R to p. In that case, the identification of R as the intentional relation is a matter of pure conceptual analysis, involving no a posteriori stage: that is, the present suggestion presupposes that the concept of intentionality, or of reference, is (or includes) the concept of R. We are no longer in the game of scientific reduction. In section 4.3 we shall see that the determination of R cannot be a conceptual matter.[13]

So, we haven't identified a property of intentional states that singles R out: that is, a property that can both be reduced to external relations (even to *weak* ones) and fit intentional realism. Since it appears that all prima facie plausible options have been examined, the scientific analogy breaks down. Unlike standard scientific reductions, in the supposed naturalistic reduction of intentionality it is not the case that we discover that some pre-theoretically given property is constituted by some underlying property (as it was discovered that watery properties are constituted by H_2O).

Would it make sense to claim that the macro analogue in question is simply intentionality, aboutness, regardless of any way in which it is given to us? This view does not fit with scientific reduction. The reduction of water to H_2O is not such. It is not the case that we reduce water regardless of any way in which it is given to us. Rather, we reduce water as given to us by some of its macro properties (specifically, those "watery properties"). Let's suppose that instead of appealing to any such properties, a philosopher who endorses some naturalistic reduction of intentionality claims that she simply identifies some external relation R

---

[12] See Chapter 1, and also Fodor (1978), Rey (1980), McGinn (1982), and Horowitz (1992). Note that on the suggestion under consideration, functional role is supposed to be what determines R rather than R itself—it belongs to the to-be-reduced level rather than to the reducing level. So the suggestion is not a functional role semantic theory of intentionality. But the charge against short-armed functional role theories to the effect that functional roles do not determine intentional objects is effective against this suggestion, in showing that short-armed functional roles do not determine R.

[13] Braddon-Mitchell and Jackson distinguish this suggestion from another, according to which the naturalistic intentional relation is an essential property of intentional states. This difference makes no difference for my arguments against naturalistic reductions of intentionality.

AGAINST NATURALISTIC REDUCTIONS OF INTENTIONALITY   103

with aboutness. What could she reply, if asked what makes the reducing property she opts for identical with aboutness?

Replying that it is a relation to an extra-mental object would obviously be too weak. She might add that this naturalistic relation underlies our practice of content ascription (and that the appeal to the practice of content ascription is what, in fact, directs her choice of a relation). But this reply would not suffice either, for if she only defends, and can defend, her choice of a specific naturalistic reduction in this way, then she does not and cannot offer a realist approach to intentionality. Relatedly, she might also add that reports of this naturalistic relation respect logical or grammatical features that are typical of (or even unique to) reports of aboutness (e.g., intensionality). However, being truly reportable in a way that satisfies logico-syntactic constraints falls short of singling out a relation as aboutness: for example, it would not distinguish an object from its permutations.[14] Thus, insofar as intentional reductive naturalism depends on the notion of simply identifying R with aboutness, regardless of its being given to us in any way, it is doomed to fail.

The line of reasoning suggested in this section is general, for "R" can stand for whatever naturalistic relation. For example, this line of reasoning undermines the idea of cashing out intentionality in terms of information (see, e.g., Dretske 1981, 1986, 1988): that is, the idea that the content possessed by a representation is the information that it carries (while the notion of information in play is, e.g., the mathematical notion of information or some variation thereof). In the absence of "macro" constraints, nothing can make the identification of intentionality and information true. Note also that the argument that has just been presented against the reductive-naturalistic approach to intentionality as a scientific reduction does not presuppose that reductions of the intentional to the non-intentional depend on any specific model of scientific reductions. The argument only assumes that some (macro-analogue) property is supposed to constrain the identity of the supposed intentional naturalistic relation for such reductions to get off the ground, and derives the conclusion that the notion of such a reduction fails from the mere unavailability of such a property.

It seems that the collapse of the scientific analogy of the naturalistic reduction of intentionality means that the very idea of such reduction is false. But before embracing this conclusion, we have to consider an alternative conception of this reduction.

---

[14] The intentional reductive naturalist may seek assistance in another aspect of the water–H_2O case, and claim that this failure to single out a specific relation is not problematic, for, as many philosophers believe, it makes sense to say that water is necessarily H_2O even if both H_2O and some different microstructure may possess watery properties. However, this analogy cannot work in our case, since such a notion of intentionality (given in terms of grammatical constraints) would yield alternative intentional objects being had *by the same intentional state*, with no way to decide among them.

104 INTENTIONALITY DECONSTRUCTED

4.3 Naturalistic Reduction and the Concept of Reference

In this section I will attempt to pay off the debt that was left in the previous section: to rule out the possibility that the identity of R is a conceptual matter. According to this idea, the connection between intentionality and the naturalistic relation to which it is reduced is conceptual. That is, it is the concept of intentionality (or of reference, or of aboutness, etc.) that determines R as the intentional relation; R is what this concept is a concept of. Thus, in explaining what makes one—among the many word–world relations—the relation of reference, Michael Devitt writes.

> Why is the relation between Bill Clinton and Chelsie Clinton, Prince Philip and Prince Charles, and...rather than the relation between Bill Clinton and Newt Gingrich, Prince Philip and Baroness Thatcher...to be identified as **being the father of**? Or the analogous question about the property **cathood**: Why is the property of Nana, Jemina, and so on...rather than the property of Fido, Bill Clinton, and...to be identified as **cathood**? We need say no more in answer to these questions than that the specified relation just *is* **being the father of** and the specified property just *is* **cathood**. Similarly, we need say no more in answer to the question about reference than that the specified relation just *is* reference. That relation and no other simply is the one we call "reference" and that's that.
>
> (Devitt 1997, pp. 332–333)

The idea is that the identity of the naturalistic relation that is supposed to constitute intentionality is a conceptual matter. The reference relation, or the intentional relation, is simply that one among the many (language–world or mind–world) naturalistic relations that obtain in the world to which concepts such as "refers to" or "thinks that" apply. It is the concept of intentionality which determines R and connects it with intentionality; it is this concept with which R is supposed to "match." (We should not interpret this suggestion as committed to there being an explicit definition of "intentionality" or "reference." Plausibly, the idea is that R is singled out by the use of ascriptions of content and reference in various circumstances.) This idea seems to make sense. We regularly apply the concept of intentionality (or the concept of reference, or that of think about, etc.), and when we apply it from the third-person perspective, then, plausibly, its application conditions are naturalistic. At any rate, intentional realism as a form of intentional naturalistic reductionism thus appears to get a clear sense.

Indeed, this is not the story of scientific reduction—this is the standard story of concept application. But the question that we have to face is whether this story can sustain a realist interpretation of intentional naturalistic reductionism. Suspicions that it cannot sustain such an interpretation emerge upon considering what the water–H_2O analogue of the present suggestion would be. It would be the idea that H_2O is simply (identified as) what we label "water." That means that the watery properties are left out of the picture; they play no essential role in the truth conditions of the identity statement "Water is H_2O." This is certainly implausible. Such implausibility pertains also to Devitt's conceptualist conception of the naturalistic reduction of intentionality. This conceptualist conception of the naturalistic intentional relation leaves out something that it shouldn't: namely, aboutness. Consider: The statement that identifies intentionality with some naturalistic relation is supposed to be about a certain phenomenon that is pre-theoretically given to us—aboutness. As such, it must be a synthetic statement, and not merely one of labeling some relation—not merely a stipulation. If the reductive-naturalistic approach is a realist approach to intentionality—if it takes intentionality to be real and aims to inform us of its real nature—then it is committed to the idea that we first encounter the phenomenon of intentionality—namely, aboutness—and then identify the naturalistic relation that underlies this phenomenon (it's not that we learn what intentionality is upon encountering R). This means that the identity statement in question cannot be a stipulation of the sort under consideration. "Intentionality" is not supposed to be just a name for some naturalistic relation, a name that could be replaced (in statements such as "This is a case of intentionality" which accompany demonstrations of R) with any arbitrary combination of letters. And this is, in fact, what the present suggestion delivers—mere labeling that has nothing to do with aboutness. Trivially, the possibility of such a labeling affirms the obtaining of R, but our issue is that of intentional realism, not that of R-realism; intentionality, or the concept of intentionality, plays no role in stipulating that a certain term—be it "intentionality," "reference," or whatever other term—denotes R.

As noted, Devitt's conceptualist approach confronts the challenge of there being a multitude of naturalistic word–world—and, similarly, mind–world—relations. The reductive-naturalist must tell us what determines one of them as the intentional relation. In fact, the macro–micro analogy can be taken to address this very question. According to that analogy, it is the (pre-theoretically given) phenomenon of aboutness that constrains those relations. I argued that this reply fails because there are no relevant macro-like phenomena in the case of intentionality. Devitt's alternative reply is that it is stipulation (though he does not use this term) that singles out the relevant naturalistic relation, and I argued that this reply in fact leaves aboutness out. So, the naturalistic reduction of intentionality fails to relate the supposed intentional phenomenon with a naturalistic relation via the concept of intentionality: it will not do to say that some R is the relation called "reference" (or, relatedly, that this is how we ascribe content). Since it leaves aboutness out, adopting the conceptualist conception of the naturalistic reduction of intentionality would leave us with no external criterion for the truth of content ascriptions: that is, it would leave us with intentional anti-realism.

Further, the assumption underlying the very idea of connecting intentionality with R via its concept is false, for the concept of any naturalistic relation whatsoever

106 INTENTIONALITY DECONSTRUCTED

is not the concept of intentionality, or of reference, or of think about, etc. For the concept of intentionality—that is, the concept of aboutness—has nothing to do with any *specific* naturalistic relation. It is neutral with respect to the identity of the naturalistic relation—it does not prefer any specific relation over any other. Again, taking the connection between intentionality and R to be conceptual, in the sense under consideration, is an empty stipulation that robs "intentionality" of any content. Note also that had the concept of intentionality been the concept of a specific naturalistic relation, then any two philosophers who differed in what they took to be their theories of intentionality—that is, who differed in their views about the identity of the naturalistic relation to be associated with "intentionality"— would not have been able to understand each other when speaking about the referent of "intentionality." In fact, they would not have been referring by "intentionality" (and "reference" etc.) to the same phenomenon.

But one might think that this consideration does not undermine the claim that the concept of intentionality (the concept of aboutness) is the concept of R. Suppose that we adopt the externalist idea that one's macro concepts (e.g., the concept of water) are the concepts of whatever micro properties (e.g., H_2O) in fact—whether or not one knows it—underlie the relevant macro properties, and apply this approach to the relations between the pre-theoretic reduced concept of intentionality and R.[15] According to this suggestion, one's concept of intentionality is the concept of whatever external relation in fact underlies ascriptions of intentionality. It may thus be the concept of R, even though no pure a priori conceptual analysis can reveal R in it.

I take this externalist idea to be flawed,[16] but anyhow it cannot rescue intentional naturalistic reductionism from an irrealist or anti-realist fate. For, on such an approach, it is the connection between the reduced and reducing properties (e.g., watery properties on the one hand and H_2O on the other) that is supposed to be responsible for the macro concept being the concept of the specific micro property in question. Thus, the truth of the claim that the concept of intentionality is the concept of R depends on the supposed connection between intentionality in its macro phase and R. But since no "macro" properties are available in the case of the alleged intentional reduction, then—unlike the water–H_2O identification— there is no possible ground for this identification, or in other words, there is no criterion for its truth. Note that the externalist characterization of the concept of intentionality, under the current suggestion, is committed to intentional

---

[15] See Putnam (1975a). It is legitimate to assume semantic externalism in criticizing my argument even if externalism is understood as a realist thesis, since the burden of proof is with me to show that intentional realism (of all varieties) cannot be true within the reductive-naturalistic framework. Note also that externalism can be construed as a thesis regarding content ascriptions (a thesis to the effect that such ascriptions are sensitive to external factors) and thus as non-committal with respect to the issue of intentional realism.

[16] See Horowitz (2001, 2005). In these papers I took the issue to concern the nature of content rather than content ascriptions, but it can also be construed as concerning the latter (see Chapter 5).

AGAINST NATURALISTIC REDUCTIONS OF INTENTIONALITY 107

anti-realism. This concept is supposed to be the concept of whatever external relation in fact underlies ascriptions of intentionality. That is, in the absence of a relevant macro analogue, R can only be constrained by content ascriptions. This means that, insofar as intentional realism depends on naturalistic reductionism construed in this externalist manner, there is no criterion that is external to the practice of content ascriptions for the truth of such ascriptions; the truth of any content ascription is practice-dependent, so intentional realism is false.

We saw that the conceptualist model of intentional naturalistic reductionism fails. Precisely like the objection against the scientific macro–micro model of intentional naturalistic reductionism, the objection brought in this section against the conceptualist conception is effective regardless of which naturalistic relation figures in it. One may call information, or indication, or whatever other naturalistic relation "intentionality"—any such conceptual identification would leave intentionality out.

4.4 Naturalistic Reduction and Indeterminacy

I shall now present another argument against the very idea of the naturalistic reduction of intentionality. This argument has as its starting point a familiar difficulty that threatens the feasibility of this idea, and I would like to show that this difficulty is insurmountable. As is well known, there are not one but many kinds of causal and other naturalistic world–mind or world–language relations. Any single mental state bears naturalistic relations to many environmental items. The ubiquity of such relations is perhaps part of what makes the naturalistic approach to intentionality appealing; it appears that securing intentionality in such a framework is simple—just pick out one world–mind (or world–language) relation. Yet, the apparent simplicity of this naturalistic framework proves to be its downfall. For, the question arises, what makes one such kind of world–mind (or world–language) relation semantic? What makes one such relation the intentional relation? Even if we limit ourselves only to world–mind relations, there still remain many such relations, and the reductive naturalist must justify her choice of one of them as the intentional relation. What may justify any such choice? In what sense does this relation, rather than another, constitute intentionality and hook up our thoughts and words to the world?[17]

These questions may seem simple. In fact, Devitt's conceptualist account, cited above, responds to them. According to Devitt, recall, "we need say no more in answer to the question about reference than that the specified relation just *is*

[17] For arguments for reference indeterminacies of this kind, see Davidson (1979) and Putnam (1980, 1981, 1988, 1989). Also of relevance are the indeterminacy arguments of Quine (1960), Schiffer (1987), and Galen Strawson (2010, appendix).

108 INTENTIONALITY DECONSTRUCTED

reference. That relation and no other simply is the one we call 'reference' and that's that" (Devitt 1997, p. 333). On this approach, one naturalistic relation simply is the reference relation. If this approach is correct, it defends reductive naturalism from any possible indeterminacy charge: define "reference" specifically enough and you can set aside all but the true reference assignment of any concept.

To me, this sounds suspicious. Indeed, this approach isn't as innocuous as it appears to be. Devitt's wording is revealing: "That relation and no other simply is the one *we call 'reference'…*" (my emphasis). This means that, among the many naturalistic relations, it is the relation that is referred to by concepts such as "refers to," "think that," and the like. Thus, by using ascriptions of content and reference (as noted, we certainly do not explicitly define "reference" and the like), we choose one relation as the reference relation. What sense can be given to this idea of choosing a relation? The only possible sense that can be given to it within a naturalistic framework is this: we choose one (world–mind or language–mind) naturalistic relation by bearing a second-level relation to it. And it is our ascriptions of content or reference that thus choose the first-level naturalistic relation as the reference relation: we choose it by using such ascriptions in such a way that they bear a certain naturalistic relation (a second-level relation) to the supposed (first-level) relation between, say, the word "dog" and dogs. (To employ a relation R in ascribing content p to S is to ascribe this content to S's mental state in those circumstances in which this mental state bears R to p.) In other words, the intentional relation, which is a naturalistic relation, is captured by our ascriptions of content and reference to subjects, and this cannot but take the form of the obtaining of a naturalistic relation between those ascriptions and the relation that constitutes intentional facts. This second-level relation captures one first-level relation—a naturalistic relation that obtains between standard words such as "dog" and "tree," and their intentional objects—and makes this first-level relation intentional; it singles it out as the reference relation.

However, once we realize that this notion of singling out one naturalistic relation as the reference relation involves—indeed, cannot but involve—another appeal to a naturalistic relation, it becomes clear that this notion cannot solve the problem, but only pushes it to another level. For exactly as there is a multiplicity of first-level naturalistic relations, there is a multiplicity of second-level naturalistic relations. So, which (second-level) relation is the one that picks out the intentional relation? The problem re-emerges: what sense can be given to picking out one second-level relation among all others? The only eligible candidates are naturalistic relations, but, again, the quest for a further naturalistic relation just invites another indeterminacy, and so on. Thus, no sense can be given to the singling out of one (first-level) relation as the intentional relation in a naturalistic framework, and we are facing intentional indeterminacy: that is, there is no matter of fact about intentionality. We are left with interrelated first-level and second-level sentences or thoughts that do not touch the realm of any supposed representata—language and thought do not hook up to the world in such a framework.

Devitt thinks that it is one and the same relation that picks out the intentional objects of both non-semantic words like "red" and "cat" and semantic words like "reference." This does not avoid the problem. For, even supposing that we confine ourselves to a framework of a single relation at both levels, the question still remains as to what sense can be given to the picking out of one relation operating at both levels over any other relation operating at both levels. We are still facing indeterminacy.

This is not a point about philosophical anthropology. I am not asking why we should—or why we do—single out one naturalistic relation and attach significance to it. I am not asking what is special about the reference relation, in contrast to schmeference, beference, etc. I am not interested here in the anthropological questions of when or why we have singled out one naturalistic relation as the intentional relation. Rather, I call into question the very meaningfulness of such singling out, of such a choice, in a naturalistic framework. This point is related to a possible objection to the line of thought I have presented: namely, that it unjustifiably shifts the question from that of reference to that of the reference of the word "reference." I believe that it is not an unjustifiable shift, since the two questions are deeply intertwined, and it is anything but accidental that Devitt himself characterizes the privileged naturalistic relation as "the one *we call 'reference'*." This point can be noticed by considering a claim made by Devitt in his later treatment of the initial charge regarding the indeterminacy of reference: namely, the charge that usages of words are related by naturalistic relations to many world-items rather than to one. At this point, Devitt is no longer satisfied with addressing this charge by saying that the intentional relation is simply that one among the many word–world relations which we call "reference," on the grounds that it does not address the real challenge that is posed by the indeterminacy problem (Devitt mainly refers to Putnam's model-theoretic argument). "This response," he says, "is naive because the problem of determining reference is not primarily to identify one word-world relation as reference but to say, *first*, how that relation *differs* from other world-word relations; and, second, what is *significant* about that difference, what is *special* about reference" (Devitt 1997, p. 336).

Devitt indeed believes that reference (rather than schmeference, beference, etc.) is special and significant. According to him, "The properties and word-world relations that we ascribe to thoughts have to be appropriate given the effects of thoughts.... It [the standard interpretation of thought] is right because the property it ascribes is part of the explanation of what the person in fact did..." (pp. 334–335). This seems to convey the idea that content ascriptions that are underlain by the naturalistic relation that is the reference relation are explanatorily better than content ascriptions that are underlain by other naturalistic relations. Let us assume that this is true (the exact details, as we shall now see, are not important). Further, let us grant that, indeed, this fact makes reference (rather than schmeference, beference, and the like) special and significant. Now, citing this supposed fact can serve as an attempt to answer the anthropological

110   INTENTIONALITY DECONSTRUCTED

question—to explain *why* our content ascriptions are sensitive to a specific naturalistic relation. The question remains, however, what sense can be given to such a relation's being reference? It is one thing to say that some special naturalistic relation that connects our words or concepts with items in the world lies out there; it is another thing to say that some naturalistic relation is the reference relation. It is essential to the reductive-naturalistic account of intentionality that it is also committed to this latter claim, which implies, as argued above, that the world–mind or world–language relation in question must be singled out by means of our ascriptions of reference (this is what is supposed to make it the relation of reference). So, any uniqueness that is not thus singled out cannot make this relation rather than any other the relation of reference. The supposed uniqueness of no relation lying out there in nature can single it out as that.[18]

Devitt thinks that the challenge posed by the question "Why identify reference with one word-world relation...rather than with any of the others?" (p. 332) is easily met—"That relation and not any other is the one we call 'reference' and that's that" (p. 333), and he shifts his attention to the "real challenge" of the determinacy problem, the challenge regarding the uniqueness and significance of reference. But it is necessary for the reductive-naturalistic accounts of intentionality to also handle the challenge of singling out reference, and, as I argued, they cannot: the requirements that the reference relation be captured by ascriptions of reference and that its being so captured must be naturalistic lead to indeterminacy of the reference relation.[19]

---

[18]   This is one of the reasons why David Lewis's reference magnetism is doomed to fail. Lewis takes the "naturalness" of certain properties to be what singles them out as referents and avoids indeterminacy (see, e.g., Lewis 1984). Even if this idea could be made to work, its application would be limited, for various indeterminacies of reference (such as the ones discussed here) are indeterminacies among properties that cannot be said to differ in terms of naturalness (whatever "naturalness" exactly means). But a deeper problem for the effectivity of this idea is that the supposed "objective" naturalness of any property, like any uniqueness lying out there, cannot single it out as our referent. Devitt's suggestion suffers from the same flaw.

[19]   I think that realizing the connection between the question concerning the determinacy of reference and the one concerning the reference of "reference," "speaks of," etc., might help see in better light Putnam's "more of a theory" claim that is part of his model-theoretic argument. (Putnam presents his argument as a *Reductio* on metaphysical realism.) Putnam's reply to the reductive-naturalistic claim that the reference of the terms of our theory about the world is determined causally was that this is only "more of a theory": that is, that this maneuver only adds another component (i.e., the causal theory of reference) to the theory about the world, and that the extended theory is indeterminate in reference exactly as the original theory has been shown to be by the model-theoretic argument. Putnam's reply was criticized on the grounds that he assumes that the causal theorists take the causal theory of reference to fix reference, while what actually fixes reference according to them is the (relevant) causal connection itself (see, e.g., Devitt 1997; Simchen 2017). I think that in light of my claim regarding the relevance of the question of the reference of "reference" to the question of the determination of reference, Putnam's reply (whether or not it turns out to prevail in the final analysis) makes better sense than it seems to make at first blush. In a nutshell, the idea is that a semantic claim like "R_1 is reference" is in as much need of interpretation as first-level (non-semantic) claims, and the interpretation of the latter presupposes an interpretation of the former. But interpreting the former, as we saw, involves indeterminacy, and thus the reductive naturalists find themselves with one extended theory

AGAINST NATURALISTIC REDUCTIONS OF INTENTIONALITY   111

But recall that Devitt takes the standard interpretation of content to be correct because the property it ascribes is part of the explanation of the action of the person to which the content is ascribed. That is, he also uses the specific significance he assigns to reference to resolve the indeterminacy of reference: one relation is singled out as the reference relation in that it is that relation the citing of which plays that explanatory role.[20]

This suggestion doesn't work. First, Devitt does not at all justify the claim that ascriptions of reference have explanatory power that ascriptions of schmeference or ascriptions of beference do not have, and so the indeterminacy in question is not resolved. Further, this claim is false: it does not hold for some of those alternative relations that map intentional states to permutations of the supposed objects to which the reference relation maps them. Second, it isn't clear why we should accept this suggestion in the first place. Why identify reference with a relation that meets this criterion, rather than any other? It is merely an arbitrary stipulation. That content ascriptions serve to explain behavior does not mean or imply that contents can be identified in terms of the explanatory roles of their ascriptions. (As we shall see in Chapter 6, the explanatory and predictive success of content ascriptions does not even imply that mental states have intentional contents.) Contents (as argued in Chapter 1) are identified in terms of their objects and the properties they are represented as possessing.[21]

4.5 Extending the Arguments' Applicability

The arguments above targeted the very idea of reductive-naturalistic accounts of intentionality, understood as reductions of this phenomenon to external (extra-mental) relations. However, these arguments also undermine functional role theories. Other considerations tell against such theories. As we saw in Chapter 1, the short-armed version cannot account for intentionality as standard-object aboutness, whereas both the long-armed version and the two-factor version are

---

(the first-level theory plus the semantic theory), to the interpretation of which they cannot give sense. (My argument does not hinge on the "more of a theory" claim.)

[20] Note the difference between the suggestion in question and intentional instrumentalism such as Dennett's (1978b, 1987c). On intentional instrumentalism, the intentional relation is the explanation relation—the relation of explaining and predicting behavior. On the present suggestion, the intentional relation is some naturalistic relation (e.g., some causal relation) whose citing enables the explanation and prediction of behavior.

[21] One may think that intentional objects are singled out by their relations to the macro analogues of intentional properties, in accordance with the scientific model of reduction, and thus that the present objection to intentional reductive naturalism depends on the previous one. However, it is not only that, as we saw, there are no such analogues, but rather, that even had there been such analogues, appealing to them would not avoid the need to appeal to the idea that the intentional relation is that one of the many word–world relations we call "reference." For one thing, without the aid of such a stipulation, no putative macro analogue of intentionality can differentiate an object from its permutations, or single out one among the various links that figure in a causal chain that is related to the presumed intentional state.

112 INTENTIONALITY DECONSTRUCTED

in conflict with the idea that intentionality consists in *nothing but* standard-object directedness. But, if the arguments of the current chapter are along the right lines, then the latter two versions not only include in intentionality what's not there, but also (like their short-armed relative) fail to account for what's in there: namely, reference to standard objects. This is clear in the case of the two-factor version, whose tracking factor is supposed to semantically relate the mind to intentional objects, but these arguments show that it fails to do so. Its functional role factor certainly cannot help its tracking factor avoid the objections raised above. Because short-armed functional roles do not determine reference, then, as we have seen, they cannot serve as the macro analogues of scientific reductions (and thus avoid the first objection), but trivially, for this very reason they cannot secure intentional determinacy (and thus avoid the second). As to the long-armed version of the functional role theory, it isn't clear whether it is even prima facie compatible with the idea of an internal component constraining the tracking of external objects, since it does not acknowledge a natural border between the inner and the outer. But at any rate, any causal-psychological role that is part of a long-armed functional role would meet the same difficulties in reaching extra-mental reality.

What about normativist accounts of content? Our concern should lie neither with theories that merely take content or its possession to have normative charac-teristics (e.g., Kripke 1982; Boghossian 2003, 2008; Gibbard 2012), nor with theo-ries that account for content in normative terms but leave its referential dimension out (Brandom 1994, 2000—see Chapter 1). Rather, it should lie with theories, if there are such, that account for the referential dimension of content in normative terms. Any possible theory of this sort would aim to reduce the content that p of a mental state S to some p-involving norm that applies to S (e.g., a norm that dic-tates that in some circumstances S has an interaction of a certain sort with p).[22] Such theories might seem to have an advantage over standard (naturalistic) track-ing theories, for norms are supposed to be right or wrong, and so reference (in contrast to schmeference etc.) is supposed to be singled out by the right norm. However, first, it is unclear whence such norms can come—Rosen (1997) raises this difficulty for norms of inference—and second, the arguments brought in this chapter against the reductive-naturalistic approach undermine such theories as well. I will be satisfied with supporting the second of these points. Any p-involving norm of the kind in question, which applies to the supposed bearer of intentionality *in virtue of a non-intentional characterization*, cannot be a categorical norm (like moral ones), but must be a conditional (and empirically based) one—a norm in the instrumental sense. That is, norms of this kind must be such that obeying them is supposed to bring about some results, having to do with supposed inten-tional objects. (One might think that norms of inference are not instrumental,

---

[22] I do not know whether anyone endorses any such theory, unless teleological theories count.

but the point is that for a norm to connect us to worldly items and constitute intentionality, it must be an object-involving norm, not an abstract one, and such norms must be empirically based instrumental norms.) That means that such normativist theories of content boil down to reductive-naturalistic theories, according to which a mental state possesses the content that p in virtue of maintaining some factual-naturalistic (even if conditional) connection with the fact that p. (In fact, such theories would resemble teleological theories.[23]) Trivially, then, such theories are subject to the objections raised against the reductive-naturalistic approach.[24]

4.6 Naturalism and Content Ascription

If the arguments presented here are along the right lines, then the very idea of the (extrinsic) naturalistic reduction of intentionality—when realistically construed—is flawed. These arguments are general. They do not target specific tracking theories, but rather the very idea that underlies such theories. Such theories, then, cannot account for the constitution of intentionality.

We may now ask what conditions underlie content ascriptions. The arguments above leave intact the possibility that naturalistic tracking theories may get it right, in the sense of yielding the same results as our practice of content ascriptions (in contrast to the sense of informing us of the contents our mental states in fact have). In other words, these arguments allow for reductive-naturalistic theories to be true when abstracted from realist aspirations—from accounting for how thought or language hooks up to the world. Such theories systemize the regularities governing our usage of semantic idioms such as "refers to" and "think of": that is, they specify circumstances under which we ascribe specific contents, and one (or some) of them may do it correctly. They could be described as theories of the practice (or practices) of ascriptions of intentionality, rather than as theories of intentionality.[25]

The question of what conditions underlie the practice of content ascription is a contingent one, but it appears that some possible naturalistic theory is true for any practice of non-vacuous content ascriptions. The ("primitivist") idea that no

---

[23] Neander (2008) takes the teleological theory of intentionality to account for the normative character of this phenomenon.

[24] Hutto and Satne (2015) propose to naturalize intentionality by invoking a primitive form of it as an intermediate stage between the non-intentional and the full-blown contentful. This primitive non-contentful intentionality consists in a creature's responding to the world selectively, without the involvement of any representations. However, it remains unclear how the gap between this non-contentful phenomenon and contentful intentionality is supposed to be bridged, and the authors do not provide a substantive account for this (see Sultanescu 2015).

[25] There is some affinity between this idea and Field's (1994) suggestion to take Kripke's observation about proper names to concern our inferential practice rather than reference.

114 INTENTIONALITY DECONSTRUCTED

conditions underlie our content ascriptions makes no sense—our ascriptions must be sensitive to something. And since the concept of intentionality (be it as flawed as I take it to be)—as that which is ascribed by content ascriptions—is the concept of standard-object aboutness, then content ascriptions must be sensitive to relations between supposed intentional states and their supposed "standard" (not mental or Meinongian) intentional objects. That is, they must be sensitive to external non-intentional relations.[26] In fact, any account that fails to explain intentionality because it fails to relate supposed representations to extra-mental reality—that is, fails to make sense of the transcending nature of intentionality— cannot be an account of the conditions underlying content ascriptions, and the reductive-naturalistic account is the only possible account that does not founder on this rock (it founders, as we saw, on other rocks). This sensitivity to non-intentional external relations holds for third-person-based content ascriptions. First-person-based content ascriptions, recall, are vacuous. So, all non-vacuous content ascriptions are sensitive to non-intentional external relations between supposed intentional states and their supposed intentional objects. And one possible theory that specifies such relations—perhaps one of those prevalent kinds (informational, causal, teleological, etc.)—is the correct theory of content ascription.

Still, I doubt that we have discovered, or that we ever will discover, this theory. For the human practice of content ascriptions is extremely varied and complicated—it is too varied and complicated to be capturable by any single elegant formula, one that is not a disjunction of conjunctions etc.—and, plausibly (this is the lesson from the history of philosophy for such cases), any theory to be actually suggested will meet counterexamples.[27]

More details regarding this idea and further support for it will be provided in Chapter 6. There we shall see that it helps intentional anti-realism to meet an important challenge.[28]

---

[26] One might think that content ascriptions can be sensitive to other content ascriptions in a holistic manner: for example, that the condition for ascribing to one the belief that p is that we ascribe to one the belief that q, and that the condition for ascribing to one the belief that q is that we ascribe to one the belief that p. Thus, content ascriptions are not sensitive to non-intentional relations. However, though some of us might occasionally ascribe contents in such a way, it cannot be the considered story about content ascription, since this story loses the connection with p (and thus with q): that is, it loses the concept of intentionality as standard-object aboutness.

[27] Plausibly, according to intentional realists, a correct theory of intentionality is also (by and large, and subject to some qualifications) a correct theory of ascriptions of intentionality—recall the method of cases. (But of course, a correct theory of ascriptions of intentionality is not necessarily a correct theory of intentionality.) Thus, the claim that the conditions for the application of content ascriptions are naturalistic is a claim that realist reductive naturalists would be inclined to accept—they would only add that those naturalistic relations constitute content.

Note also that this claim is the claim that the conditions in question are the conditions that obtain when we ascribe contents. It is not the same as, and does not presuppose, the claim that in ascribing contents we are conscious of these conditions.

[28] We shall also see there that content ascriptions need not always be *directly* responsive to external relations.

5

Intentional Anti-Realism I

5.1 Intentional Anti-Realism—The Negative Thesis

In this chapter and the following one, I present and defend a version of intentional anti-realism, some important tenets of which are already present—sometimes implicitly, sometimes explicitly—in earlier chapters. I draw in these chapters a comprehensive picture of supposedly intentional states, of content ascriptions, and of truth (or a substitute for it) in general and of content ascriptions and other semantic claims in particular. I also pursue various implications of the intentional anti-realist theory to be suggested, and further develop it by addressing objections to the repudiation of intentionality.[1]

According to the thesis of intentional realism, there are intentional states. In particular, intentional realism is committed to our having mental intentional states. Further, this thesis is usually taken to be committed to the idea that many of our actual intentional ascriptions are true (see, e.g., Fodor 1987). Among the rival theses to intentional realism, I distinguished (in Chapter 1) between the theses I call "intentional irrealism" and "intentional anti-realism." According to the former, there are no concrete intentional entities (or, in soft versions, there are not many); put differently, no concrete entities instantiate intentional properties. According to the latter, there also *cannot be* concrete intentional entities—no concrete entities can instantiate intentional properties. This is so, for the concept of intentionality— like other concepts (so important figures in the history of philosophy argued), such as the concept of substance and that of self—is inherently flawed (and so intentionality can be said to be a conceptually uninstantiable property). It appears to us to be perfectly lucid and coherent, but upon philosophical reflection, it is revealed to lack clear sense and integrity. The related concepts of reference, think-about, etc., share this predicament. I endorse the stronger thesis, that of intentional anti-realism. Repudiating the very possibility of the existence of intentional states, the thesis advanced on these pages is not a contingent and empirical thesis, such as the theses of Paul Churchland

---

[1] One of the prominent objections to views that deny intentionality—namely, that we know from our own case that there are intentional states—was already addressed in criticizing Horgan and Tienson's case for phenomenal intentionality in Chapter 3.

Intentionality Deconstructed: An Anti-Realist Theory. Amir Horowitz, Oxford University Press.
© Amir Horowitz 2024. DOI: 10.1093/oso/9780198896432.003.0005

116 INTENTIONALITY DECONSTRUCTED

(1979, 1981, 1988) and Stich (1983), but rather, a necessary, conceptual, and a priori thesis. As noted, it concerns the integrity of the concept of intentionality.[2]

We may put the theses of intentional irrealism and intentional anti-realism in terms of the truth of content ascriptions. Intentional irrealism is the thesis that such ascriptions (or the majority of them) are false,[3] whereas intentional anti-realism is the thesis that content ascriptions, in themselves, *cannot* be true and *cannot* be false (where the modality in question is conceptual). In other words, according to intentional anti-realism, content ascriptions, in themselves, lack truth conditions and truth values. I take content ascriptions to lack truth conditions and truth values, since I believe that (what appears to be) the ascription of a conceptually uninstantiable property to anything is not false but makes no sense. One might dispute this general principle and take the claim that the concept of intentionality is flawed to entail that content ascriptions are (necessarily) false. But it seems to me that no essential point hinges on this, and therefore that no damage is done if you take any of the claims expressed in this book to the effect that content ascriptions lack truth conditions as a claim to the effect that content ascriptions are necessarily false.[4]

My view concerns the (alleged) intentionality of mental states and other entities. I do not deny the existence of mental states, including the (so-called) propositional attitudes, though, trivially, my conception of their nature is different from the standard commonsense conception. I deny that there are states such as beliefs and desires only in the sense in which their being intentional is essential to them. That is, I deny that there are, and even that there can be, instantiations of intentional properties by any concrete entities. However, I affirm the existence of mental states with the characteristics typically attributed to intentional mental states—be they epistemic, phenomenological, causal, or logico-syntactic properties—*minus intentional properties*. Relatedly, I accept the common view that such mental states are causally efficacious, and that their ascriptions have explanatory and predictive power. Since these ascriptions identify the states in terms of their contents, which on my view aren't real, I will have to explain how it is possible that these ascriptions have explanatory and predictive power.

---

[2] Among other empirically motivated eliminativists are Patricia Churchland (1986), Rosenberg (MS), Ramsey, Stich, and Garon (1990), Ramsey (2007), who defends a somewhat qualified version of eliminativism, Chemero (2009), and Rowlands (2013). Hutto and Myin (2013) deny intentionality from perceptual experiences. Arguments against the very possibility of real intentionality are suggested by Quine (1960), Davidson (1984), Dennett (1978b, 1987c, 1990), Putnam (1983), and Chomsky (1995, 2000). Kripke's rule-following argument (1982) is often interpreted as an argument for intentional anti-realism.

[3] This formulation (with the parenthetical remark) makes the softer version of intentional irrealism clearer. We can further clarify it by saying that, according to it, folk psychology is radically false (a claim that allows content ascriptions to be true, occasionally).

[4] The view that a statement that ascribes to anything a conceptually uninstantiable property can be neither true nor false does not entail (though it is entailed by) the view that any statement in which a flawed concept figures is neither true nor false, for a concept can figure in statements that do not ascribe "its" property to something (e.g., ones that assert its uninstantiability).

The very thesis of intentional anti-realism as so far characterized is a negative thesis. However, the version of intentional anti-realism that I defend has positive components as well. Before presenting and defending them, let us see what supports the negative thesis. This thesis—the idea that no concrete entity can possess intentional content, or (put differently) that content ascriptions, in themselves, lack truth conditions—was supported in the previous chapters in two ways. First, it was supported by the transcendental argument presented in Chapter 2. According to this argument, recall, no sense can be given to the obtaining of "objective" practice-independent semantic facts, which are supposed to lie out there. Whether "Gödel" refers to Gödel or to Schmidt, I argued, is a difference that makes no difference. Being an argument of the "difference-that-makes-no-difference" kind, I took this argument to be tentative and to merely shift the burden of proof to other side: namely, to the intentional realist. I will supplement this argument, to make it conclusive, in Chapter 6.

This negative thesis was also established by a conjunction of arguments from previous chapters. In Chapter 1, I rejected the notion of primitive intentionality, and in Chapter 3 I rejected the two possible forms of intrinsic reduction of intentionality, the conceptual and the synthetic-empirical ones.[5] (The latter move involved rejection of the notion of phenomenal intentionality, which is the prevalent, and the prima facie most plausible, instance of intrinsic intentionality.) Since in Chapter 4 I rejected the very idea of an extrinsic reduction of intentionality (which is in fact the naturalistic reduction of intentionality), I exhausted all options in the relevant logical space. All possible notions of (real) intentionality have been undermined: primitive intentionality, reduced intrinsic intentionality, and reduced extrinsic intentionality.[6] Thus, the very idea of intentionality has been shown to lack sense, which is the message of intentional anti-realism. Note that the rejection of intrinsic and extrinsic reductions of intentionality (on the assumption that they exhaust the logical space of reductions of this supposed phenomenon) entails that intentionality cannot be "something else," as Fodor (1987) put it, whereas the rejection of intentional primitivism means that it must be something else—that it must be constituted by the non-intentional. This argument, then, exposes one manifestation of the inherent tension in the concept of intentionality.

We can see that rejecting intrinsic intentionality has special importance. For, first, because my case against the idea of intrinsic intentionality involves rejecting intentionality as accessed from the first-person perspective, it implies that a central motivation for intentional realism loses its sting. If it is not the case that

---

[5] As argued in Chapter 1, primitive intentionality +is a form of intrinsic intentionality, for its possession by entities is independent of any property other than itself possessed by whatever entity.

[6] Recall that the only prima facie plausible approach that reduces intentionality to normativity is an extrinsic-naturalistic one.

118   INTENTIONALITY DECONSTRUCTED

intentionality is that close to us—that we are acquainted with it from the inside—it is not so outrageous to maintain that it is a chimera. Once the pressure put forward by our own assurance about the reality of intentionality drops out of the picture, establishing intentional realism would only be possible by appealing to theoretical considerations (in contrast to alleged direct evidence).

The second sense in which rejecting intrinsic intentionality has special importance can be realized by noticing a characteristic of the alternative of reductive-naturalistic intentionality. In the reductive-naturalistic framework, representational truth loses its alleged unique and privileged status, and becomes just one among many world–mind or world–language relations, as Stich (1990) shows. Of course, this characteristic of truth in this framework stems directly from the fact that the intentional relation in this framework is just one among many world–mind or world–language relations. Still, pointing it out is significant since it seems more of the essence of the pre-theoretic notion of truth that being true involves having an especially intimate connection with reality, not just one among many. In this respect, the reductive-naturalistic framework, which deliberately abandons the idea of intentionality as "immanent transcendence," is a revisionist framework, and so the rejection of intrinsic intentionality—which exposes a tension in this idea—is already an especially significant step.

The arguments presented here, which form the case against intentional realism, target the intentionality of all entities—mental, linguistic, and any other (with the exception of those targeting the phenomenal intentionality thesis, which are only relevant to the mental realm). If they are along the right lines, then the very idea of intentionality breaks down. It is not only that the concept of intentionality is not instantiated. Rather, the idea of possessing an intentional property makes no sense, the concept of intentionality is inherently flawed, and content ascriptions, in themselves, lack truth conditions.

5.2 Practice-Dependence Intentional Anti-Realism

One of the positive tenets of the thesis of intentional anti-realism that I suggest concerns content ascriptions. According to it, although content ascriptions *in themselves* do not have truth conditions, they do have truth conditions (or conditions of a certain related kind, as we shall see—I suppress this issue for now) *relative to practices of content ascription*. When such a practice is taken into account, individual content ascriptions—which may conform or fail to conform to the practice under given circumstances—are, respectively, true or false under those circumstances. Let's focus on the Kripkean Gödel–Schmidt example and suppose that the name "Gödel" is used by one who only associates with this name the description "the mathematician who proved the incompleteness theorem." On this version of intentional anti-realism—"practice-dependence intentional anti-realism"—in abstraction from a practice of content ascription, the correct answer to the question "To whom does the name 'Gödel' refer?" is "To no one." When such a practice is taken into account, this name refers to that individual dictated by the assumed practice of content ascription (e.g., the actual practice of our linguistic community). It refers to Gödel if this practice is a causalist practice of the kind suggested by Kripke (1980), and it refers to Schmidt if this practice is a descriptivist practice of the kind suggested by Russell (1912, 1956). Of course, to know the nature of our actual practice (or actual practices) of content ascription, we cannot be satisfied with armchair theoretical reflection, but rather have to carry out a probe and analysis of the principles underlying our content ascription, an enterprise that must involve experimental work of the kind done in experimental philosophical semantics. Carrying out this enterprise is not among the goals of the present investigation.

This idea, regarding the practice-dependence of the truth conditions of content ascriptions, requires further elucidation, which will be provided later. Now let's see what supports this idea as so far presented. Once we accept the negative thesis of intentional anti-realism—that content ascriptions, in themselves, do not have truth conditions—the route to accepting the practice-dependence view of content ascriptions is rather short.

Consider the following reasoning against the idea that content ascriptions lack truth conditions altogether. This radical idea appears to be false, since we assign truth values to many content ascriptions, and so take them (at least implicitly) to have specific truth conditions. Perhaps we are systematically mistaken about their truth values (perhaps, that is, belief-desire psychology is radically false), but it appears that we know what makes them true and what makes them false. So, contrary to intentional anti-realism, content ascriptions appear to have truth conditions.

A few obstacles have to be overcome before this appearance can be endorsed. First, one might claim that we *merely interpret* content ascriptions as having truth conditions and truth values. Yet such a claim amounts to accepting that these ascriptions have truth conditions as interpreted by us, and the distinction between their having truth conditions and their having truth conditions as interpreted by us does not hold water. Second, it might be thought that the conditions we take to make the ascriptions true or false actually have nothing to do with truth or falsehood, for they are non-cognitive or non-assertoric (e.g., they are emotional reactions of some sort). While perhaps such an option makes sense in other domains of discourse (notably moral psychology), it makes no sense in the case of ascriptions of content.[7] One might think that such an option makes sense if some

---

[7] Note that the relevant issue in moral psychology does not concern the possibility of moral facts, but the nature of moral attitudes.

120 INTENTIONALITY DECONSTRUCTED

normativist account of intentionality is true. I doubt this, but at any rate I argued in Chapters 1 and 4 against such accounts.

Another possible obstacle for attributing truth conditions to content ascriptions is the suggestion that these ascriptions are mere gibberish. If this suggestion means that they lack meaning and content, then it provides little support for intentional anti-realism, since (as we shall see in section 5.4) lacking meaning and content is compatible with having truth conditions, or at least with having some epistemic substitutes for them, which are given in terms of coherence (call them "adequacy conditions"). If lacking meaning and content is compatible with having truth conditions, then this gibberish option forms no objection to the claim that content ascriptions have truth conditions. On the other hand, if lacking meaning and content is only compatible with having coherentist adequacy conditions, then the gibberish option does form an objection to this claim, but it leaves intact the weaker claim that content ascriptions have coherentist adequacy conditions. This is bad enough for intentional anti-realists, since for them no statement and no belief have truth conditions, and if this view is only compatible with beliefs and statements having coherentist adequacy conditions, then, in this respect, content ascriptions do not differ from all other statements and beliefs.

I will later expand both on those coherence adequacy conditions and on this prima facie predicament for intentional anti-realists, which can be motivated on independent grounds. Now I will show that the reasoning in question does not compel us to concede either that content ascriptions have truth conditions or that they have some coherence adequacy conditions.[8] Though this reasoning forms an effective objection against the idea that content ascriptions lack truth conditions *altogether*, taking it to establish that content ascriptions *in themselves* have truth conditions is to ignore the option that they have merely practice-dependent truth conditions.

Let me clarify some notions. A *scheme* of content ascription is an (abstract) set of principles (at whatever levels of generality) that underlie content ascriptions. A *practice* of content ascription is the use of a scheme of content ascription by actual ascribers. A scheme or a practice of content ascription is *relevant* to an ascription in case it has some implication for its (scheme-dependent or practice-dependent) truth value. Schemes of content ascription can be minimal—for example, they can embody low-level generality and thus be relevant to a relatively small number of ascriptions—but actual practices are (at least typically) rich. Identifying practices of content ascription is an empirical matter, and such practices—for example, corresponding to the causal-historical theory of names or to its descriptivist rival—were indeed identified among various groups of people by experimental

---

[8] For convenience, from now on, unless context demands otherwise, I omit reference to those epistemic substitutes and write in terms of truth conditions and truth values. I will return to discuss these substitutes in due course.

philosophers (see Chapter 2).[9] While some practices of content ascription may be better than others in terms of comprehensiveness or consistency (and different practices may entail conflicting judgments about individual ascriptions), according to intentional anti-realism practices of content ascription do not differ in truth values, for no practice (i.e., no principle of ascription) has a truth value.

So, to repeat, the above reasoning does not establish that content ascriptions in themselves have truth conditions. This reasoning does not and cannot rule out the option that we seem to recognize absolute, practice independent, truth values of content ascriptions because the practice of content ascription in which we are immersed evades our glance, and so we project content onto (semantics-free) reality. Furthermore, it is not only that this possibility blocks the inference. We also have good reason to take it to be actual. If one is persuaded by the arguments presented in this book that content ascriptions *in themselves* lack truth conditions, and one is also persuaded by the reasoning just presented that our actual content ascriptions do have truth conditions, one must acknowledge that we take our content ascriptions to have truth conditions in some relative way, one that helps explain the fact that we assign them specific truth values. That is, accepting the negative thesis of intentional anti-realism along with the above reasoning commits one to accept that our content ascriptions can be true or false relative to practices of content ascription, where the criterion for their truth value is relative all the way down—it is anchored in no absolute true value. Thus, the practice-dependence option readily suggests itself. Trivially, if indeed content ascriptions are such things that may be true or false—if, that is, they are cognitive—then any individual content ascription is either true or false relative to any scheme or practice of content ascription that is relevant to ascriptions of its kind. It is either true or false depending on whether or not it conforms with the scheme or practice. What is not trivial—and this is the upshot of the reasoning suggested here—is that our content ascriptions are made on the background of some practice in which we are immersed and relative to which they are (in most cases) either true or false. What is also not trivial is that our content ascriptions have *only* practice-dependent truth conditions. This is the intentional anti-realist (negative) message: our practice of content ascription itself isn't true, and so it cannot endow absolute truth upon any content ascription. Conforming with the practice is *the only criterion* for the truth of a content ascription. This is what makes this view a real practice-dependence view, one according to which the truth value of any content ascription is relative all the way down.[10]

---

[9] Recall that the difference between such practices is not a matter of the (first-level) use of expressions, but of how the practices ascribe content or meaning given the circumstances in which the expressions are used.

[10] It might be argued that the fact that content ascriptions appear to have truth values and thus truth conditions can be explained by the assumption that content ascriptions (in themselves) have verification or assertability conditions, and that the argument for their having practice-dependent

122   INTENTIONALITY DECONSTRUCTED

Thus, what seemed to be a mere possibility turns out to be the case: we indeed project content ascriptions onto absolute, or independent, or objective (semantic) reality. Those who share the Kripkean causalist intuition, precisely like their descriptivist rivals, do not (at any rate, when not in a reflective mood) take themselves or their community to legislate the meta-semantics of names—that is, to legislate what circumstances make a certain name refer to a certain individual—or to echo such legislation, but rather to reflect it. For them, given the circumstances, "Gödel" *really* refers to Gödel. According to this latter claim, the phenomenology of content ascription is realist, and so it reveals intentional anti-realism to be an error theory; and the (projectivist) error can be explained from the perspective of the practice-dependence version of intentional anti-realism.

The claim that content ascriptions have practice-dependent truth conditions does not mean that entities such as belief-states have intentional properties that are practice-relative or relational (that they have them relative to the practice), as secondary qualities are supposed to be relational properties of physical objects, or, similarly, as semantic externalism takes intentional properties of beliefs to be environment-relative (see, e.g., Putnam 1975a; Burge 1979, 1982). Both kinds of cases allow some (relationalist) form of realism with respect to the properties in question, but the practice-dependence view of content ascriptions is significantly different. This is so because, according to it, the truth values of content ascriptions depend on *nothing but* the truth values of content ascriptions. That is, there is no external criterion for the truth value of any content ascription; there is no reality that may match or fail to match such an ascription, except for the reality of a practice of content ascription. Whereas, on this view, the truth value of any content ascription is determined by its relation to the practice of content ascription, this practice in itself isn't true or false—it cannot be. (Arguments for the negative thesis of intentional anti-realism, whose soundness we now assume, show this.) In other words, the truth value of any content ascription is *only* intra-practice. The practice-dependence view's commitment to this idea reflects the fact that it is indeed a version of intentional anti-realism. It is underlain by the conviction that there are no semantic facts that lie out there, independently of there being content ascriptions; facts waiting, as it were, for content ascriptions to represent them. This conviction is conspicuously anti-realist.

It may be instructive to present the idea that the practice-dependence view does not allow a relational intentional realistic understanding in the following way. The obtaining of a practice of content ascription merely determines what

---

truth conditions is thus blocked. But, first, I do not see how the assumption that content ascriptions have verification or assertability conditions can explain the appearance of their having truth conditions unless content ascribers are taken to be immersed in a practice of content ascription. Second, the argument is anyhow not blocked by the verificationist option, since a content ascription that is made warrantedly assertable but not true by certain facts is made true by these facts relative to some practice that is assumed to be true (and such truth of an ascription is not evidence transcendent).

contents accord with the practice *that in fact obtains*. (The word "merely" salvages this sentence from being a truism.) It does not determine that entities in fact have the contents that accord with it; it does not and cannot determine that this practice itself is "binding"—that it endows any entity with content. In this respect, the obtaining practice has no advantage—as far as determining the truth values of content ascriptions is concerned—over any possible non-actual practice, which can equally form the basis for evaluations of content ascriptions. (The role of the actual practice of content ascription is different, then, from the role of the actual environment in determining content according to semantic externalism.[11]) These qualifications regarding the role of the practice according to practice-dependence intentional anti-realism are essential to its being an anti-realist position deserving of the name. They are essential to its denial of there being any external (i.e., practice-independent) criterion for the truth value of any content ascription, and they are thus essential to its commitment that no content ascription in itself has truth conditions, and that no concrete entity can have any intentional property.

It is important to emphasize that I do not take content ascriptions to play a role in constituting content, since on my view nothing has contents, and so nothing—content ascriptions included—constitutes content. Relatedly, I do not take content ascriptions to be intentional. So, critiques that were directed against ascriptivist views, such as Davidson's (1984) and Dennett's (1978b, 1987c), to the effect that they account for intentionality in terms of content ascriptions that are intentional, are inapplicable to my view.[12]

The notion of practice in question is not necessarily social—the practice of content ascription need not be shared. Evidently, people sometimes defer to ascription standards of their fellows—that is, make them their own (and we are rarely the originators of the standards we exercise)—but this fact plays no essential role in the suggested picture, which even tolerates the possibility of there being only individualistic and idiosyncratic (and even momentary) practices of ascription. Similarly, the practice-dependence view is not committed to there being a single practice of content ascriptions among humans. It would not be undermined by a diversity in practices of content ascription of the kind argued to obtain by experimental philosophers of language and mind, and further, as we saw in discussing the claim for such diversity in Chapter 2 (to be further supported in Chapter 6), the very possibility of such diversity supports the negative thesis of intentional anti-realism.

Also, this view is not committed to any such human practice being perfectly coherent and systematic. It is only to be expected that such a complicated human practice would involve various lacunas and incoherencies, which result in puzzles

---

[11] Semantic externalism faces a difficulty regarding this role (see Horowitz 2001, 2005).

[12] Among those critiques see Brandom (1994), Child (1994), Rey (1994), Baldwin (1993), and Heil (1992). For replies, see Mölder (2010).

124   INTENTIONALITY DECONSTRUCTED

and indeterminacies—that is, cases in which the practice does not dictate an (univocal) answer concerning a term's reference. Kripke's (1979) puzzle about belief is a conspicuous example: the fact that there are cases in which our practice dictates contradictory content ascriptions (or cases in which the practice leaves indeterminacies) is anything but a puzzle from the intentional anti-realist perspective, since from this perspective such cases simply reflect the nature of this vulnerable human practice. It is the (either implicit or explicit) intentional realist assumption that underlies the thought that cases such as this one point to a philosophical problem that is not just a problem for the actual practice of content ascription.[13]

The practice-dependence view of content ascription should not be confused with the view of "referential pluralism" that is examined and rejected by Mallon et al. (2009). On the latter view, the reference of a term employed by members of a group is determined by the semantic intuitions of members *of this group*, so that there may be more than one "correct" reference relation for this term. On the view advocated here, since it is possible to evaluate any content ascription relative to any possible (comprehensive) practice of content ascription, the practice of content ascription of *any* group (or individual) is relevant to the reference determination of the terms used by *any* speaker. A speaker's or a thinker's own practice of content ascription has no privileged status with respect to the truth of any ascription of content to herself. Reference and intentionality depend upon and are relative to a practice of ascription. Their relativity consists in being reference and intentionality according to an ascriber, or from an ascriber's point of view— what content she ascribes or would ascribe—and not according to a speaker or a thinker (as a speaker or a thinker).[14] It is not that "Gödel" *in the mouth of East Asians* refers to Schmidt. This makes no sense according to intentional anti-realism. Rather, according to it, "Gödel" in the mouth of East Asians refers to

---

[13] Two remarks are in order. First, to disarm Kripke's puzzle in this way is not to fully explain it. It is a worthwhile endeavor to try to identify what it is about the nature of the actual practice of content ascription that is responsible for the puzzle. But it is not among the concerns of this book to uncover the principles of the actual practice. Second, one need not be an intentional irrealist or anti-realist in order to maintain that the practice of content ascription is the source of the puzzling phenomenon described by Kripke. See, for example, Igal Kvart's dissolution of the puzzle. According to him, "since the belief construction doesn't display the beliefs in question but rather describes them in a certain way (or rather makes an existential claim under certain classificatory specifications), dealing with epistemological questions via the belief construction is comparable to watching a subject through a veil: it keeps us from a closer touch with the doxastic phenomena themselves. It would be a mistake then to attribute features that reside at the level of our doxastic phenomena to the level of the linguistic constructions that report those phenomena, and vice versa. Not keeping these two levels clearly separated is a mistake that can, and often does, easily lead us astray" (Kvart 1986, p. 295).

[14] I refrain from dubbing the suggested view "relativism" in order to avoid various connotations that surround this term. It is important to note that whether or not it is so with respect to relativistic views in other domains (e.g., the moral one), the relativity of reference according to the suggested view is anti-realist.

Schmidt *according to* East Asians.[15] At the same time, our content ascriptions are in fact made on the background of some practice in which we are immersed and relative to which they are (in most cases) either true or false.

5.3 Intentional Anti-Realism, the Existence of So-Called Intentional States, and Logico-Syntactic Structures

One reason for Stich's eliminativism (1983; see also 1978) was the thought that since no entity possesses all the properties that are supposed to be possessed by beliefs, there are no beliefs. Later, Stich (1996) realized that this reasoning presupposed a specific theory of reference and handled the issue in terms of his pragmatist epistemology. On my intentional anti-realism, there are no intentional states or attitudes, but this does not mean or imply that those mental states or attitudes to which intentionality is normally ascribed do not exist. Intentional anti-realism only maintains that such states and attitudes are not what they appear to be in one respect: they lack intentional properties and so are not intentional states and attitudes. I do not deny the existence of mental states with the characteristics typically attributed to them—such as phenomenology and functional profile—*minus intentional properties*. In fact, I take the prominent reason that intentional realists (notably Fodor) cite in favor of their view—namely, the success of ascriptions of content in explaining and predicting behavior—to be an effective reason for the existence of mental states, but not for their having intentional properties (see Chapter 6). Similarly, I believe that introspection is a relatively reliable guide for discovering mental states of various kinds and various mental properties, but (as the discussion of Chapter 3 shows) intentional properties are not among them. Those mental states that are similar to (so-called) beliefs but lack intentional properties are not states of believing—they cannot be strictly said to be *beliefs-that*. We may refer to them as "belief-states," and we may similarly speak of desire-states, and so on. These expressions would still sound to some as denoting intentionality, but this is an unimportant terminological matter—my use of these expressions is meant to be innocuous.[16]

Intentional anti-realism may be interpreted as committed to the idea that utterances of sentences are mere noise, and their inscriptions mere patches of ink; similarly, it might be interpreted as committed to the idea that mental states are

---

[15] Of course, I do not intend to rule out the possibility of a practice that takes "Gödel" in the mouth of East Asians to have a different reference from "Gödel" in the mouth of Westerners. Still, this difference obtains for ascribers (whether or not they are the speakers).

[16] Such belief-states and desire-states are similar to the B-states and D-states whose postulation in cognitive science is recommended by Stich (1983). As we shall see further in this chapter, the theory to be suggested here is similar to Stich's theory also in the important role it takes logico-syntactic properties to play.

126   INTENTIONALITY DECONSTRUCTED

mere "flat" phenomenological items. But I do not take those noises, patches of ink, and phenomenological items to be *simply* noises, patches of ink, and phenomenological items. For one thing, they are *structured* noises, *structured* patches of ink, and *structured* phenomenological items. That is, in addition to possessing phenomenological, epistemic, and causal-functional properties, those mental states that are normally taken to be intentional, or at least the so-called propositional attitudes like belief-states and desire-states, also possess logico-syntactic structures.[17]

We shall see that there are a few notions of logico-syntactic structures, and each of them encompasses structures of several forms. First, there is the notion of *thin* logico-syntactic structure. It can be standard grammatical syntax or—at another level of abstraction—standard logical form, but it can also take other forms. Such structures include no constants. There are also two notions of *thick* logico-syntactic structure. Structures of the first kind are thin logico-syntactic structures that are further individuated by the phenomenology and/or by the physical realizations of the structures' components (depending on whether the states having such structures are conscious or not). Thick structures of this kind can also take several forms (e.g., grammatical or logical). This notion is a system-relative notion of structure. The second and more abstract notion of thick structure is that of thin structure (of, e.g., grammatical or logical form) further individuated in terms of some naturalistic (yet not semantical) relations of its constants. Structures of the first thick category are determined by those of the second thick category for a given system. Structures of all these categories are real features of mental states. All this will be explicated as we proceed, in this and in the following chapter.

Consider linguistically articulated mental states. Linguistically articulated thoughts, for example, appear to have specific structures, such as that of "It never rains in Madagascar in the summer." Individuated by the grammatical syntax of specific languages, this structure is identical to that of "It seldom snows in Burkina Faso in the spring." However, individuated in another way, these structures are different: for example, "Madagascar" is an essential component of the first structure and "Burkina Faso" of the second—these components are constants rather than variables.[18] It is to this second notion of grammatical structure that I refer as

---

[17] For the purposes of this book, it is not important to decide whether mental states other than the so-called propositional attitudes—notably perceptual (and other) experiences—are structured in a sense that is similar in some respect to that in which the so-called propositional attitudes are. The notion of logico-syntactic structure in play is supposed to allow intentional anti-realism to make room for truth or a substitute for it (an issue which is discussed in this section) and to undermine the argument from the predictive and explanatory success of content ascriptions (an issue which is discussed in Chapter 6). These two tasks are concerned with the so-called propositional attitudes.

[18] It might be thought that since the suggested notion of structure applies to entities with such components, using the term "structure" is misleading. My use of this term is meant to reflect the facts that the feature in question is *structured* and that neither it nor its components are intentional. Note,

"thick." It is thicker than the standard grammatical notion. By simple abstraction—turning the constants into variables (e.g., turning both "Madagascar" and "Burkina Faso" into the same variable)—we get standard grammatical syntax, to which we may then refer as "*thin* grammatical syntax."

Similar to the pair of thick and thin *grammatical syntactic* structures, we have a pair of thick and thin *logical* structures; and again, these two are systematically related in that the same kind of abstraction leads from the former to the latter.[19] Different thin syntactic-grammatical structures may realize the same (thin) logical structure. This is the case, for example, with the (thin) syntactic-grammatical structures of "I am working now" and "Ich arbeite jetzt," sentences that belong to natural languages that have not only different words but also different (thin) syntactic-grammatical formation rules. This is also true of the relation between thick grammatical structures and thick logical structures. We may speak in this context of two axes of abstraction, a vertical one and a horizontal one. The vertical one concerns thick vs. thin structures; the horizontal one concerns grammatical vs. logical structures. But these latter two do not exhaust the horizontal axis. We can also attribute to the mental states in question structures other than the logical and the (language-specific) grammatical structures: for example, structures at the level of universal grammar. These are also subject to the thick–thin distinction.

By "logico-syntactic structure" I refer to structures of all these kinds, at all levels of abstraction. Our focus will be the *thick* notions of logico-syntactic structure, due to the theoretical fruitfulness of these notions, as will become evident later. Thick logical structures and thick grammatical structures are different—they belong to different levels of abstraction. (For example, two sentences in an active and passive form may share logical structures, but they differ in their grammatical structures.) The mental states under consideration can have structures of both kinds—structures belonging to different levels of abstraction may coexist. The fact that mental states have logical structures will play a more important role than their having grammatical ones in the defense of intentional anti-realism to be presented here.

Noting that the components of thick logico-syntactic structures are constants rather than variables is not enough. We should specify what it is that remains constant, or, in other words, what the individuation criterion of these constants is, and, accordingly, what the individuation criterion of the logico-syntactic structures as wholes is. Of course, there may be different ways of individuating such

---

also, that the term "structure" can denote structured objects or states of some kind (e.g., reasoning-related mental states, or computational states of computers), and it can denote features of such objects or states (their being structured). I mainly use this term in the latter sense but occasionally also in the former. The context indicates the relevant sense in each case.

[19] Of course, we can also speak of logical structures at different levels: for example, that of propositional calculus and that of predicate calculus. This point is not important for our purposes.

128   INTENTIONALITY DECONSTRUCTED

components and such structures. I will appeal to two such ways. In the case of conscious mental states, it appears that one criterion that underlies our individuation of their structures' components is their phenomenology (in the examples above, of "rains" and "Madagascar" vs. "snows" and "Burkina Faso"). Thus, the logico-syntactic structures are the thin structures further individuated by the phenomenology of the structures' components. A related individuating criterion is physical (it may be said to concern the physical realizations of the structures' components). This criterion is relevant to the structures of unconscious mental states, and also—under plausible psychophysical assumptions—to those of conscious mental states. I will henceforth speak in terms of phenomenological-physical logico-syntactic individuation (though, for my purposes, nothing of importance depends on taking the individuation of structures of conscious mental states to be physical).

The multiple realizability that is attributed to mentality might be thought to pose a difficulty for the idea of a physical individuation criterion of mental logico-syntactic structures, but as we shall see later, the suggested individuation is anyhow confined to the structures of single systems at a given time and, so, we can ignore this difficulty for now. Another complication for the physical individuation concerns the fact that the physical individuation that is suitable for our purposes (like physical individuations in various other contexts) is not absolute: that is, it ignores various physical differences. To take but one familiar example, "A" and "A" are taken to be the same letter under an individuation that is, by and large, physical in nature, despite their physical difference. (A similar complication applies to phenomenological individuation.) In our case, it is reasonable to maintain that the physical resolution of the components of mental logico-syntactic structures (if there are such structures) is determined by the sensitivity of the cognitive processes operating on these structures.

This point in fact shows that the physical (as well as the phenomenological) individuation of the logico-syntactic structures of mental states is only derivative. This is unsurprising. Certainly, no logico-syntactic feature deserving of the name can be understood in terms of physical shape alone. For example, the mere shape of "if…then," in abstraction from its function in a system, has nothing to do with any logical operation. Logico-syntactic structures are primarily individuated functionally. For a functional account of mental logico-syntactic properties, see the following words of Stephen Stich, which I endorse and will use to further explicate the notion of such structures:[20]

> Mental state tokens are brain state tokens. But the properties in virtue of which mental state tokens are classified into syntactic categories are not intrinsic

---

[20] Some of Stich's claims pertain directly to the methodology of cognitive science, which is not the focus of this book.

features of those brain states; they are not features which depend exclusively on the shape or form of "brute physical" properties of the states. Rather, the syntactic properties of mental states are relational or functional properties—they are properties that certain states of the brain have in virtue of the way in which they causally interact with various other states of the system. To put the point in a slightly different way, we would have no reason to view brain states as syntactically structured unless that structure can be exploited in capturing generalizations about the workings of the mind/brain's mechanisms. Attributing syntactic structures to brain state tokens—assigning them to syntactic types—is justified only if some interesting set of causal interactions among those tokens is isomorphic to formal relations among abstract syntactic objects.   (Stich 1991, p. 244)

And

the cognitive states whose interaction is (in part) responsible for behavior can be systematically mapped to abstract syntactic objects in such a way that the causal interactions among cognitive states, as well as causal links with stimuli and behavioral events, can be described in terms of the syntactic properties and relations of the abstract objects to which the cognitive states are mapped. More briefly, the idea is that causal relations among cognitive states mirror formal relations among syntactic objects.   (Stich 1983, p. 149)

Although it is impossible comprehensively to account for logico-syntactic structures in phenomenological or physical terms, the phenomenological-physical individuation of such mental structures will prove useful for some theoretical purposes. But it does not suffice for all purposes. For example, it does not take into account language differences between subjects, and it thus treats phenomenologically identical structures of subjects who speak and think in different languages (structures which play different cognitive roles) as the same. Logico-syntactic structures thus individuated are not ascribed and individuated by content ascriptions. We shall see (in Chapter 6) that the structures of belief-states and of other mental states indeed belong also to more abstract patterns on the vertical axis: that is, to patterns of structures that cut across languages and phenomenologies. These further patterns—which can be said to be functional in a broad sense—are not individuated in terms of thin logico-syntactic structures *plus phenomenology (or physical realization)*. It is these more abstract thick logico-syntactic patterns that are ascribed and individuated by content ascriptions, and for this reason they are especially important for us. The individuative role of phenomenology (or physical realization) vis-à-vis content ascription is only derivative. (The phenomenological-physical individuation is determined by the more abstract individuation relative to a system.) But in this chapter, I will focus on logico-syntactic patterns of the first (phenomenological-physical) thick kind (which I will

130 INTENTIONALITY DECONSTRUCTED

often refer to as "thick" *simpliciter*), and mostly suppress reference to patterns of the more abstract kind.

The objects of content ascriptions—what they ascribe—are structured. Content ascriptions are also, *ipso facto*, ascriptions of logico-syntactic structures to the subject's belief-states, desire-states, and other (seemingly intentional) mental states. Moreover, they are, *ipso facto*, ascriptions of *specific* logico-syntactic structures. The ascription of a specific content necessarily involves the ascription of a specific *logical* structure: sameness of content implies sameness of truth conditions and, in turn, sameness of logical structure. So, when we ascribe to Ali the belief that David loves John, we thereby ascribe to Ali a belief with a certain logical structure, that of the sentence "David loves John," which is different from that of the ascribed belief that Noah and Gadi are clever. We may then say that strictly logical properties are *conceptually implied* by content ascriptions. This does not hold for grammatical structures, since sameness of content as well as sameness of logical structure are compatible with different grammatical structures. Furthermore, this claim is true if understood to concern *thin* logical structures, but it is not true with respect to *thick* logical structures of the first (phenomenological-physical) kind. We may, for example, ascribe to Ali the belief that David loves John without assuming that his beliefs possess (thick) English structures, and so without assuming that he believes "David loves John." However, the claim in question *is* true if understood to concern thick logical structures of the second, more abstract, kind: that is, those structures that cut across languages and phenomenologies. These *are* conceptually implied by content ascriptions. I still haven't explicated, let alone defended, the notion of thick structures of this second kind, so the claim that content ascriptions are *ipso facto* ascriptions of specific logical structures of this kind is still a promise, to be fulfilled later.

Since logico-syntactic structures (at some level of abstraction) are conceptually implied by content ascriptions (e.g., ascriptions of content to a subject's belief-states)—in other words, since content ascriptions carry logico-syntactic messages (which are conceptually appropriate)—then (ironic as this may sound), when abstracted from their semantic messages, content ascriptions have truth values (or epistemic substitutes thereof) and may be true (or adequate).[21] Different

---

[21] This is not to say that content ascriptions *represent* logico-syntactic structures—they can be true or false in a non-representational way, like ascriptions of properties of any other kind (see section 5.4 and the discussion of truth makers in Chapter 6). Talk of content ascriptions as carrying messages should be similarly understood. (Specifying that the logico-syntactic messages of content ascriptions are conceptually appropriate is required since conceptually flawed messages such as semantic ones do not have truth values, or at any rate cannot be true.)

One may say that since content ascriptions carry logico-syntactic messages even when they are not abstracted from their semantic messages, then content ascriptions have (absolute) truth values and may be true in an absolute sense. Note that this would mean that *content ascriptions as such* have (absolute) truth values and may be true in an absolute sense *due to their logico-syntactic messages*. So be it. Nothing important for my view hinges on accepting or rejecting such a claim.

practices of content ascription—practices that may differ in the contents they ascribe under the same circumstances—need not differ in the *thin* logico-syntactic structures they ascribe under the same circumstances. When they are appropriate, they do not thus differ. (The inclusion of "appropriate" here is important. There may be crazy and explanatorily idle practices of content ascription that are not constrained by thin logico-syntactic structures.)[22]

The fact that the notion of thick logico-syntactic structure is more fine-grained than the standard—thin—grammatical notion (or, for that matter, the logical notion) should not tempt one to think that such structures are intentional. Whether or not the above-mentioned structure "It never rains in Madagascar in the summer" carries the intentional content that it never rains in Madagascar in the summer—an issue about which intentional anti-realism says "no"—its fine-grained nature does not make it intentional. The difference between the quoted phrase "It never rains in Madagascar in the summer" and the disquoted one *that* it never rains in Madagascar in the summer is precisely the difference between reference to the structure and reference to content. Ascribing this content to this quoted phrase is a substantive move, one that according to intentional anti-realists is doomed to fail. Thick logico-syntactic structures themselves lack any stand-for relations (even weak ones).

My claims that mental states possess no content and that ascriptions of content are also ascriptions of logico-syntactic structures might create the impression that I take content ascriptions to be based on prior conscious identification of such structures: that is, that we first recognize logico-syntactic structures and then (erroneously) attach semantic interpretations to them. But I do not succumb to this view. As noted in Chapter 3, I accept the view that no flat psychological surface is given to us in introspection in the normal course of things. That is, in introspecting our so-called intentional states we are, standardly, immediately *aware* of them as intentional (in a non-factive sense of "aware as," which does not imply that what we are aware of as being so and so *is* so and so). In the first stage of the process of forming content ascriptions via introspection, we standardly have unconscious access to flat psychological surfaces. We do not become *aware* of any flat psychological feature, logico-syntactic structures included, prior to our

---

[22] A point that is related to the one concerning the structural nature of ascribed semantics is that ascribed semantics is combinatorial. That is, the contents we ascribe to thoughts are functions of the contents we ascribe, or would ascribe, to their components. Thus, the fact that a descriptivist practice ascribes the content that Schmidt was an important mathematician to the thought that is expressed by "Gödel was an important mathematician" is to be traced to the fact that this practice takes the mental tokening of "Gödel" by the relevant subject to refer to Schmidt (and to the way it interprets this thought's other components). Note that practices of content ascription need not be structured though the actual ones are, and relatedly, they need not base combinatorial (ascribed) semantics though the actual ones do.

Reference to the combinatorial semantics of mental states might bring to mind the language of thought (LOT)–connectionist debate. I refer to it in section 6.3.

132 INTENTIONALITY DECONSTRUCTED

being aware *as if* of content. So, intentionality is "doxastically" prior to logico-syntactic structures. But this priority, as we saw, has no bearing on the existence of intentionality.

The question of the priority relation between intentionality and the logico-syntactic structures of mental states also bears on certain considerations in favor of the notion that mental states possess such structures. It even has implications regarding the very compatibility of intentional anti-realism and the attribution of such structures to mental states. While the existence of mental states with logico-syntactic structures may seem obvious, it is not so obvious (and this is the issue we should be interested in) whether there are good reasons to accept the existence of mental states with logico-syntactic properties if mental states are taken to lack intentional properties. We shall see in Chapter 6 that while the predictive and explanatory success of employing content ascriptions does not attest to there being mental states with intentional properties, it does attest to there being mental states with logico-syntactic properties. But one may also think that a short route to establishing the existence of mental states with logico-syntactic strictures yet absent intentional properties is open for the intentional anti-realist. For, one might think, such mental states are what we get once we subtract intentional properties from those mental states that (falsely) appear to be propositional attitudes.

Now, both these considerations for the view that mental states have such structures in spite of lacking intentionality take it for granted that syntax does not presuppose semantics, yet some philosophers have argued (against Stich's syntactic theory of the mind) that syntax does presuppose semantics. Of course, if they are right, then not only are these considerations ineffective, but further, this view itself is false. Why think that syntax presupposes semantics? Tim Crane argues against Stich's presupposition of "the conceptual independence" of the syntax and the semantics of the language of thought (referred by him as "LT") —"the thesis that it is possible for the LT to have syntactic structure without having any semantic interpretation" (Crane 1990, p. 196). Crane acknowledges that there can be abstract syntactic systems with no semantics, but according to him we cannot tell which properties of the states of a concrete system, such as a brain, are syntactic except by appealing to semantic interpretations. For, our mental syntactic properties are supposed to be those properties that are causally relevant to inferences and to the production of behavior, and, alas, our brain sates possess a multitude of such intrinsic properties. (A similar claim is made by Jacquette (1990).)[23]

Crane (and anyone else, to the best of my knowledge) does not in fact provide an argument to the effect that only semantic interpretations can single out logico-syntactic properties, and, so, does not conclusively establish the dependence

---

[23] One might also think that logico-syntactic categories (e.g., the category of individual constants) depend on semantic categories (e.g., the category of singular terms). However, once we realize that logico-syntactic categories are partly functional categories, we can see that this is not the case.

thesis. Rather, he notes Fodor's appeal to intentional properties to meet the challenge of explaining how syntactic properties are singled out, and then considers (on behalf of Stich's theory) and rejects two possible intentional irrealist strategies to meet this challenge. I will not dwell on these strategies or on Crane's critiques.[24] This is not required, since once we recall that intentional anti-realism can avail itself of (false) intentional *ascriptions*, it becomes clear that intentional anti-realism can account for the singling out of logico-syntactic properties. The logico-syntactic properties of mental states that figure in this view are those that are conceptually implied by explanatorily or predictively successful content ascriptions. The success of content ascriptions attests to the fact that mental states possess those properties, as we shall see, but neither the existence of such properties nor the effectivity of this inference depends on the truth of content ascriptions. Logico-syntactic properties are only singled out by content ascriptions, and there could be other ways—either having nothing to do with semantics or having to do with different schemes of semantic ascription—to single them out.

In replying to the question of what physical properties in the brain logico-syntactic properties are (or, perhaps, are realized by), we may appeal to the commonplace computer analogy. Computers perform computations, inferences, etc., and so they operate on logico-syntactic (and, most plausibly, semantics-free) structures. That is (to use Stich's words), causal-functional relations among their states mirror formal relations among logico-syntactic objects. The intrinsic physical properties whose instantiations are the relata of such causal-functional relations realize logico-syntactic properties. (This is true at list for digital computers.) So (under the plausible assumption that at least some computers lack semantics), computers are a counterexample to the thesis that syntax conceptually depends on semantics. On my view, the situation with our brains is similar. Their logico-syntactic properties are realized by those (complex) neural properties whose instantiations are the relata of those causal relations among cognitive states that mirror formal relations among logico-syntactic objects that are implied by explanatorily or predictively successful content ascriptions.[25] So, intentional

---

[24] Let me just make this brief comment. Crane criticizes one of these strategies for leaving Stich's theory with no resources to account for the semantics of language and for non-linguistic behavior. The first of these critiques does not threaten intentional anti-realism, according to which there are no linguistic meanings, and the second critique is undermined (I believe) by my account of the intentional explanation of action that is suggested in Chapter 6.

[25] Note that it also isn't clear how semantics can help someone who rejects this account. A semantic interpretation to a whole structure presupposes a logico-syntactic structure, and semantic interpretations to a structure's components do not suffice to endow structures with their logico-syntactic profiles.

In arguing against folk psychology, Patricia Churchland (1986) claims that it is hard to see where in the brain those sentence-like structures that propositional attitudes are taken to have can be found. Pylyshyn (1984), Fodor and Pylyshyn (1988), and McLaughlin and Warfield (1994) argue that the neurological level is the wrong level to look for such psychological structures. I believe that they are right—that we have to "look" at some high (functional) level of abstraction of physical structures to find logico-syntactic structures.

134 INTENTIONALITY DECONSTRUCTED

anti-realism can accommodate the existence of mental logico-syntactic structures: that is, there can be mental semantics-free logico-syntactic structures. Later on, we shall see that indeed there are such structures.

Since my view of logico-syntactic properties is committed to the notion that syntax is an intrinsic property of the mind, John Searle's objection to this notion might also be mounted against it. According to Searle, since in any sufficiently complex object we can discern some pattern of molecular movements that is isomorphic to the formal structure of any computer program, then anything sufficiently complex implements any program. Therefore, Searle concludes, computer programs are not intrinsic properties of anything. They are not discovered within the physics, but rather are assigned to the physics (see Searle 1992, pp. 207ff.; 1990; Putnam (1988) argues for a similar conclusion).

I think that we have good reason to reject the claim that anything sufficiently complex implements any program (see Chalmers 1996), but let's grant it for the sake of argument. The conclusion that programs are not intrinsic to physics does not follow, since it is possible that an object simultaneously instantiates many programs, all of which are intrinsic to it. Of course, some structures and sequences of structures that an object instantiates may be discernible more easily than others; some may be more relevant to our interests than others. We can distinguish among structures across various dimensions and can also consider some to be privileged according to some criterion. And the claim that computer programs, computational properties, and logical-syntactic structures are intrinsic to their objects is consistent with the assumption that, as a matter of fact, untrue semantic ascriptions single out syntactic characteristics.[26,27]

5.4 Intentional Anti-Realism and Truth (or Epistemic Worth) without Meaning

According to intentional anti-realism, no concrete entity can possess (and hence possesses) any intentional property. Mental states, linguistic acts and objects, pictures, computers, whatever—none of these is intentional. This all-embracing radical commitment is, of course, related to its being a conceptual thesis. I also presented intentional anti-realism as a thesis regarding content ascriptions, to the effect that they (in themselves) do not have truth conditions. But it seems that, on this thesis, not only content ascriptions lack truth conditions. Due to the

---

[26] In earlier work (Horowitz 2007) I maintained (following Shagrir 2001) that semantics is responsible for computational individuation, or, in other words, for singling out a system's computational profile among its various syntactic profiles. (A system's computational structure is the logico-syntactic structure the system implements in performing its cognitive task.) I would now say that it is *the ascription* of semantics that is responsible for computational individuation.

[27] For a *reductio* argument against Searle's and Putnam's arguments see Matthews and Dresner (2016).

INTENTIONAL ANTI-REALISM I   135

seeming connection between intentionality (or reference, or content, or meaning) and truth, intentional anti-realism seems committed to the notion that nothing— including standard non-semantic ("first-level") beliefs and utterance of sentences— has a truth value. No sentence, no utterance of a sentence, no belief (or belief-state) is ever true (or false). This seeming commitment of the view appears to be an epistemic catastrophe. It robs belief-states of their prominent epistemic asset— namely, the potential to be true—and undermines their supposed built-in aim. Further, we thus seem to lose the distinction between "good" or "adequate" belief-states and "bad" or "inadequate" ones. Similarly, intentional anti-realism seems to rob desire-states of their satisfaction conditions, and thus to take the sting out of them.

The linkage that is presupposed in this reasoning between intentionality, or reference, or meaning, or content, and truth, might seem obvious. It might seem evident that the truth of a sentence (or its falsity, for that matter) depends on the representational properties of its components.[28] This observation got theoretical backing in Tarski's (1935) analysis of truth in formal languages, and in Davidson's application of Tarski's model to a theory of meaning to natural languages (see, e.g., Davidson 1967).[29] These ideas apply to propositional attitudes precisely as they apply to sentences. However, their application to either is qualified: they are concerned with the combinatorial nature of truth understood in representational terms. The truth of a sentence or a belief must be determined by the representational properties of the sentence or the belief (say in the Tarskian manner) only if truth is (or involves) representation: in other words, only if truth is (or involves) correspondence.[30] Evidently, pointing out such a conditional linkage between truth and representational properties does not preclude intentional anti-realism from making room for truth.

Various philosophers have maintained that truth need not involve reference or representation. Donald Davidson, for example, put this idea in the following explicit form: "Beliefs are true or false, but they represent nothing" (Davidson 1989, p. 156.) Alternative conceptions of truth have been suggested throughout the history of philosophy, such as pragmatism and coherentism. Intentional anti-realism of the sort suggested here well accords with the conception of truth as coherence, due to its adherence to the idea that our belief-states and sentences, though lacking intentional properties, have thick logico-syntactic structures. According to the coherentist approach to truth, it is a belief's coherence with a

---

[28] I use here "representational properties" rather than "referential properties" because sometimes the former is understood to have a general application whereas the latter is understood to refer to the language–world semantic relations of words of some sorts.

[29] We should take this part of Davidson's philosophy of language to imply neither that he is an atomist nor that he is an intentional realist; he is a holist and interpretivist.

[30] I do not mean to suggest that Tarski offered a correspondence theory of truth. The issue is controversial (see, e.g., Davidson 1969; Field 1972; Putnam 1985).

136 INTENTIONALITY DECONSTRUCTED

large (coherent) body of beliefs that makes this belief true, and logico-syntactic properties can sustain coherence relations.[31] Thus, meaningless logico-syntactic structures may be truth bearers. Intentional anti-realism can then sever the connection between truth conditions and meaning or content, and defend truth without meaning or content.

It might be thought that formal logico-syntactic properties cannot sustain all coherence relations: for example, that they cannot sustain the notorious inference from "A is green" to "A is a color." This is true with respect to thin logico-syntactic properties, but it isn't true with respect to thick ones. No inferential power is lost when we abstract belief-states from their stand-for relations: that is, from their intentionality. We can infer the claim that A is a color from the claim that A is green coupled with the claim that everything that is green is a color, and, similarly, we can infer the structure "A is a color" from the structure "A is green" coupled with the structure "everything that is green is a color" (without taking the components of these structures to have representational properties). We can see that, in general, intentional anti-realism that acknowledges that mental states have thick logico-syntactic structures has all the resources to account for reasoning and coherence relations as does the intentional realist. Disquoting the belief-state "p" (thickly understood) to the belief *that p* adds nothing to this dimension. Note that the claim that logico-syntactic properties can sustain coherence relations does not mean or imply that coherence relations are all deductive; it is consistent with their being inductive, abductive, explanatory, and the like, for all these conform to formal patterns (in the thick sense).[32] So, logico-syntactic structures can maintain inferential relations such as coherence relations. And the thick individuation of such structures ensures that they can maintain all the coherence relations that intentional structures are supposed to maintain.

It is beyond the scope of this book to present a detailed coherence theory of truth, to defend one, or to show that only coherence theories of truth can accommodate substantive yet non-representational truth. Rather, I argue that

---

[31] Some coherentists maintain that truth is constituted by coherence among the current beliefs of actual people, others maintain that it is the beliefs of ordinary people who have reached the limit of inquiry, and there are other views on the matter (see Young 2018), but deciding on it is not important for our concerns. As will be evident later, the coherentist idea that is important for our concerns is that truth is constituted by those inferential relations that form *the test* for truth, whatever they may be.

[32] Various works in cognitive science suggest that some reasoning abilities are sensitive to content, in the sense that when subjects are confronted with formally identical cognitive tasks, different cognitive algorithms are activated, depending on the inputs. See, for example, the findings of Tversky and Kahneman (1973) concerning probabilistic thinking, or other works of theirs, and Wason's (1966) selection task and various experiments that show that success on the task is to a significant extent content-dependent (e.g., Cosmides and Tooby 1992). One might think that such research establishes the view that cognitive activities essentially involve content, but this is not so. Formulating the conclusion of these works in terms of content presupposes intentional realism. Proponents of intentional anti-realism of the kind suggested here can accommodate the findings on which this conclusion is based by saying that the reasoning abilities in question are sensitive to thick logico-syntactic structures. As long as the claim for the formal nature of reasoning is thickly construed, it is in no clash with these findings.

combining the coherence approach to truth with the version of intentional anti-realism that I defend allows the latter to preserve a substantive (non-deflationary) notion of truth for belief-states and other entities. This is so since belief-states have thick logico-syntactic structures, which allow them to maintain coherence relations with each other. We can further motivate the acceptance of the coherence approach to truth in the framework of intentional anti-realism in the following way. We have good reason to accept that coherence is a test for truth. Given this, and assuming a substantive notion of truth, it seems that the only obstacle for a coherence theory of truth—of a theory according to which truth *is* coherence—is the possibility that a correspondence theory of truth is true. Once this possibility is ruled out—and intentional anti-realism rules it out—then, assuming a substantive notion of truth, the way is paved to accepting that truth is coherence.[33] Of course, this assumption should not be taken lightly, and it might be that ruling out correspondence truth forces us, rather, to give up this assumption. I will return to this issue presently.

We can see that combining intentional anti-realism with a coherence approach to truth may even be taken to put it in a better position with respect to the pre-theoretical notion of truth than reductive-naturalistic accounts of intentionality. For truth is pre-theoretically conceived as a privileged relation between mind, or language, and reality, yet Stich (1990, ch. 5) showed that in a reductive-naturalistic framework, which takes the intentional relation to be just one among many world–mind or world–language relations, truth becomes idiosyncratic and loses its alleged unique status and importance.[34] In light of Stich's observation, we see that the issue of truth does not make intentional anti-realism more vulnerable

---

[33] For defenses of the coherence approach to truth see, for example, Bradley (1914), Blanshard (1939), Putnam (1981), and Young (1995, 2001, 2018). It is reasonable to assume that to the extent that pragmatist theories of truth can accommodate (non-representational) truth, it is only insofar as they incorporate a coherentist element. This is so, because it is implausible that accepting any true statement is beneficial. It is the system of beliefs as a whole that may be said to be beneficial, and so the criterion for a pragmatist truth involves coherence. Membership in a coherent system that is beneficial is certainly an asset for beliefs.

Arguably, an external constraint on a coherent system is required to endow members of such systems with epistemic value, and this may justify the appeal to a pragmatist element. On the other hand, one might think that, insofar as we deal with the coherence of actual beliefs (rather than of abstract propositions), characteristics such as consistent and high-resolution sensitivity to the environment could also serve as such constraints. At any rate, when I write about coherence theories of truth here, I mean to refer also to pragmatist-coherentist theories.

Just as pragmatism does not take any true belief to be beneficial, it also does not take any beneficial belief or set of beliefs to be true. For this reason, pragmatic considerations concerning the utility of the intentional stance do not vindicate intentional realism. Specifically, my arguments against this view can be taken to show that it does not meet the requirement of coherence with our body of knowledge.

Note that endorsing pragmatist-coherentist theories of truth by no means involves endorsing a pragmatist approach to meaning, such as the verificationist approach that was advocated by Peirce (1878/1992).

[34] Stich also argues against the instrumental value of having beliefs that are true relative to beliefs that bear other naturalistic relations to the world. For a critique of Stich's argument to this effect, see Loewer (1993).

138 INTENTIONALITY DECONSTRUCTED

than the reductive-naturalistic approach. Once we give up first-person based intentionality and face the choice between intentional anti-realism and the reductive-naturalistic approach, considerations pertaining to truth do not prefer the latter. And if the former is considered together with the coherence approach to truth, such considerations prefer it.[35]

However, suppose that, as various philosophers believe, coherence does not constitute truth, and further, that truth cannot be accounted for in *any* non-representational terms. Accepting this supposition is by no means detrimental to intentional anti-realism. Coherence is an epistemic merit of belief-states and statements. Moreover, it is such an epistemic merit that distinguishes good or adequate from bad or inadequate belief-states and statements. That is, since coherence with a large (coherent) body of beliefs is the test for truth (even for those who reject the coherence theory of truth), beliefs that cohere with a large (coherent) body of beliefs, and only such beliefs, are those it is important to single out as epistemically meritorious. If we wish to preserve the distinction between those beliefs that (upon sound scrutiny) we take to be true and those we take to be false, intentional anti-realism that embraces coherence delivers: it preserves precisely this distinction. It is not crucial whether the epistemic merit in question can be identified with what is pre-theoretically regarded as truth, or whether coherence only provides a substitute for this.[36] So, since intentional anti-realism can respect this distinction , the only truth-related charge that can be raised against this view is that it is committed to a counterintuitive view. But raising such a charge against a theory—and certainly against an (anyhow counterintuitive) error theory—does not weigh against arguments in its favor.

For simplicity, unless context requires otherwise, I will henceforth speak of intentional anti-realism as making room for truth in virtue of its making room for coherence, but I do not insist that coherence constitutes what is pre-theoretically regarded as truth. You can read "truth conditions" as referring to coherence conditions that need not be truth conditions and call them "adequacy conditions," and read "truth" as referring to that epistemic merit regardless of whether it is indeed truth and refer to it as "adequacy."

5.5 Coherence and the Status of Content Ascriptions

I shall now present a prima facie difficulty for coherentist intentional anti-realism, and then address it and further clarify my approach. The difficulty concerns the

---

[35] One might suggest that this advantage of intentional anti-realism vanishes once a coherence approach to truth is incorporated, similarly, into reductive naturalism. But taking beliefs to represent while taking their truth to be independent of their representing makes no sense.

[36] For this reason, it is not important to decide here whose beliefs constitute coherence (e.g., actual people or ordinary people who have reached the limit of inquiry). The coherentist idea that is important for our purpose is that truth is constituted by those inferential relations that form the test for truth, whatever they are.

epistemic status of semantic sentences or beliefs—that is, of content ascriptions—in comparison to that of non-semantic sentences and beliefs. As noted, intentional anti-realism as the thesis that content ascriptions lack truth conditions implies that no belief or sentence is representationally true (or false). If intentional anti-realism incorporates a coherentist conception of truth, and thus beliefs and sentences may be true (or false) in a coherentist sense, the question of the truth conditions of content ascription re-emerges. Do content ascriptions have coherentist truth conditions and truth values like all other beliefs and sentences, or is there a way to single them out in this respect? If content ascriptions have coherentist truth conditions, are these truth conditions practice-independent, like the truth conditions of other beliefs and sentences, which are supposed to be determined by coherence? A positive reply to this question would amount to the denial of intentional anti-realism.

To better realize the pressure to treat all beliefs and sentences as basically possessing the same epistemic status in a coherentist framework, consider Quine's coherentist-holistic-pragmatist-empiricist epistemology (1953). On Quine's picture, on the one hand, no statement—even those statements that appear to be true in virtue of meaning alone, which are located near the center of the field of knowledge—is immune to revision in the face of recalcitrant experience. On the other hand, no statement—even those statements that are located at the periphery of the field—must be given up in the face of recalcitrant experience. On this epistemic model, there can only be a difference in degree in the epistemic strength of statements, not a categorical difference. All are subject to (epistemic) indeterminacy to some degree. If content ascriptions are part of the field of knowledge, they must be subject to just such indeterminacy, and differ from non-semantic statements such as "Grass is green" only in degree. Can this (conditional) claim be squared with my claim that content ascriptions have only practice-dependent truth conditions, which suggests that they are subject to indeterminacy of a deeper kind? Is it compatible with the natural construal of intentional anti-realism as a thesis about the uniqueness of content ascriptions?[37,38]

The answers to these two questions are positive. Whereas, in many cases, considerations of coherence can favor standard (non-semantic) claims over all their alternatives, if my arguments or any other arguments for intentional anti-realism are sound, then no such considerations favor any content ascription over all

---

[37] This difference in the status of truth between content ascriptions and non-semantic statements entails a difference in the epistemic dimension pertaining to acceptability and revisability, since practice-dependence in the former dimension entails practice-dependence in the latter. In relying on this claim, I do not intend to suggest that Quine endorsed it, nor that he held a coherence theory *of truth*. Also, I do not endorse Quine's picture in its entirety. For one thing, on my view analytic statements are not located at the center of the field of knowledge but rather outside this field.

[38] These difficulties and questions are equally pressing for intentional anti-realists who give up truth and take the epistemic merit of coherence to substitute it rather than constitute it, for they are also challenged to make room for a difference in the epistemic status of content ascriptions and standard, non-semantic, statements or beliefs. We will also be able to see that the answer to be suggested below can be adjusted to fit such intentional anti-realism.

140   INTENTIONALITY DECONSTRUCTED

possible alternatives. The soundness of these arguments means that no non-semantic statement or any conjunction of such statements can justify us (remaining with the Gödel–Schmidt example) in preferring any Gödel content ascription over the corresponding Schmidt content ascription, or vice versa. In this sense, content ascriptions may be said to be radically indeterminate; they are indeterminate in a different, and stronger, sense than non-semantic statements. The arguments for intentional anti-realism establish that content ascriptions entirely lack epistemic status: being unqualified for coherence with our large body of beliefs, they lie outside the field of knowledge. No content ascription can break the circle of non-semantic knowledge and sneak in. Unlike non-semantic statements, content ascriptions lack not only correspondence-representational truth conditions, but also coherentist ones. This is the fate of all statements that include those flawed expressions such as "think that," "want that," "refers to," and the like.[39] Content ascriptions have practice-dependent truth conditions, but recall that their actually having truth conditions (and occasionally being true) in an absolute sense depends upon the truth of an assumption—namely, that a practice of content ascription is itself true—which isn't true and cannot be true.[40]

At the same time, as already noted, since logico-syntactic structures (at some level of abstraction) are conceptually implied by content ascriptions, then, when abstracted from their semantic messages—for example, when taken as "S believes 'It is raining'' rather than as "S believes that it is raining"—content ascriptions have truth values (or epistemic substitutes thereof), and may be true (or adequate). Such abstractions strip them of their "think that" (or similar) aspects: that is, of those logico-syntactic characteristics that make them content ascriptions and prevent them from cohering with the field of knowledge. They would then cohere or fail to cohere with the field of knowledge precisely like non-semantic statements.[41]

The idea that semantic ascriptions lie outside the field of knowledge is an essential aspect of intentional anti-realism, and is reflected in other characterizations of the view: for example, that according to this view practices of content

[39] The same reasoning can be taken to show that analytic statements, too, lie outside the field of knowledge, and thus that there is a sharp distinction between analytic (or semantic) statements and synthetic (or non-semantic) ones, but the issue requires further development that is beyond the scope of this book.

[40] By contrast, truths in the coherentist sense are true regardless of any assumption. It is not that we take a statement p to be true on the assumption that statements q and r, with which it coheres, are true. Rather, on the coherentist picture, logico-syntactic relations among beliefs constitute truth in the full-blown sense—from scratch, as it were.

The assumption in question is a presupposition of content ascriptions, in the sense in which one sentence presupposes another if and only if whenever the first is true or false the second is true (Strawson 1950).

[41] The fact that the unfitness of content ascriptions to cohere with the field of knowledge is rooted in their thick logico-syntactic structures does not imply that this appears on their surface and can easily be noticed. A philosophical endeavor—that is, arguments against intentional realism—was required to expose it.

ascription legislate semantic facts or truths rather than reflect them.[42] At any rate, we saw that, with the help of the epistemic attribute of coherence, intentional anti-realism can assign content ascriptions a unique status.

One might object to the idea that content ascriptions lie outside the field of knowledge by claiming that they are sources of knowledge, in that on various occasions we infer what the case is from what we take some people to believe. If we take one to believe some proposition p, then we sometimes infer from this ascription, together with some other premises (e.g., that one is an expert on the subject or happens to be well situated with respect to the relevant fact), that p. In other words, under some circumstances we take one's believing that p to be an indicator of the obtaining of p (see Field 1972, 1978; Schiffer 1981). Certainly, sometimes such inferences aren't strong, but sometimes they are. So, because the ascription that one believes that p is sometimes a source of knowledge, it seems to be integrated with the field of knowledge.

This objection pressures me to further clarify the sense of the claim that content ascriptions lie outside the field of knowledge. This claim means that content ascriptions cannot be inferred—either deductively, inductively, or abductively— from statements that are within the field of knowledge. This claim has been shown to be true—again, arguments for intentional anti-realism show just this. This claim is not shaken by the objection, because, first of all, the objection concerns inferences in the opposite direction—content-to-world. It is the claim concerning world-to-content inferences that is essential to intentional anti-realism, since intentional anti-realism is a thesis about the truth values of content ascriptions, and it is inferences in this direction that are candidates for yielding the truth of content ascriptions. So even if inferences from content ascriptions to the claims embedded in them are reliable, this does not affect the claim that content ascriptions lie outside the field of knowledge.

We may think that a similar objection is possible that does affect the claim regarding the epistemic status of content ascriptions. For similar inferences to the ones underlying the original objection, but in the opposite direction, seem to be effective as well: if one is well situated with respect to the obtaining of some fact, we may justifiably infer that one believes that this fact obtains. Such world-content inferences indeed appear justifiable, but not in a sense that endangers intentional anti-realism or the claim that content ascriptions lie outside the field of knowledge. According to intentional anti-realism, such inferences are justified only if a scheme of interpretation (a scheme of content ascription) is assumed. We can realize this by considering any example in which the belief ascribed to

---

[42] This talk of legislating semantic facts does not amount to talk of the stipulation of meanings realistically understood. No stipulation creates meaning on intentional anti-realism. Rather, talk of legislating semantic facts means that content ascriptions treat various word--object or thought–object relations as if they constitute meanings.

142 INTENTIONALITY DECONSTRUCTED

one is a Gödel belief (if to stick again to the Kripkean story). Taking any such ascriptions to be warranted presupposes the absolute truth of a scheme of interpretation, and thus of intentional realism. From a perspective that does not presuppose this view, circumstances may justify the claim that John believes "Gödel proved the incompleteness theorem," but not the claim that John believes *that* Gödel proved the incompleteness theorem. One who is not impressed by arguments for intentional realism should not therefore be impressed by the objection in question. It cannot be taken to show that content ascriptions form part of the field of knowledge.

Let us return to inferences from beliefs to worldly facts. Their reliability, in various cases, may be taken to attest to the truth of intentional realism, for one may wonder how we can explain the partial but not accidental success of such inferences without assuming that content ascriptions are sometimes true. Such inferences must rely on the obtaining of causal correlations between the instantiations of properties that are typically instantiated by subjects when we ascribe to them contents and the inferred worldly facts, and it seems natural to assume that these properties are intentional properties. However, the assumption that content ascriptions are true in these cases does not at all help to explain such correlations. It isn't clear what it is about supposedly intentional properties that can make their instantiations correlate with the worldly facts they are supposed to represent. To assume that the relation of aboutness is somehow transformed into a causal relation—that being directed at something underlies a causal relation with it— makes no sense. Furthermore, there is an alternative explanation for the correlations in question. Note what it is that requires an explanation. It is not the very existence of correlations between belief-states and worldly facts, correlations that are, in principle, quite understandable. What requires explanation is the existence of correlations between, on the one hand, belief-states to which contents are ascribed in terms of those worldly facts the obtaining of which they indicate, and, on the other hand, those worldly facts. When the requirement is so posed, the explanation readily suggests itself: our practice of content ascription is such that we ascribe contents to belief-states in terms of the worldly facts the obtaining of which they indicate. We need not postulate any contents. It is of course convenient to make inferences of the kind in question when the belief-states are described in terms of those worldly facts with which we take them to correlate under given circumstances—that is, when they are described in intentional terms (and this is an advantage of employing the intentional stance)—but this convenience by no means implies that belief-states possess intentionality.[43,44]

---

[43] It might be tempting to think that such world–mind correlations endow mental states with contents, but it is a lesson of this book, and in particular of the discussion of Chapter 4, that this cannot be true.

[44] The claim that the correlations in question can only (or best) be explained by postulating intentional properties is reminiscent of the claim that the explanatory and predictive success of content ascriptions can only (or best) be explained by postulating intentional properties. In Chapter 6, I provide an extensive reply to the latter claim, and, *mutatis mutandis*, it can be taken to address the former.

This is, then, how the coherence theory of truth incorporates intentional anti-realism: standard (i.e., non-semantic) beliefs are true if they cohere with our body of beliefs. They may be true even though they are not intentional—the coherence theory makes room for this possibility. Content ascriptions do not cohere with this body of beliefs, in that they are not implied—either deductively or inductively—by this body; they lie outside the field of knowledge. Their having practice-dependent truth values is their having merely assumed, or conditional, and not actual truth values, since their actually having truth values in virtue of according with a certain practice of content ascription or failing thereof depends upon the truth of an assumption—namely, that the principles underlying the practice of content ascription are true—that is not and cannot be true.

In addressing the difficulties that eliminative materialism faces with the notion of truth and related notions, Paul Churchland (1981) promised that replacements for these notions would arise in the future, though he did not know what these replacements would be. This position was met with the reaction that until some plausible replacements were forthcoming, we had better bet against eliminativism (see Baker 1987; Hannan 1993).[45] We can see that such an objection is not effective against my version of intentional anti-realism since it is not futuristic in such a sense. My approach to truth—or at any rate to the related epistemic virtue—only appeals to conceptual resources that are already at our disposal.

I will conclude this section by addressing a possible objection to the version of intentional anti-realism that incorporates a coherentist conception of truth. Since on this view (non-semantic) beliefs and sentences may be true, they have truth conditions (understood in coherentist terms). But then, it might be argued, this view does make room, after all, for intentionality and reference: these can be characterized (in Davidsonian spirit) as the contribution of the components (or some of the components) of beliefs and sentences to the truth conditions of these beliefs and sentences. So, the objection proceeds, this view is not really intentional anti-realism. But it is. You can refer to the components' contribution to truth conditions in whatever way you choose; the crucial point, in virtue of which this view is intentional anti-realism, is that this contribution to truth conditions is a contribution to what are in fact *non-intentional* truth conditions. Thus, this contribution too is non-intentional.[46]

---

[45] Hilary Putnam criticized Churchland's position along similar lines: "But the task of showing that a successor concept can be provided, that *it* has the kind of objectivity the scientific realist regards as characteristic of science, and that it can play a suitable role in explaining the success of scientific linguistic practice is today only a gleam in Churchland's eye" (Putnam 1988, p. 110).

Baker considers and rejects a few accounts of truth that do not assume intentionality, but the coherentist option is not among them (see Baker 1987, pp. 143–147).

[46] Intentional anti-realism may be challenged to provide sense not only to the truth of beliefs, but also to the satisfaction of desires. This is significant, for the notion of desire satisfaction appears important from various perspectives: for example, from certain approaches to morality. However, once it is realized that intentional anti-realism can provide sense to truth (or adequacy), we can see that it can provide sense to desire satisfaction. It is simply that a desire "p" is satisfied

144   INTENTIONALITY DECONSTRUCTED

I will continue to develop the suggested version of intentional anti-realism in Chapter 6. Now let me draw two implications from the theory as so far presented.

5.6 Two Implications of Intentional Anti-Realism

5.6.1 Thought and Language

As mentioned, on the standard intentional realist approach to the connection between the semantics of the mind and that of language, utterances of sentences derive their meanings from the contents of mental states. In particular, it is some kind of intention on the speaker's part—for example, an intention to produce in the hearer a belief with a certain content—that is supposed to endow our words with meaning. On this approach, the mind is taken to have original intentionality—intentionality that is not derived from the intentionality of anything. Further, the mind is the source of all intentionality. Some intentional realists who take the mind to be the source of all intentionality, such as Chisholm (in Chisholm and Sellars 1958) and Searle (1983, 1989, 1992), anchor this privileged status of the mind in its unique metaphysical nature, sometimes in its conscious aspect. Other intentional realists do not go to such metaphysical depths. Thus (as mentioned earlier), Fodor (1987) anchors the semantic priority he assigns to the mind in the mere fact that the mind–world causal chains that constitute content are shorter than the language–world causal chains that constitute meaning.[47]

Denying that any concrete entity—mental, linguistic, or any other—has content (or meaning), intentional anti-realists cannot avail themselves of the notions of content derivation and semantic priority in its realist form. But they can avail themselves of certain notions of content derivation and semantic priority. The intentional anti-realist sense of mind–language content derivation is that—as a matter of (contingent) fact—we interpret language in terms of the contents we ascribe to the mind. That is, our practice of content ascription is such that it systematically matches the contents ascribed to language to those ascribed to the mind. The practice of content ascription may also be such as to legislate that the (ascribed) intentionality of entities of a certain kind (e.g., mental ones) does not depend on the (ascribed) intentionality *of anything else*. We thus give sense .to the idea of *original* (i.e., non-derived) intentionality in an intentional anti-realist framework. According to intentional anti-realism, what kinds of entities "possess" original (ascribed) intentionality and what kinds "possess" derived (ascribed)

---

under those circumstances, and only under those circumstances, in which a belief-state "p" would be true (or adequate). The circumstances in question pertain to coherence.

[47]   As we saw in Chapter 4), a reductive account that gives priority to the intentionality of the mind may be an account of content derivation, but it need not be.

intentionality is a deeply contingent matter, one that is determined by the form that the practice of content ascription in fact takes, while it could have taken another path.[48] I neither assume nor argue for the mind–language priority thesis in the ascriptivist sense. I refer to this thesis as a mere example, and it is not part of the intentional anti-realist view that is defended on these pages. Intentional anti-realism can give sense to this thesis precisely as it can give sense to the converse one. It is an implication of intentional anti-realism that the way to find out whether linguistic intentionality depends on mental intentionality—that is, whether *ascribed* linguistic intentionality depends on *ascribed* mental intentionality—is to probe and analyze our actual practice (or practices) of content ascription. Performing such an analysis (which is not guaranteed to discover that there is a homogeneous practice in this regard) lies beyond the scope of this book.[49]

In providing those senses to derived intentionality, original intentionality, and the source of intentionality, I do not mean to suggest that they are the correct interpretations of the linguistic expressions of the ideas in question, or to rule out the possibility that these ideas are standardly construed realistically (e.g., that the notion of original intentionality is understood as implying real intentionality). Rather, I mean to suggest that if we construe these ideas in the way suggested here, then, whether these senses can be said to reflect the original ideas or to be revisionist suggestions as to what we can make of the original ideas while abstracting away from their realist commitments, the senses provided suggest a substantive issue to pursue.

Note that my case for thorough intentional anti-realism does not depend on any thesis of semantic priority. Specifically, I do not argue against (real) linguistic intentionality by arguing for the dependence of linguistic intentionality on mental intentionality and undermining the latter. With one exception (the argument against phenomenal intentionality from Chapter 3), which is irrelevant to linguistic intentionality, the arguments for intentional anti-realism that have been suggested here are intended to have general applicability and to undermine the possession of contents by any concrete entity—mental, linguistic, or any other—irrespective of its connection to the (presumed) intentionality of any other entity.[50]

---

[48] For an extended discussion of this issue that does not presuppose intentional anti-realism, see Horowitz (2021).

[49] Nothing said here is meant to suggest that there are no constraints on good or plausible practices of ascription in this regard. It might be, for example, that a practice that assigns priority to ascriptions of intentionality to mental states is more efficient in explaining behavior since mental states cause behavior, or that it better serves our use of others as sources of knowledge regarding their environments since mental states are "closer" to environmental events than the utterances to which they give rise.

[50] Like the issue of semantic priority, the issue of semantic externalism vs. semantic internalism (standardly understood as an issue of content determination) can also be presented in terms of the actual practice of content ascription. The issue then becomes whether content ascriptions are sensitive to external factors or only to internal ones. In fact, the prominent externalist arguments of Putnam (1975a) and Burge (1979) involve analyses of (what they take to be) our practices of content ascription. For my criticism of these arguments, see Horowitz (1996, 2001, 2005).

146 INTENTIONALITY DECONSTRUCTED

Let me add a brief remark on another dimension of the thought–language relations. It seems that on my approach the linguistically articulated belief-state "p" and the corresponding sentence ("p") cannot share thick logico-syntactic structures since the notion of logico-syntactic structure that is in play has functional aspects and the functional profiles of mental states and of linguistic utterances differ. (I referred, in this context, to mental functions.) However, I do not consider it to be a fact that these do share their structures. Plausibly, we simply *take* sentences to be of the same thick structures as the corresponding belief-states. When I speak of belief-states and sentences or their utterances as sharing logico-syntactic structures, I do not assume more than this. This also suffices to make sense of our taking beliefs-states and the corresponding sentences to have the same truth values. (Note that the notion of coherence that figures in coherentist accounts of truth, as well as in my discussion of the issue, is, first and foremost, coherence among beliefs or belief-states.)

5.6.2 The Turing Test and the Alleged Ubiquity of Intelligence

It might be thought that according to the view here presented, intelligence is cheap, indeed ubiquitous. What seems to indicate that this view has this implication is the fact that this view may legitimate the Turing test for intelligence (Turing 1950). If the adequacy of this test is challenged by its dismissal of intentionality as an aspect of intelligence (see Searle 1980), then intentional anti-realism legitimizes it.[51] On the kind of intentional anti-realism suggested in this book, intelligence may seem to be present everywhere, since logico-syntactic structures and processes connecting their instantiations seem to be everywhere. Is this a problem for intentional anti-realism? I do not think so. If one wishes to say that every process over logico-syntactic structures instantiates intelligence, then one must use "intelligence" in such a loose sense in which great stupidity might count as a case of intelligence. The ubiquity of intelligence in such a sense is not a problem for the view. It would have been a problem had a rock come out *very* intelligent on this view, or had it come out as intelligent as a regular (say) human being. I do not find the implication that a rock has intelligence, if minimal (for all we know), to be problematic, precisely as I do not consider problematic the fact that a theory of art implies that some charlatan drawing is an artwork, as long as it does not imply that it is good artwork. (If you are not sympathetic to this example, I bet you can find one to which you are.) For all we know about

---

[51] Of course, it might be claimed that a view that gives up intentionality rather gives up intelligence. I think that this claim can only be based on a terminological consideration. My treatment of the claim for a linkage between rationality and intentionality in Chapter 6 applies to this claim as well.

rocks, the intentional anti-realism defended in this book, precisely like the Turing test, does not imply that a rock is very intelligent. Intelligence that is embodied in a system's sophisticated processing and in its high sensitivity to its environment, so that it produces a variety of useful responses to environmental stimuli in changing circumstances, is anything but ubiquitous.[52]

---

[52] Note that a rock doesn't come out very intelligent on this approach even for one who believes that every object instantiates any logico-syntactic structure.

6

Intentional Anti-Realism II

Objections and Further Developments

6.1 Intentional Anti-Realism and the Success of Content Ascription

A prominent objection to eliminative materialism that appears to apply to intentional anti-realism as well is based on the following idea. Explanations and predictions of human behavior (and perhaps also of animal behavior) in terms of the contents of mental states work extremely well, and this fact can be best (if not only) explained on the assumption that behavior is caused by intentional mental states (perhaps in virtue of their intentional contents). So, we have good reason to assume that we have intentional mental states, mental states with intentional contents (see, e.g., Fodor 1987; Pylyshyn 1980). I begin addressing this argument in the present section, but its full rejoinder awaits further development of the suggested intentional anti-realist theory and will extend to the next three sections.

In addressing this argument, I grant the assumption that explanations and predictions of behavior expressed in intentional terms systematically succeed in predicting and explaining behavior. Indeed, some philosophers—notably, Paul Churchland (1981) (see also Rosenberg MS)—downplay the soundness of folk psychology, but it seems hard to deny that, though limited in force, those intentional explanations and predictions that we daily employ with respect to our fellow subjects enjoy remarkable systematic success.[1] It is their systematic success that enables our social interactions (see Fodor (1987) for examples). When this assumption is coupled with the assumption that predictive and explanatory success indicates that the predictions and explanations in question are true, intentional realism is vindicated.

Baker's argument from rationality and justification against eliminative materialism (Baker 1987, pp. 135–136) is similar in an important respect to the argument from the explanatory and predictive success of content ascriptions.

---

[1] Curiously, while intentional irrealists discuss the issue of mental causation (see, e.g., Dennett 1987c, 1991; Davidson 1980, 1993; Mölder 2010), they hardly discuss this argument, which poses a serious challenge to their view. Note that arguments to the effect that knowledge of people's internal states does not play an extensive role in human interactions (e.g., Maibom 2007) do not undermine the success argument, since it needs only to focus on those interactions in which such knowledge is involved.

Intentionality Deconstructed: An Anti-Realist Theory. Amir Horowitz, Oxford University Press.
© Amir Horowitz 2024. DOI: 10.1093/oso/9780198896432.003.0006

According to Baker, denying that we have intentional states undermines the ideas of justification and rational acceptability—indeed, the very idea of a good argument. Thus, one who argues that eliminative materialism is justified or rationally acceptable is caught in a pragmatic incoherence: one claims that one's view is rationally acceptable, but one is committed to the claim that, like any other view, it is not rationally acceptable. (For a similar argument, see Swinburne (1980).) This charge is presented by Baker as an instance of the "cognitive suicide" family of objections, another instance of which will be discussed in section 6.4. The significance of the instance now under consideration lies in its insistence on the role of intentional properties in reasoning, and its relevance to the general idea of rational acceptability. From this perspective, we can notice a clear affinity between this charge and the one from the explanatory and predictive success of content ascriptions; it is just that the former applies not only to practical reasoning (i.e., action-oriented reasoning), but also to theoretical reasoning. Let me start by addressing the charge raised by Baker.

Recall that the suggested version of intentional anti-realism does not amount to, and does not entail, mental (ontological) eliminativism: it acknowledges the existence of mental states with the properties standardly attributed to them, minus intentional properties. Such a version of intentional anti-realism does not undermine the notions of justification or rational acceptability, for these can be understood in logico-syntactic terms. Reasoning, justification, and the like, need not involve intentional properties. It is possible to account perfectly for the appropriateness, justifiability, or rationality of a transition from a statement (or a set of statements) to another statement in purely logico-syntactic terms. Intentional anti-realism can thus account for the validity of arguments, and since, as we saw, this view makes room for truth (or at any rate for epistemic merits that distinguish between belief-states in a way that corresponds to the true–false distinction), it can also account for the soundness of arguments (or at any rate for epistemic merits that distinguish between sound and unsound arguments). Remember that the notion of logico-syntactic structure in play is thick; it is sensitive to the differences between, for example, Da and Pb (where such fine-grained sensitivity need not involve semantics, i.e., *standing for* other entities). We can also account in such terms for "analytic" transitions, such as from "a is a mother" to "a is a parent"— the transition appears smooth when represented as a transition from "a is FP" to "a is P"; it works regardless of what, if anything, these letters stand for.[2] We can also account for transitions such as the one from "a is green" to "a is a color." As the discussion of coherence in Chapter 5 shows, every reasoning that is described in intentional terms can be carried out by means of thick

---

[2] This claim implies that analytic statements, such as "A mother is a parent," which are standardly taken to be true in virtue of meaning alone, have their epistemic merit in virtue of thick logico-syntactic structures.

150   INTENTIONALITY DECONSTRUCTED

logico-syntactic structures, parallel to the ascribed semantic objects. We can account for arguments and justifications in such terms whether they conform to a deductive or to an inductive pattern. As far as arguments and justifications are concerned, syntacticization (thickly understood) is always possible, and it suffices to account for their appropriateness. Thus, the intentional anti-realist can reply to the objection from rational acceptability that all arguments—including the arguments for intentional anti-realism itself—need not involve intentionality. Logico-syntactic characteristics can do the job. So intentional anti-realism does not rob any claim, including the claim for intentional anti-realism itself, of justifiability and rational acceptability. This reply to Baker's objection holds for practical reasoning precisely as it holds for theoretical reasoning.[3]

Now, even if we can account for both theoretical and practical reasoning by merely postulating logico-syntactic properties, it might be that the explanatory and predictive success of content ascriptions attests that *in fact* intentional properties are involved in reasoning. The reply to Baker's argument falls short of addressing this possibility, to which I now turn. Crucial to this argument is the idea—familiar from discussions of scientific realism—that explanations and predictions of a certain kind that are systematically successful are (most plausibly) true. Thus, Hilary Putnam (1975b) and Richard Boyd (1983) argue that unless our scientific theories were true, their explanatory and predictive success should

---

[3] This consideration also undermines Baker's contention that a conception that denies intentionality denies rationality. It sometimes seems that Baker's idea is that contentless processes aren't rational processes *by definition*. If so, she merely argues about words. It seems to me that Hannan's argument against eliminative materialism to the effect that "rational capacities (*qua* rational, *qua* cognitive) cannot be explained except by reference to states described as possessing propositional content" (Hannan 1993, p. 173) boils down to such a terminological claim. Employing an example of Pylyshyn (1980), Hannan argues: "[S]uppose that Patricia has encountered any one of the myriad stimuli that might mean 'the building is on fire'. Now suppose that some internal state occurs in Patricia's head, and Patricia subsequently runs out of the building.... Surely, it is of no help to be given a syntactic or neurophysiological description of the internal state that occurred in Patricia's head. The fact that a system prints an uninterpreted syntactic string subsequent to being exposed to some stimulus and prior to performing some action points to no *rationality* connection between the fact and the stimulus. What is essential to seeing the rationality connection is seeing whatever occurs in the head as symbolic, as having interpretation, as meaning something (such as that the building is on fire)" (pp. 173–174). I can identify no argument here except for this terminological one.

A related charge that is sometimes raised against intentional anti-realism is that it cannot account for communication. This objection can be understood in two ways. On the first, intentional anti-realism is charged for making no room for the very existence of communication since communication is (by definition) the transference of meaning between people (and perhaps other creatures). However, assuming that there is communication in the sense of transferring meaning is begging the question against intentional anti-realism. On the second understanding, the charge is that the linguistic processing involved in communication cannot be explained without assuming the processing of meaning. But what has been argued in this chapter suffices to show that postulating logico-syntactic processing (i.e., moving from one mental state to another in accordance with purely formal rules) well explains the facts of communication, exactly as it accounts for any psychological processes. Further, it isn't clear what the idea of processing meaning can be; it seems to be committed to the weird notion that our mental processes involve (bidirectional) transitions between symbols and their abstract meanings.

Another possible charge is that a logico-syntactic account of practical reasoning leaves the action itself out. I discuss it in section 6.3.

be considered a miracle. Applied to the present discussion, this idea implies that explanatorily and predictively successful content ascriptions are (most plausibly) true, and so (most plausibly) there are intentional states—instantiations of intentional properties.

How can intentional anti-realism rebuff this challenge? Its first move is to deny the general principle that systematically successful explanations and predictions are (most plausibly) true. Among the objections that have been raised against this principle, let me mention objections of one kind that appear to be specifically relevant to the success of belief-desire explanations and predictions. According to Philip Kitcher (1993), we need not consider all parts of successful theories true, but only those parts that play an explanatory role (dubbed by Kitcher "active"). Psillos (1999) adopts a similar approach. Commenting on the anti-realist claim that history suggests ample cases of successful but false theories, he argues that the success of those false theories was due to true parts that they included.

I think that selective realism of this genre has much to recommend it. Many scientific theories (if not all) are committed to more than is required to account for their explananda (as is attested by the existence of many cases of different but empirically equivalent theories), and so their success does not require that all of their commitments be true. This point can be illustrated simply: if claim p explains some phenomenon, so does the conjunction of p&q, even if q is false (unless, perhaps, it is self-contradictory or contradicts p). So, the theory that endorses the conjunction p&q cannot be argued to be true merely by appeal to its success in explaining the phenomenon in question. This might seem too simplistic, for usually scientists are not so bored as to add irrelevant conjuncts to their theories. Nonetheless, theories implicitly possess such a characteristic, and have aspects that are inessential to their explanatory and predictive powers. What is important for us is that this is so in the case of content ascriptions, as we shall now see.

Blocking the path from success to truth amounts to blocking the argument from success in favor of intentional realism. As it stands, this argument is unsound. However, we should consider whether it can be supplemented. For the selective realist approach just mentioned cannot be automatically applied to any successful theory or set of explanations and predictions. Whether this approach is applicable to any specific theory or set of explanations and predictions depends on whether we can distinguish within the theory or set in question parts or aspects that are explanatory (or "active") and parts or aspects that are not or, at any rate, need not be. Now comes the second move of the intentional anti-realist rejoinder to the argument from success. According to it, intentional realists cannot show that the selective realist approach is inapplicable to the case of folk psychology and intentional predictions and explanations of behavior since folk psychology and intentional predictions and explanations do allow for such a distinction. In Chapter 5, I argued that by ascribing contents we also ascribe logico-syntactic structures. I also argued that logico-syntactic properties are apt for the job of

152   INTENTIONALITY DECONSTRUCTED

rationalizing our theoretical and practical reasoning. Still, it must be logico-syntactic properties of the same kind that are both ascribed by content ascriptions and apt for rationalizing our theoretical and practical reasoning, and this has yet to be shown. Thin logico-syntactic properties were shown to be conceptually implied by content ascriptions, whereas only thick logic-syntactic properties are apt for rationalizing reasoning and behavior. However, thick logico-syntactic properties of the second, more abstract, kind will prove to meet both requirements.[4] I will now turn to discuss them.

6.2 Intentional Anti-Realism and Naturalistic Patterns

Content ascription involves subtleties. We often ascribe content to people's belief-states and utterances by simply disquoting the sentences in question. That is, we ascribe to the utterance "p" the content *that p* (in these terms). But this is not always the case. Reflection on the inter-linguistic issue yields an example. We sometimes ascribe content to people's belief-states and utterances in a language different from that to which the sentences that are believed or uttered belong.[5] Another example concerns indexical and demonstrative expressions or thoughts: when reporting on one's saying "This dog is so cute" we often replace "this dog" with some definite description of the dog, with "that dog," etc. In the context of intentional anti-realism, such examples raise the question of whether there are non-intentional patterns common to such expressions or thoughts, and if there are, what they are. What patterns, if any, are conceptually implied by content ascriptions? What further individuates those logico-syntactic structures beyond their thin structural features? The patterns sought would not be shared by, for example, the belief-states "Dan is pretty" and "John is pretty" (for these patterns are not thin), but would be shared by, for example, "Dan is pretty" and "Dan est beau," for the practice of content ascription (in English) standardly ascribes to both the content *that Dan is pretty*.

---

[4] One might think that the conceptual implication requirement is too strong, and that appealing to (low-level) properties that are in fact instantiated when predictively or explanatorily successful content ascriptions are made can account for their success. However, in order to account for the success of content ascriptions in predicting and explaining various possible actions that differ physically from each other—ones that fall under non-physical generalizations—mere correlations are not enough. I discuss this point in section 6.3.

[5] Plausibly, disquotation is also involved in cases of inter-language content ascriptions. Thus, according to Kripke (1979), the ascription in such cases results from the operation of both the "disquotation principle" and the "principle of translation." But the role of the disquotation principle in content ascriptions does not undermine the motivation for the present discussion since this motivation is based on the claim that we do not *merely* disquote in ascribing content. (Nothing that is written here is meant to claim that we are aware of our engaging in disquotation.)

There are further subtleties regarding content ascription in general and disquotation in particular, but they are not important for the concerns of this book.

The issue of the availability of such patterns proves important for intentional anti-realism when looked at from the perspective of explanation and prediction of behavior. The same content ascriptions can succeed in predicting and explaining behavior of subjects whose mental states share thin logico-syntactic structures but differ phenomenologically (and physically), as is the case (*inter alia*) with subjects who think in different languages. What common features ascribed by content ascriptions may be responsible for the success in question? Reflecting on this question reveals not only that thin logico-syntactic structure plus phenomenology (or physical realization) is not necessary for the individuation of thick structures implied by content ascriptions (for structures that are supposed to play the same predictive and explanatory role may differ in phenomenology), but also that it is not sufficient, since words and even sentences with the same phenomenology will differ with respect to this role when they figure in systems that differ linguistically. Similarly, postulated logico-syntactic structures of unconscious mental states are not individuated in terms of thin logico-syntactic structures plus physical realization. So, another individuating factor is required.

As long as content ascriptions are concerned with explaining or predicting the behavior *of a single individual or system at a given time*, taking them to ascribe thin structures further individuated by phenomenology or physical realization can account for their explanatory or predictive success. There is a consistency constraint regarding the components of the structures in play: an ascription of a cognitive process (such as an inference) enjoys predictive or explanatory success only if the relevant subject instantiates the ascribed thin logico-syntactic structures, and those features of these structures' components to which cognitive processes are sensitive are consistent vis-à-vis the ascription. That is, a structure of the ascribed process may instantiate either "pretty" or "beau" (etc.) when the predictively or explanatorily successful ascription is expressed in terms of "pretty" and all structures that take part in the process that are ascribed in terms of "pretty" instantiate (in the "right" place) the same effective feature (i.e., a feature to which cognitive processes are sensitive). This consistency constraint is a significant constraint, since cognitive processes are not isolated but are substantively interrelated: for example, the conclusion of a theoretical inference often serves as a premise in a practical inference.

So, for a single individual at a given time, individuation of thick logico-syntactic structures in terms of thin structures plus phenomenological or physical characterizations that respects the consistency constraint is appropriate. In fact, the formal characterizations that are relevant to Turing machines are system-relative in a similar way: different machines that are classified as the same Turing machines (i.e., different machines that compute the same functions according to the same rules) may treat typographically different inscriptions as identical, depending on the sensitivity of the machine's operations.

154   INTENTIONALITY DECONSTRUCTED

However, that consistency constraint, as presented here, may not apply to unrelated cognitive processes: for example, to those of different subjects. Nonetheless, identical content ascriptions often succeed in predicting and explaining the behaviors of subjects who think in different languages and thus instantiate phenomenologically and physically different logico-syntactic structures. So, we still face the question of what is common among those structures whose postulation can account for the predictive and explanatory success of content ascriptions? Put simply, what is common to "pretty" and "beau" when instantiated in systems that differ linguistically, for example?

The intentional realist has a ready-made answer to this question: she simply characterizes the common pattern in question as the intentional content of the belief-states or utterances, and she may or may not characterize content in other terms (e.g., in terms of some naturalistic function). The intentional anti-realist has at her disposal an alternative reply (one which may be said to be extensionally equivalent to that of some reductive naturalist intentional realist). As we saw in Chapter 4, the intentional anti-realist can provide a sense to the notion of a (correct) reductive-naturalistic theory of intentionality. The idea is that such theories specify circumstances under which we ascribe specific contents—they systemize our practice (or practices) of content ascription—and one such theory (or more than one) may do this correctly. Not only did I specify this intentional anti-realist sense, I also argued that naturalistic relations underlie all non-vacuous content ascriptions. Whereas according to reductive-naturalistic intentional realism the world–mind or world–language relation that is specified by a correct reductive-naturalistic theory is the intentional relation, according to my intentional anti-realism such a naturalistic relation underlies content ascriptions without being the alleged intentional relation. Combining this claim with the claim that *thin* logico-syntactic structures are conceptually implied by content ascriptions, we arrive at the view that the patterns that underlie our making content ascriptions (and are thus conceptually presupposed and implied by them) are individuated in terms of thin logico-syntactic structures plus some naturalistic relations of the components of these structures.[6]

I will not attempt to specify what the naturalistic relation in question is (and so decide which theory of intentionality, if any, is correct, when considered as a theory of content ascriptions). As I said in Chapter 4, since the practice of content ascription is a varied and complex human practice, the naturalistic relation that underlies content ascriptions is a complex relation that cannot be expressed by a simple formula; plausibly it can only be expressed by a disjunction of conjunctions

---

[6] The naturalistic relations must be applied to the components of these structures and not to the structures as wholes, for a holistic individuation scheme of content ascriptions would leave the structures' logico-syntactic characters out and consequently deprive the ascriptions of the ability to account for reasoning.

etc. It seems to me to be a fair bet that this complex relation will never be known. It also makes sense to assume that the notion of this relation is open-ended, so that its application to various cases is indeterminate. Note also, that as this relation is supposed to underlie content ascriptions, then, first, the search for it consists of an empirical probe and analysis of the actual practice(s) of content ascription and, therefore, cannot be a pure armchair enterprise. Second, if there are different practices of content ascription, then, trivially, each of them is linked with its unique relation.

Let me mention two constraints that apply to the naturalistic individuation in question. First, since intentionality is standard-object aboutness and the concept of intentionality is a concept of an (either strong or weak) external (transcending) relation, then content ascriptions must be responsive to an (either strong or weak) external relation that relates components of thoughts to (actual or merely possible) objects. The conditions underlying the ascription of p-involving content should relate that to which such content is ascribed to p (though this relation to p need not be simple, and may well be counterfactual, involve complex circumstances, etc.). But the concept of intentionality does not require that all mental items to which contents are ascribed be *directly* related to objects by means of external relations. It allows that an indirect function relates a mental item to which some content p is ascribed to p: that is, that it relates this item to another item that is connected to p, where the former is connected to the latter by means of some (internal) naturalistic relation. Thus, it is possible that content ascriptions are responsive to some intra-mental causal or functional condition.

This point brings us to the second constraint. There is reason to believe that many content ascriptions are indeed responsive to such a causal or functional condition. For thoughts that are ascribed the same contents by predictively or explanatorily successful content ascriptions have, in most cases, the same psychological causal powers (though they need not actually be involved in identical causal interactions), and this is the case even if they differ phenomenologically and physically (as in the case of subjects who think in different languages).[7] So, predictively and explanatorily successful content ascription is sensitive to something that ensures this phenomenon: that is, to some causal-psychological connection. We can conclude that content ascriptions are constrained not only by external relations but also by such causal-psychological features.[8]

---

[7] Of course, in some sense of "causal powers," thoughts that differ physically do not share causal powers. The discussion of Jackson and Pettit's view in section 6.3 relates to this issue.

[8] Four brief remarks can be made about this naturalistic conception of content ascriptions and the patterns in question. First, though there is certainly good reason to treat these two kinds of features underlying content ascriptions as naturalistic (in some sense that concerns the natural sciences), treating them so expands the naturalistic notion that figured earlier, which only concerned external non-intentional relations. Second, a theory of content ascription that obeys the constraints in question is neither a short-armed nor a long-armed functional role theory of content ascription, for the causal constraint in question need not apply to all mental states or to all concepts, and it is not

156 INTENTIONALITY DECONSTRUCTED

We saw that the (thick) pattern that is implied by content ascriptions is the thin logico-syntactic structure of the mental state further individuated by some (specific) naturalistic relation, which is either direct or indirect. The other thick individuation of the structures in question—the one involving phenomenological or physical individuation—may be said to play a derivative role vis-à-vis content ascriptions, as it is determined by that relation relative to a system. That is, for any given system, there are specific phenomenological or physical constraints on the possession of the naturalistic relational property ascribed by a content ascription, and thus the consistency constraint for any given system takes also a phenomenological or physical form.

According to the common practice of content ascription, "Dan is pretty" is different in thick logico-syntactic structure from "Tom is pretty" despite their sharing thin structure, as—so the naturalistic notion of logico-syntactic structures has it—they do not share that naturalistic relation (since "Dan" and "Tom" differ in this regard). In contrast, "Dan is pretty" and "Dan est beau" are identical in thick logico-syntactic structure—despite their phenomenological or physical difference—as they share thin structure *and* the relevant (anything but simple) naturalistic relation. It is their identity in both these respects that makes them have the same thick structure and thus apt for being ascribed the same content according to the common practice. So, "Alice believes that Dan is pretty" is (practice-dependently) true if and only if Alice has a belief-state that has the thin structure of "Dan is pretty" (or of "Dan est beau," which is the same thinly individuated structure), and its components possess some (specific) naturalistic relational properties, as required by the assumed practice of content ascription. And content ascriptions that succeed in predicting or explaining the behavior of some subject would succeed in predicting or explaining the behavior of another subject whose relevant mental states share thin logico-syntactic structures with those of the first but differ phenomenologically (and physically)—for example, subjects who think in different languages—as long as these states possess the same relevant naturalistic relational properties. (Parts of the naturalistic mental profiles of subjects play a role in constituting their mastery of language(s) and individuate logico-syntactic structures, so that phenomenologically or physically identical structures need not be identical logico-syntactic structures, and vice versa.)

---

concerned with total causal role. Third, the external relation constraint does not mean that semantic externalism, understood as an approach to content ascription, is true. I cannot dwell on this issue here, but let me only mention that this naturalistic constraint is compatible with semantic internalism if the naturalistic relation in question is construed as a relation in the weak sense, as characterized in Chapter 1. Relatedly, a descriptive theory of names meets the naturalistic constraint if it treats the components of descriptions' naturalistically. (On dissociating semantic naturalism from semantic externalism see Luntley (1999). Also relevant to this issue are Farkas (2008a) and Horowitz (2001, 2005).) Fourth, this external relation constraint applies only to the ascription of contents that supposedly concern concrete entities, and not abstract ones. Relatedly, this constraint is irrelevant to logical connectives or operators.

So, the thick naturalistic individuation of logico-syntactic structures allows for multiple realizability: that is, for the phenomenological or physical constraints to take different phenomenological or physical forms in different systems—for example, in subjects who think in different languages. (Further, this individuation allows for some phenomenological or physical leeway even within a given system, depending on the sensitivity of the processes operating on the system's logico-syntactic structures.) However, the full-blown naturalistic individuation is not necessary for multiple realizability. Its two elements—the external and the internal—as well as their ascriptions, can come apart. And thus, two practices of content ascription can differ in the contents they ascribe under the same circumstances—that is, they can take the same external relations to determine different semantic interpretations—yet imply the same causal-psychological features, which, in themselves, individuate logico-syntactic structures in a non-phenomenal and non-physical way.

Note that the individuation of mental logico-syntactic structures in terms of naturalistic relations—which is how content ascriptions individuate them—is relevant *only* to content ascriptions: that is, to employing the intentional stance. It is irrelevant to the truth of non-semantic belief-states, in the sense that we need not—although we may—appeal to that individuation in terms of naturalistic characteristics that include external-environmental elements in order to account for the truth values of such belief-states. Belief-states are true if they possess the required coherence, which is rooted in their logico-syntactic structures *the components of which are considered constants*, and that is all. The full-blown naturalistic individuation guarantees this but goes beyond what is necessary, precisely as it guarantees multiple realizability but goes beyond what is necessary for it. Truth is thus independent of that naturalistic individuation. Similarly, truth is independent of content. This independence is also manifest in the fact that while the having of content by an entity is practice-dependent (in a sense that makes it unreal), being true isn't. The thought that the truth value of "Gödel is pretty" depends, *inter alia*, on whether "Gödel" refers to Gödel (or, say, to Schmidt) is a remnant of the intentional realist conviction. "Gödel" refers to nothing, and so does this structure, yet the latter may nevertheless be true. (That it may differ in truth value from "Schmidt is pretty" is a purely logico-syntactic matter in the sense just mentioned.)[9]

It might be thought that allowing those naturalistic relations allows intentionality to sneak into the picture. The fact that what individuates the patterns that are implied by content ascriptions is what some (whether actual or merely possible) reductive-naturalistic theory of intentionality would take to constitute intentionality might raise the worry that these patterns are simply intentional patterns, and

---

[9] Recall that "true" refers to the epistemic merit secured by coherence (or perhaps by coherence that involves a pragmatist element), regardless of whether it constitutes what is pre-theoretically taken to be true (and this applies, *mutatis mutandis*, to "truth").

158 INTENTIONALITY DECONSTRUCTED

thus that some naturalistic relation is the intentional relation. Isn't the picture according to which mental states to which we ascribe contents possess logico-syntactic structures, individuated by our content ascriptions in terms of environment-involving naturalistic relations, simply the realist reductive-naturalistic picture of intentionality?

It is not. Though this picture is compatible with a realist reductive naturalism of intentionality, it does not entail it. The fact that my account of the patterns in question is committed to the idea that mind–world or language–world correlations underlie content ascriptions (and, a fortiori, to the obtaining of such correlations) does not compromise its intentional anti-realist commitment. The idea that content ascriptions have conditions of application is trivial—clearly, ascriptions of content to people are underlain by circumstances in which they engage their environment—and taking these conditions to be naturalistic makes no difference in this regard. The picture presented here embodies a commitment concerning the practice of content ascriptions and nothing more, and the move from acknowledging those patterns to acknowledging the (absolute, practice-independent) truth of content ascriptions is a *non sequitur*. The fact that one human practice of content ascription, among many possible (and perhaps actual) ones, is responsive to some world–mind or world–language correlations, by no means makes those correlations constitutive of content and does not at all matter to the issue of intentional realism versus intentional anti-realism. Taking these correlations to be, necessarily, the conditions for the instantiation of intentional properties and for the *truth* of content ascriptions, which amounts to denying the possibility that (realist) intentional reductive naturalism is false yet content ascriptions are underlain by naturalistic conditions, erases the distinction between intentional anti-realism and intentional realism.[10]

Thus, taking the naturalistic relations in question to underlie content ascriptions does not allow intentionality to sneak into the picture, and cannot ground a reason against the intentional anti-realist view defended here. Recalling the previously suggested arguments against intentional realism—and the case against intentional reductive naturalism, in particular—we should resist any temptation to supplement the suggested account of the individuation of thick logico-syntactic patterns with intentional realism and take those naturalistic patterns to constitute intentionality. Specifically, since this case does not concern the extensional adequacy of intentional reductive naturalism, it implies that even an extensionally adequate naturalistic theory of content would be false if construed realistically.

---

[10] Intentional realism also does not have any advantage in explaining the fact that naturalistic relations underlie content ascriptions. This fact is simply a human practice, probably rooted in human needs and interests, and so its explanation need not appeal to any metaphysical ideas. Considerations of parsimony certainly do not lend any probability to a realistic version of intentional reductive naturalism, since such a version is certainly no more parsimonious than its ascriptivist counterpart: the two differ in that the former takes some naturalistic relation to be the intentional relation, whose existence the latter denies.

INTENTIONAL ANTI-REALISM II   159

Extensional adequacy is adequacy relative to the principles of a practice of content ascription: different practices single out different naturalistic relations, no practice can be said to be true, and no naturalistic relation can be said to be the intentional relation. We should bear this in mind: The identity of the naturalistic relation that figures in a theory of content ascription is practice-dependent. So, a naturalistic account of content does not make room for intentional realism.

6.3 Back to the Success Argument

As we saw, those naturalistically individuated logico-syntactic properties underlie our making content ascriptions and are thus conceptually implied by them. At the same time, those properties are apt for rationalizing our theoretical and practical reasoning. As argued in Chapter 5, thick logico-syntactic properties of the phenomenological-physical kind are appropriate for this job. So are thick logico-syntactic properties of the naturalistic kind, sharing the former's thin structural properties and being as fine-grained with respect to any given system. It follows that the predictive and explanatory success of belief-desire psychology and content ascriptions can be attributed to the truth of the logico-syntactic messages of the ascriptions. This success can be accounted for by postulating the existence of mental states with logico-syntactic structures and without intentional properties.

Clearly, the rejoinder suggested here to the argument from the predictive and explanatory success of content ascription depends on the separability of the logico-syntactic structures in question and intentionality. Had these structures been inseparable from intentionality, then the facts that mental states have such structures and that these can account for the success in question would have supported the argument rather than undermined it. But thick logico-syntactic structures are separable from intentionality. As we saw, though such structures may be said to be "doxastically" dependent upon intentional ascriptions, they are not ontologically dependent upon intentional contents. (And, as noted in section 6.2, allowing naturalistic relations into the picture does not allow intentionality to sneak in with them.)

Can proponents of the success argument for intentional realism salvage it from the logico-syntactic rejoinder by claiming that logico-syntactic properties are not causally efficacious, and are therefore not active (in Kitcher's sense)? I think they cannot. Suppose, first, that accounting for the predictive and explanatory success of content ascriptions in terms of properties of any kind depends on these properties' being causally efficacious. In that case, for the argument from success to intentional realism to get off the ground it must be the case that intentional properties are causally efficacious. However, it is implausible to take logico-syntactic properties to lack causal efficacy while taking intentional properties to possess causal efficacy. If those reasons that seem to undermine the notion that

160   INTENTIONALITY DECONSTRUCTED

logico-syntactic properties' are causally efficacious—the reasons that concern these properties' being abstract or higher-level properties and their supposed efficacy being excluded by the causal efficacy of physical properties—indeed undermine this notion, they certainly undermine the notion that intentional properties' are causally efficacious. Many philosophers would say that the causal status of intentional properties is shakier than that of logico-syntactic properties due to the externalist nature of the former, but the rejoinder that appeals to logico-syntactic properties does not depend on taking this status to be shakier. So proponents of the success argument for intentional realism certainly cannot salvage it from the logico-syntactic rejoinder by claiming that logico-syntactic properties are not causally efficacious, since such a move would in itself undermine their argument.

But I will not be satisfied with this reply. I will argue that accounting for the predictive and explanatory success of content ascription in terms of logico-syntactic properties does not depend on their being causally efficacious. Showing this is important not only as a step in my objection to the success argument, but also for defending the claim that the predictive and explanatory success of content ascriptions is effectively accounted for by the postulation of logico-syntactic properties of those mental states that appear intentional but that (so I argue) are not. In other words, showing this is a step in establishing the existence of mental logico-syntactic properties.

I believe that logico-syntactic properties, being multiply realizable and thus high-level and abstract, are not causally efficacious: only concrete and low-level properties can be causally efficacious. However, logico-syntactic properties are causally relevant in some sense, and their being causally relevant in this sense allows them to figure in an account of the predictive and explanatory success of content ascription. The sense in question is the one suggested by Jackson and Pettit. According to them, what makes a non-efficacious property causally relevant to the causal production of an event is the fact that its realization "ensures—it would have been enough to have made it suitably probable—that a crucial productive property is realized and, in the circumstances, that the event, under a certain description, occurs" (Jackson and Pettit 1990, p. 214). Jackson and Pettit use the metaphor of programming in this context and dub the explanations that are given in terms of causally relevant yet non-productive properties "program explanations." The realization of the causally relevant but non-productive property "programs for the appearance of the productive property and, under a certain description, for the event produced.... The analogy is with a computer program which ensures that certain things will happen—things satisfying certain descriptions—though all the work of producing those things goes on at a lower, mechanical level" (p. 214; see also Jackson and Pettit 1988, 2004a, 2004b).[11]

---

[11]   Casual relevance in this sense might be said to be grounded in causal powers in a weak sense. In this sense, physically different realizations of the same algorithm may be said to share causal powers. Causal powers in this sense are not reducible to physical causal powers, though they supervene on them. For an extended discussion of this issue, see Horowitz (2015b).

INTENTIONAL ANTI-REALISM II   161

Belonging to a high level, such causal relevance is in no conflict with causal efficacy at the lower mechanical level and is not excluded by it. Though they are not physical patterns, high-level patterns of processes are real patterns of transitions between states or events, high-level properties are real properties, and statements about them may be strictly true. Since the realizations of high-level properties ensure the realizations of causally efficacious low-level properties, the realizations of the former may underlie behavior. Logico-syntactic properties are such high-level properties: their realizations ensure the realizations of causally efficacious low-level properties, and so may underlie behavior. So indeed, accounting for the predictive and explanatory success of content ascription by postulating logico-syntactic properties does not depend on these properties being causally efficacious; it is sufficient that these properties are causally relevant in the Jackson–Pettit sense.

One (though not a defender of the success argument in favor of intentional properties) might wonder why we need to postulate these properties and cannot be satisfied with low-level physical properties. In a sense, appealing to low-level physical properties always suffices for explaining behavior—the very occurrence of any individual instance of behavior, which belongs to a physical pattern, can be explained in this way. But if we are interested in explaining instances of behavior as belonging to behavioral patterns, which are not physical patterns (even though their instances are physical), appealing to low-level physical properties cannot do: high-level patterns of behavior cannot be accounted for by appealing to low-level properties. We are often interested in explaining behavior as belonging to non-physical patterns (recall well-known examples such as stopping a cab or buying a share in the stock market). Furthermore, cases in which instances of behavior that we individuate as identical regardless of whether they are physically identical are often successfully explained by employing content ascriptions: that is, by appealing to mental states that are type-identical according to some intentional individuation. This success can only be accounted for by postulating properties that are not only causally relevant (or even causally efficacious) vis-à-vis behavior, but also conceptually implied by these ascriptions. Low-level physical properties do not satisfy the second requirement.

It might be natural to think that when we wish to account for those higher-level patterns of transitions that are captured *by content ascriptions*, we must appeal to intentional contents. Referring to Stich's syntactic theory of mind, which recommends that cognitive science avoid semantic interpretations of mental states, Zenon Pylyshyn argues that indeed we must:

> I don't believe we could get away with it and still have explanatory theories. It simply will not do as an explanation of, say, why Mary came running out of the smoke-filled building, to say that there was a certain sequence of expressions computed in her mind according to certain expression-transforming rules. However true that might be, it fails on a number of counts to provide an

162   INTENTIONALITY DECONSTRUCTED

explanation of Mary's behavior. It does not show how or why this behavior is related to very similar behavior she would exhibit as a consequence of receiving a phone call in which she heard the utterance "The building is on fire!", or as a consequence of her hearing the fire alarm or smelling smoke, or in fact following any event interpretable (given the appropriate beliefs) as generally entailing that the building was on fire. The only way to both capture the important underlying generalizations (which hold across certain specific nonverbal inputs as well as certain classes of verbal ones, but only when the latter are in a language that Mary understands) *and* to see her behavior as being rationally related to certain conditions, is to take the bold but highly motivated step of interpreting the expressions in the theory as goals and beliefs... (Pylyshyn 1980, p. 161)

This challenge does not concern the explanation of the predictive and explanatory success of intentional ascription. It concerns the explanation of behavior itself, and in fact it is made in a scientific-methodological context, rather than in an ontological one.[12] But it is relevant to the ontological issue of the existence of intentional contents, since if it is successful, then intentional anti-realists cannot reject the success argument by appealing to logico-syntactic properties. Nonetheless, we need not appeal to intentional contents to explain patterns of behavior of the kinds Pylyshyn mentions. The reason is that those patterns of mental transitions that are captured by content ascriptions are also (thick) logico-syntactic patterns: that is, they follow (thick) logico-syntactic regularities. Furthermore, content ascriptions do not ascribe patterns of mental transitions that are different from the patterns of those thick logico-syntactic structures in relation to which they are appropriate. For employing the intentional terminology—that is, affixing intentional characteristics to the postulated cognitive states—is just a different way of capturing the same patterns. Intentional generalizations pertain to the same (higher) level as logico-syntactic generalizations, to which we can assign different semantic interpretations (such that are dictated by different practices). That is, we can affix to them different intentional characteristics, or avoid assigning any. Affixing such characteristics has its utility (as detailed in section 6.4), but it does not affect the algorithms to which the generalizations apply. The applicability of intentional talk may be said to be narrower, for it glues a specific environment or environmental aspect to the algorithm, but the algorithm is the same, and so it does not depend on there being any intentional property. The same-generalization claim is even more obvious—indeed, it is trivially true—in relation to the full-blown naturalistic individuation of logico-syntactic properties, since on this individuation the logico-syntactic properties are those that are taken by (realist) intentional reductive naturalists to constitute mental contents. But this claim does not depend on this naturalistic individuation.

---

[12] For Stich's reply to Pylyshyn's challenge, see Stich (1983, pp. 172–178).

It also holds in relation to the internal (causal-psychological) individuation of logico-syntactic properties (recall that the causal-psychological feature and the external relation can come apart): affixing intentional characteristics—in accordance with any practice of content ascription we like—to mental logico-syntactic structures that are thus conceived does not affect the algorithm.

So, postulating intentional properties is not needed. It is needed neither for the explanation of the occurrence of tokens of mental causal processes nor for the explanation of the patterns of transitions that are captured by content ascriptions. Postulating logico-syntactic properties suffices for both purposes: we saw that they are causally relevant in a way that makes them apt to account for behavior at the token level, and we have just seen that their postulation suffices to account for the success of predictions and explanations of behavior at the type level, that of those patterns. But it is not only that their postulation suffices for this purpose and therefore we need not postulate intentional properties. Rather, since the postulation of logico-syntactic properties is the minimal postulation that can account for the success of intentional ascriptions, which are also ascriptions of logico-syntactic properties, we have good reason to postulate mental states with such properties.

Thus, it is possible to account for the predictive and explanatory success of content ascription by merely postulating logico-syntactic properties. In one stroke, reasons are provided both for blocking the success argument for mental states' having intentional properties and for the notion of mental states' having logico-syntactic properties. In section 6.4 I will shed further light on this issue. Apart from further explicating the idea that the logico-syntactic level and the intentional level are one and the same, I will show how intentional anti-realism and the consideration that was presented against the success argument make room for the intentional stance.

Let me close this section by addressing two possible objections. The first concerns the consideration brought above for postulating mental states with logico-syntactic properties. It might be argued that whether mental states that are causes of behavior have logico-syntactic structures—or perhaps structures of different kinds—cannot but be an empirical matter, as is attested by the dispute between the language of thought (LOT) hypothesis and connectionism.[13] Let's see the precise argumentative form that this concern may take, while bearing in mind that the case for postulating mental states with logico-syntactic properties relies on the predictive and explanatory success *of content ascriptions*. This success, I argued, can be accounted for by postulating such properties, so it does not support the claim that mental states instantiate intentional properties. Now one may agree that this move undermines the success argument's conclusion that mental

---

[13] For this debate see, for example, Smolensky (1987, 1988), Fodor and Pylyshyn (1988), Pinker and Prince (1988), Horgan and Tienson (1989), Fodor and McLaughlin (1990), Chalmers (1993), Fodor (1996), Aizawa (1997), Matthews (1997), and Hadley (1997).

164 INTENTIONALITY DECONSTRUCTED

states instantiate intentional properties but argue that this success might also be explained without appealing to logico-syntactic properties. It might be explained simply by postulating causal-functional properties, or by postulating some other cognitive architecture (e.g., of some connectionist variety). However, both options cannot deliver the required goods. Causal-functional properties can only vacuously account for causal processes. The question is what properties of the mental states in question underlie their causal interactions, and citing causal-functional properties is no answer; it merely mentions the regularities of those interactions. So causal-functional properties belong to the wrong level. Architectural properties such as connectionist ones do not qualify for a different reason: namely, that they are not conceptually implied by content ascriptions, and so postulating them cannot account for the success of such ascriptions. Except for intentional properties, only logical properties are conceptually implied by such ascriptions. We may say that the success argument for postulating logical properties bypasses the LOT–connectionism debate: it arrives at a non-semantic variation of the LOT hypothesis—that is, it supports the notion that our reasoning involves non-intentional states with logico-syntactic structures—without referring to any specific cognitive ability. Rather, a fundamental feature of cognition is inferred from the success of ascriptions of contentful cognitive states.

Note two points regarding this consideration for postulating logico-syntactic properties. First, it (indirectly) undermines connectionist models of cognition insofar as they are taken to concern the cognitive-psychological level, and it does not undermine such models insofar as they are taken to concern some level of implementation of cognitive process, lower than the cognitive-psychological level.[14] Second, this reasoning relies on an empirical assumption: namely, that content ascriptions, which are also ascriptions of logico-syntactic properties, systematically succeed in predicting and explaining behavior.

The second objection is that even if we can explain reasoning without assuming intentionality, we cannot explain the connection between mental states and actions without assuming intentionality. In a sense, actions are intentional: they are directed toward objects. I lift my suitcase, I eat this apple, and so forth. Indeed, such actions are not intentional in the exact same sense that beliefs and desires are supposed to be: certainly, my eating the apple is not about the apple. However, the point of the objection is that we can only explain my eating the apple or my lifting my suitcase if we assume that I have a desire (or perhaps an intention) to eat an apple or to lift my suitcase.[15]

---

[14] For conceptions of connectionism of the first ("radical") kind, see, for example, Smolensky (1988), Patricia Churchland (1986), Patricia Churchland and Sejnowsky (1989), and Paul Churchland (1990). For conceptions of connectionism of the latter ("implementational") kind, see, for example, Broadbent (1985) and Marcus (2001).

[15] I thank Assaf Weksler for raising an objection along such lines to an earlier version of this chapter. Stich (1983, pp. 178–181) addresses a similar objection that was raised against his syntactic theory of mind by Patricia Churchland (as the devil's advocate). I think there is some affinity in spirit between

This claim for the connection between actions and intentional states is tempting, but we should resist the temptation. For one thing, appearance to the contrary notwithstanding, it isn't true that we can only explain my eating the apple if we assume that I have a desire (or an intention) to eat the apple, because, first and foremost, we simply cannot explain what makes the (supposed) fact that my desire (or intention) is a desire (or intention) that I eat the apple bring about my eating the apple. To assume that the affinity between the desire (or intention) and the action—their being "directed" at the same state of affairs—can be some-how transformed into a causal connection makes no sense (and as noted, they are not even directed at the same state of affairs in the same sense—actions lack content and cannot be said to be directed at objects in the semantic/intentional sense of "directed"). Now it might be thought that while taking the cause of an action to be directed toward the object of the action cannot (causally) explain the occurrence of the event that is the action, it can explain the action as an action (i.e., as a goal-directed, object-involving event). But we need not be realists about taking causes of actions to be intentional for this purpose. From a perspective that does not assume intentional realism, what is required is an explanation of the relation between actions "toward" objects (e.g., my eating the apple) and desires *that are ascribed* the contents of performing actions toward objects (e.g., the desire to eat the apple). When the requirement is so posed, the explanation readily suggests itself: our practice of content ascription is such that we ascribe contents to desires in terms of the actions they tend to bring about.[16] We need not postulate any contents. In section 6.4 we shall see, from another direction, that affixing intentional characteristics to causes for such explanatory purposes need not be understood realistically.[17]

6.4 Explananda, Intentional Characterizations, and Roles of Content Ascription

The goal of this section is to further clarify and defend points that arose in section 6.3. This will involve discussing an important role played by content ascription, and I will use this opportunity to refer to several other roles.[18]

Stich's reply and mine. Churchland's objection as well as Stich's reply pertain not only to the connection between desires and actions (the output side) but also to the connection between beliefs and perceptual objects (the input side). My discussion here concerns only the output side, but it can be applied to the input side as well.

[16] Given this, one may wonder why not say that the content of a desire is determined by the action to which it tends to give rise, and thus give a sense to (reductive) intentional realism? However, there are good reasons against saying this: namely, those presented in Chapter 4 against reductive-naturalistic theories of content.

[17] John Collins (2000) shows that evolutionary considerations too do not support the idea that the success of folk psychology indicates its truth.

[18] In speaking of various roles played by content ascription, I do not mean to imply that people employ the intentional stance because they assign any role to it. I only mean that content ascription in fact plays these roles. No teleology is implied.

166 INTENTIONALITY DECONSTRUCTED

The present discussion of the issue is not meant to be comprehensive. The methodological issue of the advantages and disadvantage of employing the intentional stance is not an important target of this book.

The rationale of the argument that it is the logico-syntactic properties that underlie the explanatory and predictive success of content ascriptions holds not only for folk psychology, but also for any scientific psychology that employs content ascriptions. Though cognitive science employs content ascriptions, (intentional) relations to the world play no essential—that is, indispensable—role in it, as Stich (1983), Chomsky (1995, 2000), and Ramsey (2007) argue. If so, what (dispensable) role can the assignment of content in cognitive science play? Frances Egan, who endorses this view of Stich and Chomsky along with Chomsky's related claim that to take representational talk at face value rather than as loose talk is to conflate the cognitive theory with its informal presentation, criticizes Chomsky for not allowing content to play any explanatory role in computational cognitive models.[19] Egan argues that the notion of representation is needed "to preserve the idea that cognitive theories describe some cognitive capacity or competence" (Egan 2014, p. 119). These are the explananda of scientific cognitive theories and they are described in intentional terms. As Egan writes, "the intentional interpretation of the process serves as a bridge between the abstract characterization provided by the theory and the environment-specific intentional characterization that constitutes the theory's explananda" (Egan 1995, p. 193). To explain how computing the value of some cognitive function "contributes to the exercise of the cognitive capacity that is the explanatory target of the theory" (Egan 2014, p. 123), we have to characterize the input and output that define this capacity (to characterize the chosen explananda) in a way that reflects our pre-theoretical (cognitive) "parochial interests" (Chomsky's expression), and then characterize the intermediate stages of the postulated cognitive process accordingly. That is, we should affix intentional characteristics to the postulated stages of the cognitive process. It is the ("pragmatic") choice of those types of explananda that are of interest to us that constrains the interpretation of the cognitive process. Egan (2020) characterizes her view of mental representation as a conjunction of a realist account of representational vehicles and a pragmatic account of representational content, and dubs the resulting package "a deflationary account of mental representation" (see also Egan 2009, 2010, 2018).

I think Egan's view has much to recommend it, and even though it is not one of the concerns of this book to account for the nature of theories and explanations in cognitive science,[20] my approach can benefit from her observations, which

---

[19] On Chomsky's anti-representationalism, see also Collins (2007).

[20] For this reason, I do not discuss various critiques of Egan's picture of cognitive science, such as Ramsey's (2007) doubts about the presence of a substantial notion of representation in cognitive science (see Sprevak 2013 and Shagrir 2012 for replies), Bechtel's (2016) charge that Egan does not adequately characterize how the notion of representation is employed in cognitive science (see Mollo

hold for content ascription in general. For our "parochial interests" in explananda of various kinds figure not only in scientific contexts; rather, they are salient features of ourselves and are significant to us in our social interactions with fellow subjects. We can see that Egan's account serves my account along two dimensions. First, it sharpens the point that intentional ascriptions capture precisely the same patterns of transitions of mental states that would have been captured by those thick logical ascriptions that are conceptually implied by content ascriptions. All content ascriptions are like content ascriptions in cognitive science, in that they simply affix environmental characteristics to those same patterns that those logico-syntactic ascriptions would have ascribed, and thus they do not ascribe different cognitive algorithms. They only tie the algorithms to the environment (*as if* semantically). The (high) level of intentional generalizations and the (high) level of syntactic generalizations are one and the same level.

Second, the standard (folk) employment of content ascriptions basically plays the same role that the employment of content ascriptions plays in the scientific context: affixing intentional characteristics to mental states allows for the explanation of types of explananda that are of interest to us in our daily interactions with our fellow subjects. There are aspects of the environment—kinds of objects, properties of objects—that affect us (via various causal relations, of course) in ways that are important for us, and our psychological capacities are conceived in relation to those aspects. In other words, the inputs and outputs of the exercise of these capacities are conceived in terms of those aspects, or, in still other words, we treat them as intentional (in a way that reflects our "parochial interests").[21] In turn, this interpretation of the inputs and outputs constrains the characterization of the psychological processes that serve to explain the input–output correlations: that is, as Egan explains, it implies affixing intentional characteristics to the mediating states of the processes. This explication is true of content ascriptions in all the contexts in which they are made.

2017 and Egan 2020 for replies), and Stich's (2009) similar critique. Works earlier than Egan's relevant papers that can be taken to challenge her view are Stich (1983), which contains a comprehensive case against employing content ascriptions in cognitive science, and Cummins (1989), according to which the kind of content that is required and is used in scientific psychology is not the kind of intentional content that is used in folk psychology.

[21] It might be thought that talk of interests here presupposes intentionality; Neander (2015) criticizes Egan's view along such lines. However, as far as my account is concerned, the appeal to interests is dispensable. It is sufficient to speak here of a function that, as a matter of fact, is served by employing the intentional stance (or, we may say, the specific intentional stance, for we could have chosen different relations to the environment), where the intentional anti-realist accounts for our choice to employ the intentional stance as she accounts for every choice: that is, in terms of a logico-syntactic structure in a certain psychological mode (a mode that is functionally construed). It also makes sense to assume that many of our parochial interests are interests from an evolutionary point of view, an assumption that sits well with the idea that our being content ascribers endows us with an evolutionary advantage. This is an issue that deserves extensive treatment, which cannot be provided in this book.

Recall that intentional anti-realism is not committed to denying (the obvious fact) that there are naturalistic relations between our mental states and aspects of the environment.

168 INTENTIONALITY DECONSTRUCTED

Since affixing intentional characteristics to mental states that are cited in the explanation of behavior is external to the cognitive algorithms, which are environment neutral and intentionality free,[22] we can accept the claim that to account for the predictive and explanatory success of content ascriptions we need only assume that mental states instantiate thick logico-syntactic properties (and the low-level properties that realize them); we need not assume the instantiations of the ascribed (or any other) intentional properties.[23] On my view, this pragmatic maneuver cannot be understood realistically: affixing any intentional characteristics to mental states may, at times, be more useful or less useful in some respects, but it makes no sense to take any such attribution to be true. That is, it makes no sense to take the relations to the environment, which underlie content ascriptions according to some practice and individuate the logico-syntactic structures they imply, to constitute intentional content. At the same time, my view acknowledges, as we saw, the important (though pragmatic and dispensable) role that employing content ascriptions plays in predicting and explaining behavior; specifically, in predicting and explaining behavioral patterns that are significant to us.

I by no means deny that adopting the intentional stance has disadvantages, which weigh against employing content ascriptions in cognitive science. But, again, it is no part of this book to assess strengths and weaknesses of the intentional stance. In contrast to the scientific theorizing about cognition, where adopting the intentional stance is an option, it seems that in our mundane encounters with fellow subjects, exercising the intentional stance is second nature to us, if not first; that in our ordinary encounter with people (and, in fact, not only with *other* people and not only with *people*) we cannot help but take them to have intentional

---

[22] The claim that affixing intentional characteristics to mental states is external to the (intentionality free) cognitive algorithms does not clash with the view (sometimes referred to as "computational externalism") that external factors impact computation, as long as this view does not take the formal-syntactic profiles of cognitive systems to involve any environmental factors. Proponents of this view indeed do not maintain that environmental factors impact the formal-syntactic profiles of cognitive systems, and it is hard to see how such an idea may be defended. For different versions of this view, see Burge (1986, 1989), Shagrir (2001, 2020, 2022), and Horowitz (2007). On Wilson's (1994) wide functionalism there are computational (formal) descriptions of the environment, and so there are wide cognitive algorithmic processes that extend beyond the boundaries of the individual and reach out to the environment. This view is in no tension with the objection I raised against the argument from the success of content ascriptions. If the syntactically relevant environmental factors are taken to be semantically relevant—relevant, that is, to the truth of content ascriptions—the objection remains effective as is; and if those factors are not relevant, the objection only needs to clarify that it is the narrow parts of the wide algorithms that can account for the success of content ascriptions.

[23] Adhering to a pragmatic tenet of the sort discussed here does not make my intentional anti-realism an instrumentalist view of intentionality such as Dennett's (1978b, 1987c), or, similarly, an interpretivist view, along the lines suggested by Davidson (1984), Lewis (1974), Mölder (2010), or Williams (2020), which has also a naturalistic aspect. I do not take the individuation of ascribed contents—that is, the principles underlying content ascription—to be instrumentalist or interpretivist. As mentioned, this book does not aim to identify the principles that underlie the (contingent) practice of content ascription, which are quite complicated and sensitive to various factors. I am satisfied with having argued that these principles are naturalistic in a broad sense and pointed out, in general terms, what constrains them.

properties. This practice is far from perfect, and, as mentioned, involves various lacunas and incoherencies, which result in indeterminacies and puzzles. It also has epistemic limitation. As Stich (1983) showed, in many cases we cannot decide what contents and concepts people possess according to our practice of content ascription, due, for example, to their "ideological distance" from us and our resulting failure to apply in such cases standard working hypotheses such as the principle of charity. (That is, our practice of content ascription is inapplicable in such cases.) But at the same time, the practice of content ascription plays important roles in our life. I already mentioned that it is convenient to gain information about the world by making belief-world inferences when the belief-states are described in terms of worldly facts: that is, when they are characterized in intentional terms. And we have just seen that affixing intentional characteristics to mental states enables the explanation of types of explananda that are of interest to us. Further roles for the intentional stance have been famously pointed out by Dennett, who, in various writings (1978b, 1984, 1987c), has emphasized the roles of content ascription in viewing people as responsible, free, and rational agents. I will not discuss these roles here.[24] I will now point out another role that the intentional stance plays in our life; a role that may appear trivial, but that is, at the same time, deep.

In ascribing content rather than phenomenology to a fellow subject's mind, we employ the familiar (first-level) language by which we take ourselves to be describing the extra-mental and extra-linguistic world. And it is not the words we use that are essential—the ascriptions may but need not be expressed in the words that run in the other's mind or in the words she utters—but the fact that they are taken to describe worldly items. It is convenient to use a familiar resource such as those "worldly" words, but there is more to it than convenience. In ascribing content to others, we use their minds as a models of the world. This point might be viewed as a reformulation of Brentano's point about intentionality as directedness toward the world (and herein lies its triviality), but what I am emphasizing is that the intentional stance suggests a model of the mind as a (possible) worlds projector. By adopting it—that is, by ascribing contents to others—we enrich our cognition by acquainting ourselves with a multiplicity of worlds; worlds from the perspective of those others. Intentional psychology may then be said to significantly extend our cultural horizons. But we do not get just worlds; rather, we get worlds linked with subjects, and the more interesting a subject's worlds and their interconnections are, the more interesting the subject is. Intentional psychology may then be rich and interesting psychology. Indeed, according to intentional anti-realism, subjects are not intentionally linked with possible worlds, but rather we only *take them* to be thus linked. That is, we merely ascribe these worlds to

---

[24] Recall that on my view rationality does not require intentionality.

170 INTENTIONALITY DECONSTRUCTED

them (where such ascriptions themselves are to be understood in thick logico-syntactic terms). It is our phenomenology that is thus enriched by employing the intentional stance. But should I care that it is an imaginary healer who expels the imaginary evil demon that is after me?[25] You might care about this. If you do care and have been convinced that intentional anti-realism is true, then you will be less impressed by this role of the intentional stance. Still, you might appreciate one or more of its other roles, as I do.

6.5 Intentional Suicide, and Intentional Anti-Realism as Radical Philosophy

The truth of statements according to intentional anti-realism stands at the focus of a more specific charge, or family of charges, against this view, to the effect that it is incoherent, or self-defeating, or involves cognitive suicide, in the words of Baker (1987, 1988). Usually, this objection is raised against eliminative material-ism, but what it in fact targets is this view's denial of intentionality, and so, trivi-ally, it challenges intentional anti-realism too. As we shall see, there are differences between these two views in addressing the charge in question.

We should note that neither intentional irrealism nor intentional anti-realism can plausibly be charged with being inconsistent. For an intentionality-free world is certainly logically possible. Nothing in the idea that no concrete entity in the world possesses any intentional property is conceptually problematic. (Perhaps some radical intentional naturalist would claim that intentionality is instantiated in any world in which some causal interaction occurs, but a critique of intentional anti-realism cannot rely on a realist approach to intentionality such as intentional naturalism.) Indeed, intentional anti-realism maintains that no logically possible world contains intentionality, but there is no difficulty with this idea either: if the idea of one intentionality-free possible world is self-consistent, so is the idea that all possible worlds are intentionality-free.

Of course, it might be argued that intentional anti-realism is incompatible with some (contingent) truth about this world. If arguments to this effect are sound, they show that intentional anti-realism itself is merely false, rather than inconsist-ent. The argument from the success of belief-desire explanations may be viewed as falling into such a category. The cognitive suicide arguments are not strictly of this pattern. They charge the target view with more than mere falsity. Thus, Baker argues that eliminative materialism is "pragmatically incoherent" in this sense: "If this thesis is true, it has not been shown to be assertable. If the view that no one ever believed anything is true, its assertability is problematic without some

---

[25] I heard this fable in an Indian philosophy course as an undergraduate student.

INTENTIONAL ANTI-REALISM II   171

account of how there can be assertion without belief" (Baker 1988, p. 13). And "without a new account of how language can be meaningful in the absence of belief and intention, we have no way to interpret the claim denying the common-sense conception" (p. 15). Baker is skeptical of the very possibility of such an account. Thus, she maintains that according to eliminative materialism this view itself cannot even be asserted. It is obvious that insofar as this objection threatens (ontological) eliminativism, it also threatens intentional anti-realism, since the presumed obstacle for expressibility is the presumed absence of intentionality. Further, intentional anti-realism of the sort I defend is explicitly committed to denying that language has meaning and so seems to be in an especially vulnerable situation vis-à-vis the charge in question. We may well refer to this charge as the "intentional suicide charge."[26]

How should we understand this charge? Consider the standard understanding of Baker's cognitive suicide charge, on which its basic idea is that the conjunction of eliminative materialism and *presuppositions of its own articulation and defense* is inconsistent (see Cling 1989). The logico-syntactic account of reasoning, justifi-cation, and rational acceptability suggested in section 6.1 in fact addresses the charge concerning the thesis' defensibility, so let me focus here on the issue of its articulation. The relevant presupposition is that the thesis of eliminative material-ism (or similarly, the thesis of intentional anti-realism) is meaningful. So, the charge, as applied to intentional anti-realism, is that according to this thesis, which denies that any assertion is intentional and meaningful, the thesis itself cannot be articulated. In other words, intentional anti-realism is committed to the notion that it cannot be thought and cannot be expressed in language, for its being thought or expressed presupposes its being meaningful and intentional, a presupposition that is in conflict with this very thesis.

Is this situation indeed problematic? Of course, according to intentional anti-realism the fact that this view itself cannot be thought and cannot be expressed in language is an instance of the claim that *no one* can claim that, or believe that, *anything* is the case. This claim follows straightforwardly from the intentional anti-realist idea that no concrete entity is intentional and meaningful.[27] We shall shortly consider whether this (general) commitment of intentional anti-realism is

---

[26] Baker (1988, pp. 15–17) also attributes to eliminativism pragmatic incoherence of a second kind: namely, its being unable to make sense of the error that it imputes to everyone who exercises the intentional stance. My treatment, below, of the first pragmatic incoherence charge straightforwardly applies to this second one as well.

[27] Note that opponents of intentional anti-realism cannot tackle its proponents by claiming that claims and views—and, significantly, the view of intentional anti-realism itself—are in fact expressed, for its proponents deny that linguistic acts that appear to be meaningful and to express claims indeed are meaningful and express claims. So, to claim that intentional anti-realism founders on the rocks of such presumed expressions—or contentful thoughts, for that matter—is to beg the question against it.

Paul Churchland (1981) raises a complaint of question-begging (different from this one) in address-ing a possible charge of the cognitive suicide variety against eliminative materialism. Baker (1987 pp. 138ff.) criticizes Churchland's argument, Cling (1989) replies to her, and Reppert (1992) argues

172 INTENTIONALITY DECONSTRUCTED

problematic, but, for now, let us dwell further on its specific implication—that in asserting "Intentional anti-realism is true" or "There can be no intentional states" we fail to express the thesis of intentional anti-realism. Does this fact constitute a *reductio* of this view? Is it not an absurdity that according to one's view one cannot express this very view? Herein lies the gist of the *self*-defeat and intentional *suicide* charge. The questions press: Does the (so-called?) proponent of intentional anti-realism indeed argue for this view? Isn't what we see on these pages, for example, a defense of the view that there can be no intentional states, and so, a fortiori, an expression of the view? Is it not about intentional anti-realism? Don't intentional anti-realists differ from intentional realists in that the former believe that intentional anti-realism is true whereas the latter believe that intentional realism is true? In uttering, "There can be no intentional states," don't I claim that it is true and believe that it is? It seems that, according to intentional anti-realism, all these questions must be answered negatively. It seems that, according to this thesis, my various statements and arguments to the contrary notwithstanding, this book does not suggest a case for the thesis that there can be no intentional states and is not at all about intentionality. This seems to mark self-defeat for intentional anti-realism.

Indeed, according to intentional anti-realism, belief-states and statements (which are not mere phenomenology or noise, respectively—they are structured) can be true although they have no meanings. Truth, on this view, does not presuppose meaning and intentionality. It is a matter of coherence, which is a matter of (thick) syntax. So, on intentional anti-realism, many assertions are true, and, trivially, the assertion "There can be no intentional states" is true. Like other true assertions, it is coherently true—it has the right logico-syntactic structure relative to other statements that comprise the field of knowledge. The fact that, on the suggested version of intentional anti-realism, belief-states and utterances of declarative sentences can be true despite lacking intentional content, meaning, and reference is significant for the issue under consideration. This is so because, even if we reject the view that truth conditions and truth values are everything there is to meaning, it is plausible that the potential of making its possessor true is a crucial aspect of meaning. But then, if I give you truth, why bother with meaning? Still, since this reply only addresses one aspect of the charge in question, and I haven't ruled out the option that intentional anti-realism only makes room for (coherentist) adequacy rather than truth, as pre-theoretically conceived, I do not wish to rely on it in rebuffing the charge. Further, tackling the charge head on will, I believe, shed important light on intentional anti-realism and its radical nature.

According to intentional anti-realism, the intentional anti-realist can be said to believe the statement (or the structure) "There can be no intentional states," in the

---

that this charge of question-begging cannot be sustained. Other supporters of this charge are Patricia Churchland (1986) and Ramsey (1991).

sense of having a belief-state—a state whose psychological mode is that of believing—with this thick structure. Similarly, her asserting it implies that she believes it (in this sense of believing the statement in question). It appears that the (so-called) intentional anti-realist is compelled to admit that she does not believe and does not claim or express the claim *that* there are no intentional states; that her stating (or having the belief-state with the structure) "There can be no intentional states" has no connection whatsoever to the proposition (and to the alleged fact) that there can be no intentional states. It is here that the intentional suicide charge appears to make its strongest claim.

In the standard sense of "believe that," according to the intentional anti-realist, she cannot be said to believe *that* there can be no intentional states, for there are and can be no such things as "claim that" and "believe that." This is precisely the idea of intentional anti-realism. This is what the arguments for this view purport to show. They purport to show that the "believe that" and "claim that" talk, when standardly construed (i.e., as ascribing content), cannot be true. Intentional anti-realism rejects the traditional talk—that of "claim that" and "believe that"—in its standard sense and replaces it with the "new" talk of "quoted" thick logico-syntactic structures. (This talk is new as a way of ascribing claims and belief-states.) This view rejects this traditional talk as presupposing the false ontology of intentionality, and, consequently, that of representational truth (if not that of truth *simpliciter*). But, to take the fact that intentional anti-realism rejects talk of "claim that" and "believe that," and thus the notion that an intentional anti-realist may claim that or believe that there can be no intentional states, to be problematic for this view, is precisely to ignore this view, with its radical nature. Replacing a traditional talk with a new talk is a legitimate characteristic of radical and revisionist philosophy. It changes the rules of the game and should not be assessed in light of the old rules.[28] A radical view concerning the very essence of language and thought, such as intentional anti-realism, has implications concerning itself: as part of rejecting the traditional talk, it also denies the possibility (or, we may say, the sense) of thinking or expressing the specific view that there can be no intentional states. This, however, is not a flaw of the view. It rejects the traditional conception of how views are to be understood, and we should not expect it to be framed in the very way that it rejects. If it suggests a defensible alternative, there is nothing to worry about.

This might have been puzzling had intentional anti-realists found themselves with no resources to make sense of the epistemic merit and superiority of their view, but this is not the case. As part of their alternative talk of "quoted"

---

[28] Fricker's following words seem to express a close idea: "To cite the indisputable incoherence of the statement 'I believe that I have no beliefs' proves nothing, since it does not address the crucial issue of whether our self-conception can be rewritten in terms of other concepts" (Fricker 1993, p. 255). We shall see in the following paragraphs how the other concepts resolve the prima facie incoherence.

logico-syntactic structures as a way of ascribing claims and belief-states, they endorse "There can be no intentional states" (and other structures of its thick logico-syntactic pattern). And because this talk makes room for epistemic attributes that underlie ordinary judgments of truth and falsehood but that do not depend on the truth or other epistemic merits of the view of intentional anti-realism itself, it allows for an assessment of this view. That is, "There can be no intentional states"—to which intentional anti-realism's denial of representational truth (if not of truth *simpliciter*) applies as well—can be assessed on grounds of coherence, and it is a substantive issue whether the verdict of such an assessment is positive or negative. I endeavored to show that it is positive (recall that intentional anti-realism also makes room for the notion of a good argument). It is about this substantive issue that intentional realists and intentional anti-realists disagree, according to intentional anti-realism, and so, on this view, there is a clear sense to their dispute, as well as to its own superiority. Thus, it is unproblematic that, due to its commitment that no one believes or claims *that* anything is this or any other way, intentional anti-realism implies that intentional anti-realists do not believe and do not claim *that* intentional anti-realism is true (or adequate, or whatever).

This issue of epistemic merits bears on another version of the self-defeating charge against eliminative materialism, which was raised by Boghossian (1990, 1991). For our purposes we can ignore various details of Boghossian's argument and focus on its main idea, which is as follows. First, "arguments for irrealism about the content of propositional attitudes work just as well in support of irrealism about all forms of content, including the content of ordinary linguistic expressions." Second, "different forms of irrealism about linguistic content presuppose robust semantic notions, such as realist conceptions of truth and reference. This leads to the incoherent position that, for example, there are no truth conditions and yet certain sentences (or beliefs) about content are false." (This concise presentation of the argument is taken from Ramsey (2020)).

Since on the view I presented here neither mental states nor linguistic events are intentional, I accept the first of Boghossian's two points. It is the second point that is supposed to make intentional anti-realism's commitment to the first point problematic. However, if intentional anti-realism makes room for truth as coherence, so that irrealism (or anti-realism) about intentionality and reference does not entail deflationism about truth, then intentional anti-realism is caught in no contradiction or incoherence. In such a case, intentional anti-realism can maintain that the criterion for the truth of all assertions that can be true—including assertions of the view itself—is the same: namely, coherence with the body of knowledge. But intentional anti-realists can avoid contradiction and incoherence even if they maintain that coherence—as well as any other non-representational substantive property of beliefs and statements—does not constitute truth. In this case, intentional anti-realism does not presuppose any realist conception of truth (and, of course, of reference), and no inconsistency or incoherence is involved. Intentional anti-realists would avoid commitment to the truth of the statement of their own view precisely as they would avoid commitment to the truth of any other statement. At the same time, they would insist that the statement of their view has an epistemic advantage over that of its negation, and moreover, that even proponents of representational truth take this advantage to be had by all and only true statements.[29] If my case for intentional anti-realism is sound, then this thesis indeed coheres with our body of knowledge—it might be said to have a "correct" or "adequate" logico-syntactic structure—and has that epistemic merit that underlies judgments of truth (even if, as it is according to the suggestion being considered, it is not true). It does not differ in this respect from any other statement that is taken to be true.

Of course, intentional anti-realists do not express themselves only in terms of "quoted" logico-syntactic structures. They also express themselves in the traditional standard "believe that" and "claim that" way, and they do so even when talking and writing about their own view (as this book itself exemplifies). But unless *ad hominem* reasoning is authorized, this fact poses no difficulty for intentional anti-realism. Intentional anti-realism is an error theory, and its proponents are not—and need not take themselves to be—exempt from the error, when not in a reflective mood.

Furthermore, talking in terms of "believe that" and "claim that" has its justification. It is both useful and can get a revisionist sense. Let us focus on the second point. An intentional anti-realist can give a revisionist sense to her talking in these traditional terms, including to her saying "I believe that there are no intentional states." In this revisionist sense, her uttering that sentence means that she has a belief-state such that a practice of content ascription takes it to have the content that there are no intentional states, nothing more. In other words, this talk describes belief-states and utterances whose structures is "There can be no intentional states" as, respectively, the beliefs and utterances that there can be no intentional states, without taking such a description itself to be true. The claim (or view, or proposition, or content) that there are no intentional states is the claim that is ascribed to this structure (not the one that is expressed by this structure).

---

[29] Crispin Wright (1993) shows that Boghossian presupposes his monistic approach to truth—to which he gives an explicit expression in Boghossian (1990), p. 165, n. 17)—and claims that Boghossian thus avails himself to a thesis which is in tension with any form of non-factualism regarding content talk. This would have been fine had it been shown that there is no alternative conception of truth—or an appropriate substitute for it—to which eliminative materialism or intentional anti-realism can appeal, but there is. According to Wright, the eliminative materialist "may cheerfully and consistently grant both that 'true' does not refer to a property—meaning thereby just that instances of 'S is true' are only correctness-apt—and that 'true' does refer to a property, thereby signaling his repudiation of globally deflationist account of true" (Wright 1993, pp. 322–323). Price's (2013) critique of Boghossian's argument is along similar lines. For another critique of Boghossian's argument, to the effect that it begs the question, see Devitt (1990) and Devitt and Rey (1991).

176 INTENTIONALITY DECONSTRUCTED

This applies to any sentence. In uttering or believing the sentence "p," one does not express or believe the claim that p. Rather, the connection between the belief-state or the utterance of the sentence "p" and the ("disquoted") claim that p is merely that of ascription according to a practice of ascription—nothing more. That is, our practice of content ascription takes this belief-state to have this content, or this utterance to express it. The "Claim that" and "believe that" talk (as the embodiment of a practice of content ascription) is a rhetorical device. It is a rhetorical device that captures logico-syntactic patterns, such that are common to various sentences and belief-states.[30] The "claim that" and "belief that" talk is parasitic on talk of "quoted" logico-syntactic structures—its truth value (or the alternative epistemic attribute) depends on that of those structures, the original truth bearers.

Insofar as "claim that" talk is thus construed, it involves no philosophical error. Specifically, under such a construal, the intentional anti-realist cannot be charged with suicide or self-sabotage. The intentional anti-realist who makes statements such as "I claim that there are no intentional states" or "I claim that no one claims anything" construes them as involving a rhetorical device of the mentioned sort. She construes the latter statement, for example, as "I claim* [in the ascriptivist/ rhetorical sense] that no one claims [in the standard intentionalistic sense] anything," thus freeing herself of any inconsistency or incoherence. The intentional anti-realist also avails herself of other rhetorical devices, such as "about," "refer," "mean," and "express." To stress: talk of "claims that" or "believes that" (like talk of "about," or of "refer," or of "express," etc.) *as standardly understood* is out of the game according to intentional anti-realism. It is only in the rhetorical sense of such talk that it can capture real patterns (i.e., can be true). As content-talk, it captures nothing real. Belief-states are not propositional, and utterances of sentences do not express propositions. We believe and claim "p," we do not believe or claim *that p*. This also holds for statements of intentional anti-realism itself. Intentional anti-realists are committed to the truth of "There can be no intentional states" (and of other structures of its thick logico-syntactic pattern), and take themselves to believe and claim "There can be no intentional states." But they take themselves to believe and claim *that* there can be no intentional states only in the rhetorical sense, as described above, and not as expressing intentionality.

What is the usefulness of employing a "meaning/content" rhetorical device? What roles are played by the employment of a rhetorical device that generalizes

---

[30] Taking "claim that" talk to be a rhetorical device echoes deflationism about truth. See, for example, Field (1994) for examples for the utility of using the "truth" device, and also Quine (1970) and Horwich (1990, 1993, 1998, 2010). This view is best expressed by the following words of Horwich: "[I]t is a mistake to think that truth is a substantive property with some unified underlying nature awaiting philosophical articulation. Rather, our truth predicate is merely a logical device enabling simple formulations of certain kinds of generalizations" (Horwich 1993, p. 28). Some of the claims that are made in this chapter parallel claims made by deflationists about truth.

over patterns of logico-syntactic structures that cut across languages? These are the roles played by employing the intentional stance, for employing this device and employing the intentional stance are one and the same. I discussed different roles of content ascription. Probably, the most prominent among them is that of predicting and ascribing behavior characterized in a way that reflects our pre-theoretical "parochial interests." Using rhetorical devices that capture those patterns—devices that generalize over patterns of logico-syntactic structures that cut across languages—allows for explanations of our behavioral explananda thus conceived.[31,32]

Let me briefly refer to other rhetorical devices in the same vicinity. Like its rejection of the mental "believe that p" and the linguistic "claim that p" (when they are not taken to operate as rhetorical devices), intentional anti-realism also rejects "the view that p" and "the claim that p" in their abstract senses. For, since, according to intentional anti-realism, the logico-syntactic structure "p" does not have "that p" as its content, using "p" in "that p" in such locutions says nothing—it is utterly uninformative—so "that p" is vacuous. But intentional anti-realists may use "the view that p" and similar locutions in a rhetorical sense, precisely as they use the mental "believe that p" and the linguistic "claim that p." For them, a view is a pattern of thick logico-syntactic structures. Intentional anti-realism itself is a view in this sense: it is a specific pattern of thick logico-syntactic structures, the pattern shared by "There can be no intentional states," its translations, and its paraphrases. The dispute between intentional realists and intentional anti-realists is a dispute concerning the truth (or adequacy) of this logico-syntactic pattern.

To talk of *the fact* that p is also to employ a rhetorical device, this time a rhetorical device for referring to the *truth* of belief-states or utterances of sentences or views. (The belief-state or the utterance of "p," which is ascribed as the belief or the utterance that p, is of course not about *the fact that p*, according to intentional anti-realism.) The claim that "fact that" talk is merely a rhetorical device for referring to the truth of belief-states or sentences or views means that this talk is not concerned with extra-mental or extra-linguistic truth makers of the belief-states or sentences in question. If intentional anti-realism is true, then there are no segments of extra-mental and extra-linguistic reality that make true belief-states or statements true. This idea is an essential commitment of intentional anti-realism.

---

[31] Beside those substantive reasons for employing the rhetorical device in question, there are technical reasons having to do with simplifying language (such as those pointed out by deflationists about truth).

[32] The cultural diversity in content ascription that was discovered by experimental philosophers (e.g., MMNS, 2004; see Chapter 2) might appear surprising. While it is natural to expect cultural diversity with respect to moral, aesthetic, or religious matters, it isn't natural to expect cultural diversity in semantic matters. But perhaps a semantic cultural diversity will not appear as surprising once we realize that intentional characterizations reflect our ("parochial") interests—our interest in explananda of certain sorts—and these, in turn, might reflect various values. I shall be satisfied with raising this speculation.

178   INTENTIONALITY DECONSTRUCTED

According to my version of this view, if anything can make belief-states and sentences true, it is coherence.[33]

While intentional anti-realism rejects the "fact that" talk in its literal understanding, and, relatedly, the idea of there being extra-mental and extra-linguistic segments of reality that are truth makers of belief-states or utterances of sentences, it is not committed to idealism. It is not committed to rejecting extra-mental and extra-linguistic facts, and it is also not committed to denying that belief-states and utterances of sentences are causally related to such facts. Intentional anti-realism thus makes room for the idea that what belief-states we come to have, and what true (or adequate) belief-states we come to have, is influenced by the extra-mental and extra-linguistic reality: that is, by how things in that reality are. A further discussion of the relations between belief-states and reality would involve delving into epistemic and metaphysical issues that go far beyond the issue of intentional realism and intentional anti-realism, and so I will be satisfied with these brief remarks.

Note that it is a feature of our actual practice(s) of content ascription that the rhetorical devices in question would not be applied by us to all belief-states and utterances of declarative sentences. We refrain from ascribing contents to belief-states and utterances of declarative sentences if their (thin) logical structures are inappropriate, or if their components do not fall into "legitimate" patterns: that is, on my view, they do not maintain some privileged naturalistic relations to environmental items. In fact, this claim is quite trivial: cases of the former kind are instances of standard syntactically based meaninglessness; cases of the latter, of standard semantically based meaninglessness. But this characterization reveals that intentional anti-realism respects the distinction between those sentences we pre-theoretically take to be meaningful and those that we pre-theoretically take to be meaningless (for either of the two reasons).[34] Thus, intentional anti-realism does not clash with anything done in linguistic semantics. But of course, this view takes all sentences to be meaningless. Meanings, on this view, are in the eye of the ascriber.[35]

---

[33] However, we can say that there are *practice-dependent* representational truth makers. Just as there are world–mind relations that *we take* to constitute thinking of things in the world, there are states of affairs in the world that *we take* to make belief-states true. In both cases, those relations and states do not really constitute thinking-of and truth, respectively.) Note that our taking relations to constitute thinking-of and our taking states of affairs to be truth makers of belief-states are third-person attitudes: they concern the thinking-of and the truth of belief-states of others, or of ourselves at a different time.)

[34] It is likely that the semantically "illegitimate" patterns are largely those that do not figure in the scheme of our parochial interests (only largely—because we should not expect our practice of content ascription to be perfect).

[35] In this respect, intentional anti-realism is analogous to hard determinism, which makes room for a distinction between, for example, actions that are externally forced upon us and actions that are not, though, strictly speaking, no action is free according to it.

Its adherence to the distinction in question is one of a few ways in which the suggested intentional anti-realism has affinity to intentional realism. Also worth mentioning here are the fact that

Let me recap the main tenets of the picture suggested on these pages regarding meaningfulness and truth. Since nothing is meaningful on the intentional anti-realist picture, then, of course, the claim that meanings are in the eye of the ascriber does not mean that content ascriptions themselves—whether linguistic ones or mental ones—are meaningful. Further, content ascriptions, in themselves, lack not only meaning but also truth conditions. (More precisely, content ascriptions do not have truth conditions as content ascriptions; they do have them as ascriptions of logico-syntactic structures, which they also are.) They have truth conditions (or adequacy conditions) and can be true (or instantiate that substitute for truth) relative to schemes or practices of content ascription. Further, our content ascriptions are made on the background of a practice in which we are immersed and relative to which they are (in most cases) either true or false. Yet, content ascriptions are not about belief-states, utterances of sentences, or people who have them or make them, respectively. They are syntactically related to the belief-states and utterances they seem to be about, but their logico-syntactic relations with all first-level (non-semantic) statements cannot make them cohere with such statements—that is, with our field of knowledge—and be true (or epistemically adequate) independently of any practice of content ascription.

In contrast, standard first-level non-semantic statements, in themselves, do have truth conditions in the coherentist sense. They can be true—or at any rate have adequacy conditions and can instantiate that substitute of truth—although they lack meaning and are about nothing. What about the view of intentional anti-realism itself, in this regard? Since according to intentional anti-realism there is no such thing as a view that p or a claim that p, then, trivially, this view is not committed to the claim *that* there can be no intentional states. Intentional anti-realism takes the utterance and the belief-state "There can be no intentional states" (and other utterances or belief-states that share their thick logico-syntactic pattern) to have a "correct" logico-syntactic structure. That is, it takes such utterances and belief-states to be true, or adequate, even though they are meaningless and contentless. And if the claim that there can be no intentional states is construed as a rhetorical device of the kind explicated above, it is also true (or adequate): its truth (or adequacy) is derived from the truth (or adequacy) of the thick logico-syntactic structure "There can be no intentional states," the truth (or adequacy) of which I have argued for in this book.

intentional anti-realism makes room for a reductive-naturalistic theory of intentionality considered as a theory of content ascriptions, and the fact that the logico-syntactic structures to which this theory gives pride of place are as fine-grained as ascribed contents. Due to these affinities, we may refer to this version of intentional anti-realism as "intentional quasi-realism," in the spirit of Blackburn's (1993, 1998) moral quasi-realism. But, most emphatically, this view is anti-realist concerning intentionality. Indeed, according to it, mental states have various attributes that intentional realism takes them to have in virtue of their (alleged) intentionality, but, as I showed, none of them requires the spooky stand-for relation, against which I have argued.

180 INTENTIONALITY DECONSTRUCTED

6.6 Still Another Argument for Intentional Anti-Realism

Rebuffing the objections against the repudiation of intentionality paves the way for another argument in favor of intentional anti-realism. This argument is an application of Ockham's razor. I considered in this book various possible reasons in favor of the claim that intentional states exist and rejected them all. Thus, I argued that we have no reason to postulate intentional states in order to account for our recognizing (what appears to be) the truth values of content ascriptions, for the predictive and explanatory success of employing the intentional stance, for reasoning, for the success of inferences from intentional states to states of the environment and vice versa, for introspective beliefs about contents,[36] for our claiming and thinking "There can be no intentional states," and for communication.[37] It seems that there is no phenomenon that calls for the postulation of intentionality, or even such that becomes more probable or comprehensible in light of such postulation. And it also seems that these phenomena cover all aspects that may be of relevance to intentionality. (Intentional realists are challenged to provide other such data.) If this is so, if intentional properties are dispensable for all purposes to which they might be relevant, then, in the absence of any effective argument in favor of the existence of intentional states, it is reasonable to conclude that there are no intentional states.

This argument gets further support from the transcendental argument from Chapter 2. According to this latter argument, recall, supposed practice-independent semantic facts, lying out there, are unknowable, make no difference to theoretical considerations, to first-level linguistic use or to second-level linguistic use, and have no explanatory power. Hence, no sense can be given to the postulation of practice-independent semantic facts: in other words, nothing *can* be intentional. (This is an argument for intentional anti-realism, and not only for intentional irrealism.) As noted there, it is of the nature of this argument—as one that rules against "differences that make no difference"—that, on the one hand, reasons for intentional realism not only add evidential support for this thesis but also undermine the argument itself, and that, on the other hand, removing the obstacles to intentional anti-realism strengthens the argument. We can now see that the latter case prevails.[38] If no datum calls for the postulation of intentionality

---

[36] Since. as I argued, introspection isn't a reliable indicator of contents, postulating contents can play no role in accounting for such beliefs.

[37] See section 6.1.

[38] Other difficulties for the original argument were also removed. The possibility that there can be direct evidence—introspective evidence—in favor of intentionality was rejected in Chapter 3, and clarifications for issues pertaining to the claim that supposedly practice-independent semantic facts lack explanatory power were provided in the present chapter in discussing the argument from the predictive and explanatory success of content ascriptions.

or becomes more probable or comprehensible in light of such postulation, then intentional realists cannot carry the burden of proof that the original argument shifted upon them. Thus, we get a powerful argument against the possible existence of intentionality, one that joins the argument that intentionality must but cannot be something else, which unfolds throughout this book. We can conclude that nothing can be intentional.

References

Aizawa, K. 1997. "The Role of the Systematicity Argument in Classicism and Connectionism." In S. O'Nuallain (ed.), *Two Sciences of Mind: Readings in Cognitive Science and Consciousness*. Amsterdam: John Benjamins, pp. 197–218.

Aizawa, K. and Adams, F. 2005. "Defending Non-Derived Content." *Philosophical Psychology* 18, pp. 661–669.

Alexander, J. 2012a. *Experimental Philosophy: An Introduction*. Cambridge: Polity Press.

Alexander, J. 2012b. "Is Experimental Philosophy Philosophically Significant?" In J. Horvath and T. Grundmann (eds.), *Experimental Philosophy and Its Critics*. London: Routledge, pp. 95–107.

Alexander, J. and Weinberg, J. M. 2007. "Analytic Epistemology and Experimental Philosophy." *Philosophy Compass* 2, pp. 56–80.

Artiga, M. 2021. "Beyond Black Dots and Nutritious Things: A Solution to the Indeterminacy Problem." *Mind and Language* 37, pp. 71–90.

Bailey, A. and Richards, B. 2014. "Horgan and Tienson on Phenomenology and Intentionality." *Philosophical Studies* 167, pp. 313–326.

Baker, L. R. 1987. *Saving Belief: A Critique of Physicalism*. Princeton: Princeton University Press.

Baker, L. R. 1988. "Cognitive Suicide." In R. H. Grimm and D. D. Merrill (eds.), *Contents of Thought (Proceedings of the 1985 Oberlin Colloquium)*. Tucson: University of Arizona Press, pp. 401–413.

Baldwin, T. 1993. "Two Types of Naturalism." *Proceeding of the British Academy* 80, pp. 171–199.

Bayne, T. and Montague, M. (eds.). 2011. *Cognitive Phenomenology*. Oxford: Oxford University Press.

Bechtel, W. 2016. "Investigating Neural Representations: The Tale of Place Cells." *Synthese* 193, pp. 1287–1321.

Beebe, J. R. and Undercoffer, R. 2016. "Individual and Cross-Cultural Differences in Semantic Intuitions: New Experimental Findings." *Journal of Cognition and Culture* 16, pp. 322–357.

Blackburn, S. 1993. *Essays in Quasi-Realism*. New York: Oxford University Press.

Blackburn, S. 1998. *Ruling Passions: A Theory of Practical Reason*. Oxford: Clarendon Press.

Blanshard, B. 1939. *The Nature of Thought*. London: George Allen and Unwin.

Block, N. 1986. "Advertisement for a Semantics for Psychology." *Midwest Studies in Philosophy* 10, pp. 615–678.

Block, N. 1995. "On a Confusion about a Function of Consciousness." *Behavioral and Brain Sciences* 18, pp. 227–287.

Boghossian, P. 1990. "The Status of Content." *Philosophical Review* 99, pp. 157–184.

Boghossian, P. 1991. "The Status of Content Revisited." *Pacific Philosophical Quarterly* 71, pp. 264–278.

Boghossian, P. 2003. "The Normativity of Content." *Philosophical Issues* 13, pp. 31–45.

Boghossian, P. 2008. "Is Meaning Normative?" In *Content and Justification*. Oxford: Oxford University Press, pp. 95–107.

184 REFERENCES

BonJour, L. 1998. *In Defense of Pure Reason*. Cambridge: Cambridge University Press.

Bordini, D. 2017. "Is There Introspective Evidence for Phenomenal Intentionality?" *Philosophical Studies* 174, pp. 1105–1126.

Bourget, D. 2010. "Consciousness Is Underived Content." *Noûs* 4, pp. 32–58.

Bourget, D. 2019a. "Implications of Intensional Perceptual Ascriptions for Relationalism, Disjunctivism, and Representationalism about Perceptual Experience." *Erkenntnis* 84, pp. 381–408.

Bourget, D. 2019b. "Relational vs. Adverbial Conceptions of Phenomenal Intentionality." In A. Sullivan (ed.), *Sensations, Thoughts, Language: Essays in Honor of Brian Loar*. London: Routledge, pp. 137–166.

Boyd, R. 1983. "The Current Status of the Issue of Scientific Realism." *Erkenntnis* 19, pp. 45–90.

Braddon-Mitchell, D. and Jackson, F. 1997. "The Teleological Theory of Content." *Australasian Journal of Philosophy* 75, pp. 474–489.

Bradley, F. 1914. *Essays on Truth and Reality*. Oxford: Clarendon Press.

Brandom, R. M. 1994. *Making It Explicit*. Cambridge, MA: Harvard University Press.

Brandom, R. M. 2000. *Articulating Reasons: An Introduction to Inferentialism*. Cambridge, MA: Harvard University Press.

Brentano, F. C. 1874. *Psychologie von Empirischen Standpunkt*. Leipzig: Felix Meiner. English translation: *Psychology from an Empirical Standpoint* (trans. A. C. Rancurello, D. B. Terrell, and L. L. McAlister). London: Routledge, 1973 (2nd ed., intr. by P. Simons, 1995).

Brentano, F. C. 1911. *Wahrheit und Evidenz*. Leipzig: Felix Meiner. English translation: *The True and the Evident* (trans. R. M. Chisholm, I. Politzer, and K. Fischer). London: Routledge, 1966.

Broadbent, D. 1985. "A Question of Levels: Comment on McClelland and Rumelhart." *Journal of Experimental Psychology: General* 114, pp. 189–197.

Burge, T. 1979. "Individualism and the Mental." *Midwest Studies in Philosophy* 4, pp. 73–121.

Burge, T. 1982. "Other Bodies." In A. Woodfield (ed.), *Thought and Object*. Oxford: Clarendon Press, pp. 97–120.

Burge, T. 1986. "Individualism and Psychology." *Philosophical Review* 95, pp. 3–45.

Burge, T. 1988. "Individualism and Self-Knowledge." *Journal of Philosophy* 85, pp. 649–663.

Burge, T. 1989. "Individuation and Causation in Psychology." *Pacific Philosophical Quarterly* 70, pp. 303–322.

Byrne, A. 2001. "Intentionalism Defended." *Philosophical Review* 110, pp. 199–240.

Byrne, A. and Tye, M. 2006. "Qualia Ain't in the Head." *Noûs* 40, pp. 241–255.

Cappelen, H. 2012. *Philosophy without Intuitions*. Oxford: Oxford University Press.

Carruthers, P. 1996. *Language, Thought and Consciousness*. Cambridge: Cambridge University Press.

Carruthers, P. 2000. *Phenomenal Consciousness: A Naturalistic Theory*. Cambridge: Cambridge University Press.

Carruthers, P. 2005. *Consciousness: Essays from a Higher-Order Perspective*. Oxford: Oxford University Press.

Chalmers, D. 1993. "Connectionism and Compositionality: Why Fodor and Pylyshyn were Wrong." *Philosophical Psychology* 6, pp. 305–319.

Chalmers, D. 1996. "Does a Rock Implement Every Finite-State Automaton?" *Synthese* 108, pp. 309–333.

REFERENCES   185

Chalmers, D. 2004. "The Representational Character of Experience." In B. Leiter (ed.), *The Future for Philosophy*. Oxford: Oxford University Press, pp. 153–181.

Chalmers, D. 2006. "Perception and the Fall from Eden." In T. S. Gendler and J. Hawthorne (eds.), *Perceptual Experience*. Oxford: Oxford University Press, pp. 49–125.

Chalmers, D. 2010. *The Character of Consciousness*. Oxford: Oxford University Press.

Chemero, A. P. 2009. *Radical Embodied Cognitive Science*. Cambridge, MA: MIT Press.

Child, W. 1994. *Causality, Interpretation and the Mind*. Oxford: Clarendon Press.

Chisholm, R. M. and Sellars, W. 1958. "Intentionality and the Mental: Chisholm–Sellars Correspondence on Intentionality." In H. Feigl, M. Scriven, and G. Maxwell (eds.), *Minnesota Studies in the Philosophy of Science*, vol. 2. Minneapolis: University of Minnesota Press, pp. 521–539.

Chomsky, N. 1995. "Language and Nature." *Mind* 104, pp. 1–61.

Chomsky, N. 2000. "Internalist Explorations." In *New Horizons in the Study of Language and Mind*. Cambridge: Cambridge University Press, pp. 164–194.

Churchland, P. M. 1979. *Scientific Realism and the Plasticity of Mind*. Cambridge: Cambridge University Press.

Churchland, P. M. 1981. "Eliminative Materialism and the Propositional Attitudes." *Journal of Philosophy* 78, pp. 67–90.

Churchland, P. M. 1988. *Matter and Consciousness* (2nd ed.). Cambridge, MA: MIT Press.

Churchland, P. M. 1990. *A Neurocomputational Perspective: The Nature of Mind and the Structure of Science*. Cambridge, MA: MIT Press.

Churchland, P. S. 1986. *Neurophilosophy: Toward a Unified Science of the Mind-Brain*. Cambridge, MA: MIT Press.

Churchland, P. S. and Sejnowski T. J. 1989. "Neural Representation and Neural Computation." In L. Nadel, L. A. Cooper, P. Culicover, and R. M. Harnish (eds.), *Neural Connections, Neural Computation*. Cambridge, MA: MIT Press, pp. 15–48.

Cling, A. 1989. "Eliminative Materialism and Self-Referential Inconsistency." *Philosophical Studies* 56, pp. 53–75.

Cohnitz, D. 2015. "The Metaphilosophy of Language." In J. Haukioja (ed.), *Advances in Experimental Philosophy of Language*. London and New York: Bloomsbury, pp. 85–108.

Cohnitz, D. and Haukioja, J. 2015. "Intuitions in Philosophical Semantics." *Erkenntnis* 80, pp. 617–641.

Collins, J. 2000. *Theory of Mind, Logical Form and Eliminativism. Philosophical Psychology* 13, pp. 465–490.

Collins, J. 2007. "Meta-scientific Eliminativism: A Reconsideration of Chomksy's Review of Skinner's *Verbal Behavior*." *British Journal for the Philosophy of Science* 58, pp. 625–658.

Cosmides, L. and Tooby, J. 1992. "The Psychological Foundations of Culture." In J. H. Barkow, L. Cosmides, and J. Tooby (eds.), *The Adopted Mind: Evolutionary Psychology and the Generation of Culture*. Oxford and New York: Oxford University Press, pp. 19–136.

Crane, T. 1990. "The Language of Thought: No Syntax without Semantics." *Mind and Language* 5, pp. 187–212.

Crane, T. 2001. *Elements of Mind: An Introduction to the Philosophy of Mind*. Oxford: Oxford University Press.

Crane, T. 2013. *The Objects of Thought*. Oxford: Oxford University Press.

Culbertson, J. and Gross, S. [2009]: "Are Linguists Better Subjects?" *British Journal for the Philosophy of Science* 60, pp. 721–736.

Cummins, R. 1989. *Meaning and Mental Representation*. Cambridge, MA: MIT Press.

186   REFERENCES

Davidson, D. 1967. "Truth and Meaning." *Synthese* 17, pp. 304–323.

Davidson, D. 1969. "True to the Facts." *Journal of Philosophy* 66, pp. 748–764.

Davidson, D. 1975. "Thought and Talk." In S. Guttenplan (ed.), *Mind and Language*. Oxford: Oxford University Press, pp. 7–23.

Davidson, D. 1979. "The Inscrutability of Reference." *Southern Journal of Philosophy* 10, pp. 7–19.

Davidson, D. 1980. "Mental Events." In *Essays on Actions and Events*. Oxford: Clarendon Press, pp. 207–228.

Davidson, D. 1984. *Inquiries into Truth and Interpretation*. Oxford: Oxford University Press.

Davidson, D. 1989. "The Myth of the Subjective." In M. Krausz (ed.), *Relativism: Interpretation and Confrontation*. Notre Dame, IN: University of Notre Dame Press, pp. 159–171.

Davidson, D. 1993. "Thinking Causes." In J. Heil and A. R. Mele (eds.), *Mental Causation*. Oxford: Clarendon Press/Oxford University Press, pp. 3–17.

Dennett, D. C. 1978a. "A Cure for the Common Code?" In *Brainstorms: Philosophical Essays on Mind and Psychology*. Cambridge, MA: MIT Press, pp. 90–108.

Dennett, D. C. 1978b. *Brainstorms: Philosophical Essays on Mind and Psychology*. Cambridge, MA: MIT Press.

Dennett, D. C. 1984. *Elbow Room: The Varieties of Free Will Worth Wanting*. Cambridge, MA: MIT Press.

Dennett, D. C. 1987a. "Fast Thinking." In *The Intentional Stance*. Cambridge, MA: MIT Press, pp. 323–337.

Dennett, D. C. 1987b. "Evolution, Error, and Intentionality." In *The Intentional Stance*. Cambridge, MA: MIT Press, pp. 287–321.

Dennett, D. C. 1987c. *The Intentional Stance*. Cambridge, MA: MIT Press.

Dennett, D. C. 1990. "The Myth of Original Intentionality." In K. A. Mohyeldin Said, W. H. Newton-Smith, R. Viale, and K. V. Wilkes (eds.), *Modelling the Mind*. Oxford: Oxford University Press, pp. 43–62.

Dennett, D. C. 1991. "Real Patterns." *Journal of Philosophy* 88, pp. 27–51.

Deutsch, M. 2009. "Experimental Philosophy and the Theory of Reference." *Mind and Language* 24, pp. 445–466.

Deutsch, M. 2010. "Intuitions, Counterexamples, and Experimental Philosophy." *Review of Philosophy and Psychology* 1, pp. 447–460.

Devitt, M. 1990. "Transcendentalism about Content." *Pacific Philosophical Quarterly* 71, pp. 247–263.

Devitt, M. 1997. *Realism and Truth* (2nd ed., with a new afterword). Princeton: Princeton University Press.

Devitt, M. 2006a. *Ignorance of Language*. Oxford: Oxford University Press.

Devitt, M. 2006b. "Intuitions in Linguistics." *British Journal for the Philosophy of Science* 57, pp. 481–513.

Devitt, M. 2010. "Linguistic Intuitions Revisited." *British Journal for the Philosophy of Science* 61, pp. 833–865.

Devitt, M. 2011. "Experimental Semantics." *Philosophy and Phenomenological Research* 82, pp. 418–435.

Devitt, M. 2015. "Relying on Intuitions: Where Cappelen and Deutsch Go Wrong." *Inquiry* 58, pp. 669–699.

Devitt, M. and Rey, G. 1991. "Transcending Transcendentalism: A Response to Boghossian." *Pacific Philosophical Quarterly* 72, pp. 87–100.

REFERENCES   187

Devitt, M. and Sterelny, K. 1987. *Language and Reality: An Introduction to the Philosophy of Language*. Oxford: Basil Blackwell.

Dretske, F. I. 1981. *Knowledge and the Flow of Information*. Cambridge, MA: MIT Press.

Dretske, F. I. 1986. "Misrepresentation." In R. Bogdan (ed.), *Belief: Form, Content and Function*. Oxford: Oxford University Press, pp. 17–36.

Dretske, F. I. 1988. *Explaining Behavior*. Cambridge, MA: MIT Press.

Dretske, F. I. 1995. *Naturalizing the Mind*. Cambridge, MA: MIT Press.

Dretske, F. I. 1996. "Phenomenal Externalism or If Meanings Ain't in the Head, Where Are Qualia?" *Philosophical Issues* 7, pp. 143–158.

Dummett, M. 1973. *Frege: Philosophy of Language*. London: Duckworth.

Earlenbaugh, J. and Molyneux, B. 2009. "Intuitions Are Inclinations to Believe." *Philosophical Studies* 145, pp. 89–109.

Egan, F. 1995. "Computation and Content." *Philosophical Review* 104, pp. 181–203.

Egan, F. 2009. "Is There a Role for Representational Content in Scientific Psychology?" In D. Murphy and M. A. Bishop (eds.), *Stich and His Critics*. Oxford: Wiley-Blackwell, pp. 14–29.

Egan, F. 2010. "Computational Models: A Modest Role for Content." *Studies in History and Philosophy of Science Part A* 41, pp. 253–259.

Egan, F. 2014. "How to Think about Mental Content." *Philosophical Studies* 170, pp. 115–135.

Egan, F. 2018. "The Nature and Function of Content in Computational Models." In M. Sprevak and M. Colombo (eds.), *The Routledge Handbook of the Computational Mind*. London: Routledge, pp. 247–258.

Egan, F. 2020. "A Deflationary Account of Mental Representation." In J. Smortchkova, K. Dolega, and T. Schlicht (eds.), *What Are Mental Representations?* New York: Oxford University Press, pp. 26–54.

Enoch, D. 2010. "The Epistemological Challenge to Metanormative Realism: How Best to Understand It, and How to Cope with It." *Philosophical Studies* 148, pp. 413–438.

Enoch, D. 2011. *Taking Morality Seriously: A Defense of Robust Realism*. Oxford: Oxford University Press.

Evans, G. 1982. *The Varieties of Reference* (ed. J. McDowell). Oxford: Oxford University Press.

Farkas, K. 2008a. "Phenomenal Intentionality without Compromise." *The Monist* 91, pp. 273–293.

Farkas, K. 2008b. *The Subject's Point of View*. Oxford: Oxford University Press.

Farkas, K. 2013. "Constructing a World for the Senses." In U. Kriegel (ed.), *Phenomenal Intentionality*. Oxford: Oxford University Press, pp. 99–115.

Field, H. 1972. "Tarski's Theory of Truth." *Journal of Philosophy* 69, pp. 347–375.

Field, H. 1975. "Conventionalism and Instrumentalism in Semantics." *Noûs* 9, pp. 375–405.

Field, H. 1978. "Mental Representations." *Erkenntnis* 13, pp. 9–61.

Field, H. 1994. "Deflationist Views of Meaning and Content." *Mind* 103, pp. 249–285.

Fischer, E. and Collins, J. 2015. "Introduction." In E. Fischer and J. Collins (eds.), *Experimental Philosophy, Rationalism, and Naturalism: Rethinking Philosophical Method*. London: Routledge, pp. 3–48.

Fischer, E., Engelhardt, P. E., and Herbelot, A. 2015. "Intuitions and Illusions: From Explanation and Experiment to Assessment." In E. Fischer and J. Collins (eds.), *Experimental Philosophy, Rationalism, and Naturalism: Rethinking Philosophical Method*. London: Routledge, pp. 259–292.

188   REFERENCES

Fodor, J. A. 1978. "Tom Swift and His Procedural Grandmother." *Cognition* 6, pp. 229–247.

Fodor, J. A. 1981. *Representations*. Cambridge, MA: MIT Press.

Fodor, J. A. 1985. "Fodor's Guide to Mental Representations: The Intelligent Auntie's Vade-Mecum." *Mind* 94, pp. 76–100.

Fodor, J. A. 1987. *Psychosemantics: The Problem of Meaning in the Philosophy of Mind.* Cambridge, MA: MIT Press.

Fodor, J. A. 1990. "A Theory of Content II: The Theory." In *A Theory of Content and Other Essays*. Cambridge, MA: MIT Press, pp. 89–136.

Fodor, J. A. 1994. *The Elm and the Expert*. Cambridge, MA: MIT Press.

Fodor, J. A. 1996. "Connectionism and the Problem of Systematicity (Continued): Why Smolensky's Solution Still Doesn't Work." *Cognition* 62, pp. 109–119.

Fodor, J. A. and Lepore, E. 1994. "What Is the Connection Principle?" *Philosophy and Phenomenological Research* 54, pp. 837–845.

Fodor, J. A. and McLaughlin, B. 1990. "Connectionism and the Problem of Systematicity: Why Smolensky's Solution Doesn't Work." *Cognition* 35, pp. 183–204.

Fodor, J. A. and Pylyshyn, Z. W. 1988. Connectionism and Cognitive Architecture: A Critical Analysis. *Cognition* 28, pp. 3–71.

Frege, G. 1892. "Über Sinn und Bedeutung." In *Zeitschrift für Philosophie und philosophische Kritik*, 100, pp. 25–50; translated as "On Sense and Reference" by M. Black in P. Geach and M. Black (eds. and trans.), *Translations from the Philosophical Writings of Gottlob Frege* (3rd ed.). Oxford: Blackwell, 1980, pp. 56–78.

Fricker, E. 1993. "The Threat of Eliminativism." *Mind and Language* 8, pp. 253–281.

Garson, J. and Papineau, D. 2019. "Teleosemantics, Selection and Novel Contents." *Biology and Philosophy* 34: 36.

Gennaro, R. 1996. *Consciousness and Self-Consciousness*. Amsterdam: John Benjamins.

Georgalis, N. 2006. *The Primacy of the Subjective*. Cambridge, MA: MIT Press.

Gertler, B. 2001. "The Relationship between Phenomenality and Intentionality: Comments on Siewert's *The Significance of Consciousness*." *Psyche* 7(17), http://journalpsyche.org/files/0xaa9a.pdf

Gibbard, A. 2012. *Meaning and Normativity*. Oxford: Oxford University Press.

Gopnik, A. 1993. "How We Know Our Minds: The Illusion of First-Person Knowledge of Intentionality." *Behavioral and Brain Sciences* 16, pp. 1–14.

Grice, P. 1957. "Meaning." *Philosophical Review* 66, pp. 377–388.

Gross, S. and Culbertson, J. 2011. "Revisited Linguistic Intuitions." *British Journal for the Philosophy of Science* 62, pp. 639–656.

Grundmann, T. 2012. "Some Hope for Intuitions." In J. Horvath and T. Grundmann (eds.), *Experimental Philosophy and Its Critics*. London: Routledge, pp. 199–228.

Hadley, R. F. 1997. "Cognition, Systematicity, and Nomic Necessity." *Mind and Language* 12, pp. 137–153.

Hales, S. D. 2006. *Relativism and the Foundations of Philosophy*. Cambridge, MA: MIT Press.

Hannan, B. 1993. "Don't Stop Believing: The Case against Eliminative Materialism." *Mind and Language* 8, pp. 165–178.

Harman, G. 1973. *Thought*. Princeton: Princeton University Press.

Harman, G. 1982. "Conceptual Role Semantics." *Notre Dame Journal of Formal Logic* 23, pp. 242–256.

Harman, G. 1987. "(Nonsolipsistic) Conceptual Role Semantics." In E. LePore (ed.), *New Directions in Semantics*. London: Academic Press, pp. 55–81.

REFERENCES 189

Harman, G. 1990. "The Intrinsic Quality of Experience." *Philosophical Perspectives* 4, pp. 31–52.

Harman, G. 1999. *Reasoning, Meaning and Mind*. Oxford: Oxford University Press.

Heil, J. 1992. *The Nature of True Minds*. Cambridge: Cambridge University Press.

Hill, C. 2009. *Consciousness*. Cambridge: Cambridge University Press.

Horgan, T. and Graham, G. 2012. "Phenomenal Intentionality and Content Determinacy." In R. Shantz (ed.), *Prospects for Meaning*. Amsterdam: de Gruyter, pp. 321–344.

Horgan, T. and Tienson, J. 1989. "Representations without Rules." *Philosophical Topics* 17, pp. 147–174.

Horgan, T. and Tienson, J. 2002. "The Intentionality of Phenomenology and the Phenomenology of Intentionality." In D. J. Chalmers (ed.), *Philosophy of Mind: Classical and Contemporary Readings*. New York: Oxford University Press, pp. 520–533.

Horgan, T., Tienson, J., and Graham, G. 2004. "Phenomenal Intentionality and the Brain in a Vat." In R. Schantz (ed.), *The Externalist Challenge: New Studies in Cognition and Intentionality*. Berlin: De Gruyter, pp. 297–318.

Horowitz, A. 1992. "Functional Role and Intentionality." *Theoria* 58, pp. 197–218.

Horowitz, A. 1994. "Searle's Mind: Physical, Irreducible, Subjective and Non-computational." *Pragmatics and Cognition* 2, pp. 207–220.

Horowitz, A. 1996. "Putnam, Searle and Externalism." *Philosophical Studies* 81, pp. 27–69.

Horowitz, A. 2001. "Contents Just Are in the Head." *Erkenntnis* 54, pp. 321–344.

Horowitz, A. 2005. "Externalism, the Environment, and Thought-Tokens." *Erkenntnis* 63, pp. 133–138.

Horowitz, A. 2007. "Computation, External Factors, and Cognitive Explanations." *Philosophical Psychology* 20, pp. 65–80.

Horowitz, A. 2011. "Plantinga on Materialism and Intentionality." *Analysis and Metaphysics* 10, pp. 113–120.

Horowitz, A. 2015a. "Experimental Philosophical Semantics and the Real Reference of 'Gödel'." In E. Fischer and J. Collins (eds.), *Experimental Philosophy, Rationalism and Naturalism: Rethinking Philosophical Method*. London and New York: Routledge, pp. 240–258.

Horowitz, A. 2015b. "Functionalism, the Computer Model of the Mind, and Causal Connections." *Analysis and Metaphysics* 14, pp. 59–67.

Horowitz, A. 2021. "On the Very Idea of (Real) Content Derivation." *Philosophia* 49, pp. 171–187.

Horvath, J. 2012. "How (Not) to React to Experimental Philosophy." In J. Horvath and T. Grundmann (eds.), *Experimental Philosophy and Its Critics*. London: Routledge, pp. 165–198.

Horwich, P. 1990. *Truth*. Oxford: Blackwell.

Horwich, P. 1993. "In the Truth Domain" (a review of Crispin Wright, *Truth and Objectivity*). *Times Literary Supplement* (July 16).

Horwich, P. 1998. *Meaning*. Oxford: Oxford University Press.

Horwich, P. 2005. *Reflections on Meaning*. Oxford: Oxford University Press.

Horwich, P. 2010. *Truth–Meaning–Reality*. Oxford: Oxford University Press.

Husserl, E. 1913. *Logische Untersuchungen*. Halle: Niemeyer.

Hutto, D. D. and Satne, G. L. 2015. "The Natural Origins of Content." *Philosophia* 43, pp. 521–536.

Hutto, D. M. and Myin, E. 2013. *Radicalizing Enactivism: Basic Minds without Content*. Cambridge, MA: MIT Press.

190   REFERENCES

Ichikawa, J., Ishani, M., and Weatherson, B. 2012. "In Defense of a Kripkean Dogma." *Philosophy and Phenomenological Research* 85, pp. 56–68.

Jackman, H. 2009. "Semantic Intuitions, Conceptual Analysis, and Cross-Cultural Variation." *Philosophical Studies* 146, pp. 159–177.

Jackson, F. 2003. "Narrow Content and Representation, or Twin Earth Revisited." *Proceedings and Addresses of the American Philosophical Association* 77, pp. 55–70.

Jackson, F. 2004. "Representation and Experience." In H. Clapin (ed.), *Representation in Mind*. Amsterdam: Elsevier, pp. 107–124.

Jackson, F. and Pettit, P. 1988. "Functionalism and Broad Content." In F. Jackson, P. Pettit, and M. Smith (eds.), *Mind, Morality and Explanation*. Oxford: Oxford University Press, pp. 95–119.

Jackson, F. and Pettit, P. 1990. "Program Explanation: A General Perspective." *Analysis* 50: 107–117.

Jackson, F. and Pettit, P. 2004a. "Causation in the Philosophy of Mind." In F. Jackson, P. Pettit, and M. Smith (eds.), *Mind, Morality and Explanation*. Oxford: Oxford University Press, pp. 45–69.

Jackson, F. and Pettit, P. 2004b. "Structural Explanation and Social Theory." In F. Jackson, P. Pettit, and M. Smith (eds.), *Mind, Morality and Explanation*. Oxford: Oxford University Press, pp. 131–163.

Jacquette, D. 1990. "Intentionality and Stich's Theory of Brain Sentence Syntax." *Philosophical Quarterly* 40, pp. 169–182.

James, W. 1909/1975. *The Meaning of Truth*, part of the series *The Works of William James* (eds. F. H. Burkhardt, F. Bowers, and I. K. Skrupskelis). Cambridge, MA: Harvard University Press.

Kant, I. 1772/1967. "Kant's Letter to Herz," Feb. 21, 1772. In *Kant's Philosophical Correspondence, 1759–99* (trans. and ed. A. Zweig). Chicago: University of Chicago Press, 1967, pp. 70–76.

Kaplan, D. 1989. "Demonstratives: An Essay on the Semantics, Logic, Metaphysics, and Epistemology of Demonstratives and Other Indexicals." In J. Almog, J. Perry, and H. Wettstein (eds.), *Themes from Kaplan*. Oxford: Oxford University Press, pp. 481–563.

Kitcher, P. 1993. *The Advancement of Science*. Oxford: Oxford University Press.

Knobe, J. and Nichols, S. 2008. "An Experimental Philosophy Manifesto." In J. Knobe and S. Nichols (eds.), *Experimental Philosophy*. New York: Oxford University Press, pp. 3–14.

Kriegel, U. 2003. "Is Intentionality Dependent upon Consciousness?" *Philosophical Studies* 116, pp. 271–307.

Kriegel, U. 2007. "Intentional Inexistence and Phenomenal Intentionality." *Philosophical Perspectives* 21, pp. 307–340.

Kriegel, U. 2008. "Real Narrow Content." *Mind and Language* 23, pp. 304–328.

Kriegel, U. 2009. *Subjective Consciousness: A Self-Representational Theory*. Oxford: Oxford University Press.

Kriegel, U. 2011. *The Sources of Intentionality*. Oxford and New York: Oxford University Press.

Kriegel, U. 2013. "The Phenomenal Intentionality Research program." In U. Kriegel (ed.), *Phenomenal Intentionality*. Oxford: Oxford University Press, pp. 1–26.

Kriegel, U. 2016. "Brentano's Mature Theory of Intentionality." *Journal for the History of Analytical Philosophy* 4, pp. 1–15.

Kripke, S. 1979. "A Puzzle about Belief." In A. Margalit (ed.), *Meaning and Use. Synthese Language Library* (Texts and Studies in Linguistics and Philosophy), vol. 3. Dordrecht: Springer, pp. 239–283.

Kripke, S. 1980. *Naming and Necessity*. Oxford: Basil Blackwell.

Kripke, S. 1982. *Wittgenstein on Rules and Private Language*. Cambridge, MA: Harvard University Press.

Kvart, I. 1986. "Kripke's Belief Puzzle." Midwest Studies in Philosophy 10, pp. 287–325.

Lewis, D. 1969. *Convention: A Philosophical Study*. Cambridge, MA: Harvard University Press.

Lewis, D. 1974. "Radical Interpretation." *Synthese* 21, pp. 331–344.

Lewis, D. 1984. "Putnam's Paradox." *Australasian Journal of Philosophy* 62(3), pp. 221–236.

Loar, B. 1981. *Mind and Meaning*. Cambridge: Cambridge University Press.

Loar, B. 1982. "Conceptual Role and Truth-Conditions." *NotreDame Journal of Formal Logic* 23, pp. 272–283.

Loar, B. 1987. "Subjective Intentionality." *Philosophical Topics* 15, pp. 89–124.

Loar, B. 1988. "Social Content and Psychological Content." In R. H. Grimm and D. D. Merrill (eds.), *Contents of Thoughts*. Tucson: University of Arizona Press, pp. 99–110.

Loar, B. 1995. "Reference from the First-Person Perspective." *Philosophical Issues* 6, pp. 53–72.

Loar, B. 2003. "Phenomenal Intentionality as the Basis of Mental Content." In M. Hahn and B. Ramberg (eds.), *Reflections and Replies: Essays on the Philosophy of Tyler Burge*. Cambridge, MA: MIT Press, pp. 229–258.

Loewer, B. 1993. "The Value of Truth." *Philosophical Issues* 4, pp. 265–280.

Loewer, B. 2017. "A Guide to Naturalizing Semantics." In B. Hale, C. Wright, and A. Miller (eds.), *A Companion to the Philosophy of Language* (2nd ed.). Oxford: Wiley Blackwell, pp. 174–196.

Ludwig, K. 2007. "The Epistemology of Thought Experiments: First Person versus Third Person Approaches." *Midwest Studies in Philosophy* 31, pp. 128–159.

Luntley, M. 1999. *Contemporary Philosophy of Thought: Truth, World, Content*. Oxford: Blackwell.

Lycan, W. G. 1996. *Consciousness and Experience*. Cambridge, MA: MIT Press.

Lycan, W. G. 2001. "The Case for Phenomenal Externalism." *Noûs* 35, pp. 17–35.

McAlister, L. L. 1970. "Franz Brentano and Intentional Inexistence." *Journal of the History of Philosophy* 8, pp. 423–430.

McDowell, J. 1977. "On the Sense and Reference of a Proper Name." *Mind* 86, pp. 159–185.

McDowell, J. 1984. "*De Re* Senses." *Philosophical Quarterly* 34, pp. 283–294.

McDowell, J. 1986. "Singular Thought and the Extent of 'Inner Space.'" In J. McDowell and P. Pettit (eds.), *Subject, Thought, and Context*. Oxford: Clarendon Press, pp. 137–168.

McDowell, J. 1992. "Putnam on Mind and Meaning." *Philosophical Topics* 20 (*The Philosophy of Hilary Putnam*), pp. 35–48.

McDowell, J. 1994. *Mind and World*. Cambridge, MA: Harvard University Press.

McGinn, C. 1982. "The Structure of Content." In A. Woodfield (ed.), *Thought and Object*. Oxford: Clarendon Press, pp. 207–258.

McGinn, C. 1991. "Consciousness and Content." In *The Problem of Consciousness: Essays Towards a Resolution*. Oxford: Blackwell, pp. 219–239.

Machery, E. 2012. "Expertise and Intuitions about Reference." Theoria 27, pp. 37–54.

Machery, E. 2015. "The Illusion of Expertise." In E. Fischer and J. Collins (eds.), *Experimental Philosophy, Rationalism, and Naturalism: Rethinking Philosophical Method*. London: Routledge, pp. 188–203.

Machery, E. 2017. *Philosophy within Its Proper Bounds*. Oxford: Oxford University Press.

Machery, E., Mallon, R., Nichols, S., and Stich, S. P. 2004. "Semantics, Cross-Cultural Style." *Cognition* 92: B1–B12.

192 REFERENCES

Machery, E., Mallon, R., Nichols, S., and Stich, S. P. 2013. "If Folk Intuitions Vary, then What?." *Philosophy and Phenomenological Research* 86, pp. 618–135.

Machery, E., Olivola, C. Y., and De Blanc, M. 2009. "Linguistic and Metalinguistic Intuitions in the Philosophy of Language." *Analysis* 69, pp. 689–694.

McLaughlin, B. P. and Warfield, T. 1994. "The Allure of Connectionism Reexamined." *Synthese* 101, pp. 365–400.

Maibom, H. 2007. "Social Systems." *Philosophical Psychology* 20, pp. 1–22.

Mallon, R., Machery, E., Nichols, S., and Stich, S. P. 2009. "Against Arguments from Reference." *Philosophy and Phenomenological Research* 79, pp. 332–356.

Marcus, G. A. 2001. *The Algebraic Mind: Integrating Connectionism and Cognitive* Science. Cambridge, MA: MIT Press.

Martí, G. 2009. "Against Semantic Multi-Culturalism." *Analysis* 69, pp. 42–48.

Martí, G. 2020. "Experimental Semantics, Descriptivism and Anti-Descriptivism: Should We Endorse Referential Pluralism?" In A. Bianchi (ed.), *Language and Reality from a Naturalistic Perspective*. Verlag: Springer, pp. 329–341.

Martínez, M. 2013. "Teleosemantics and Indeterminacy." *Dialectica* 67, pp. 427–453.

Masrour, F. 2013. "Phenomenal Objectivity and Phenomenal Intentionality: In Defense of a Kantian Account." In U. Kriegel (ed.), *Phenomenal Intentionality*. Oxford: Oxford University Press, pp. 116–126.

Matthews, R. 1997. "Can Connectionists Explain Systematicity?" *Mind and Language* 12, pp. 154–177.

Matthews, R., and Dresner, E. 2016. "Measurement and Computational Skepticism." *Noûs* 51, pp. 832–854.

Maynes, J. and Gross, S. 2013. "Linguistic Intuitions." *Philosophy Compass* 8, pp. 714–730.

Mendelovici, A. 2018. *The Phenomenal Basis of Intentionality*. Oxford: Oxford University Press.

Mendelovici, A. and Bourget, D. 2020. "Consciousness and Intentionality." In U. Kriegel (ed.), *Oxford Handbook of the Philosophy of Consciousness*. Oxford: Oxford University Press, pp. 520–536.

Mendola, J. 2008. *Anti-Externalism*. Oxford: Oxford University Press.

Millikan, R. G. 1984. *Language, Thought, and Other Biological Categories: New Foundations for Realism*. Cambridge, MA: MIT Press.

Millikan, R. G. 1989. "Biosemantics." *Journal of Philosophy* 86, pp. 281–297.

Millikan, R. G. 1993. *White Queen Psychology and Other Essays for Alice*. Cambridge, MA: MIT Press.

Millikan, R. G. 2004. *Varieties of Meaning: The 2002 Jean Nicod Lectures*. Cambridge, MA: MIT Press.

Mölder, B. 2010. *Mind Ascribed: An Elaboration and Defense of Interpretivism*. Amsterdam/ Philadelphia: John Benjamins.

Mollo, D. C. 2017. "Content Pragmatism Defended." *Topoi* 39, pp. 103–113.

Montague, M. 2009. "The Content of Perceptual Experience." In B. Mclaughlin, A. Beckerman, and S. Walter (eds.), *The Oxford Handbook of Philosophy of Mind*. Oxford: Clarendon Press, pp. 494–511.

Montague, M. 2016. *The Given: Experience and Its Content*. Oxford: Oxford University Press.

Neander, K. 2008. "Teleological Theories of Mental Content: Can Darwin Solve the Problem of Intentionality?" In M. Ruse (ed.), *The Oxford Handbook of Philosophy of Biology*. Oxford: Oxford University Press, pp. 381–409.

Neander, K. 2015. "Why I'm Not a Content Pragmatist." *The 2015 Minds Online Conference—the Brains Blog*: https://mindsonline.philosophyofbrains.com/2015/session4/ why-im-not-a-content-pragmatist/.

REFERENCES 193

Neander, K. 2017. *A Mark of the Mental: In Defense of Informational Teleosemantics.* Cambridge, MA: MIT Press.

Nichols, S., Pinillos, N. Á., and Mallon, R. 2016. "Ambiguous Reference." *Mind* 125, pp. 145–175.

Nimtz, C. 2012. "Saving the Doxastic Account of Intuitions." In J. Horvath and T. Grundmann (eds.), *Experimental Philosophy and Its Critics.* London: Routledge, pp. 357–375.

Papineau, D. 1984. "Representation and Explanation." *Philosophy of Science* 51, pp. 550–572.

Papineau, D. 1987 *Reality and Representation.* Oxford: Blackwell.

Papineau, D. 1993. *Philosophical Naturalism.* Oxford: Blackwell.

Papineau, D. 2001. "The Status of Teleosemantic, or How Stop Worrying about Swampman." *Australasian Journal of Philosophy* 79, pp. 279–289.

Papineau, D. 2006. "Naturalist Theories of Meaning." In E. Lepore and B. Smith (eds.), *Oxford Handbook of the Philosophy of Language.* Oxford: Oxford University Press, pp. 175–188.

Papineau, D. 2014. "Sensory Experience and Representational Properties." *Proceedings of the Aristotelian Society* 114, pp. 1–33.

Papineau, D. 2016. "Teleosemantics." In D. Smith (ed.), *How Biology Shapes Philosophy.* Cambridge: Cambridge University Press, pp. 95–120.

Papineau, D. 2021. *The Metaphysics of Perceptual Experience.* Oxford: Oxford University Press.

Papineau, D. 2022. "Swampman, Teleosemantics and Kind Essences." *Synthese* 200, pp. 1–19.

Pautz, A. 2008. "The Interdependence of Phenomenology and Intentionality." *The Monist* 91, pp. 250–272.

Pautz, A. 2013. "Does Phenomenology Ground Mental Content?" In U. Kriegel (ed.), *Phenomenal Intentionality.* Oxford: Oxford University Press, pp. 194–234.

Pautz, A. 2021. "Consciousness Meets Lewisian Interpretation Theory: A Multistage Account of Intentionality." In U. Kriegel (ed.), *Oxford Studies in Philosophy of Mind*, vol. I. Oxford: Oxford University Press, pp. 263–313.

Peacocke, C. 1981. "Demonstrative Thought and Psychological Explanation." *Synthese* 49, pp. 187–217.

Peacocke, C. 1983. *Sense and Content.* Oxford: Clarendon Press.

Peirce, C. S. 1878/1992. "How To Make Our Ideas Clear." In N. Houser and C. Kloesel (eds.), *The Essential Peirce*, vol. 1. Bloomington: Indiana University Press, pp. 124–141.

Peregrin, J. 2008. "An Inferentialist Approach to Semantics: Time for a New Kind of Structuralism?" *Philosophy Compass* 3, pp. 1208–1223.

Perry, J. 1977. "Frege on Demonstratives." *Philosophical Review* 86, pp. 474–497.

Piccinini, G. 2020. "Non-natural Mental Representations." In J. Smortchkova, K. Dołęga, and T. Schlicht (eds.), *What Are Mental Representations?* Oxford: Oxford University Press, pp. 254–286.

Pinker, S. and Prince, A. 1988. "On Language and Connectionism: Analysis of a Parallel Distributed Processing of Model of Language Acquisition." In S. Pinker and J. Mehler (eds.), *Connections and Symbols.* Cambridge, MA: MIT Press, pp. 73–193.

Pitt, D. 2004. "The Phenomenology of Cognition, Or, What Is It Like to Think That P?" *Philosophy and Phenomenological Research* 69, pp. 1–36.

Pitt, D. 2009, "Intentional Psychologism." *Philosophical Studies* 146, pp. 117–138.

Plantinga, A. 2006. "Against Materialism." *Faith and Philosophy* 23, pp. 3–32.

Price, H. 2013. *Expressivism, Pragmatism and Representationalism.* Cambridge: Cambridge University Press.

194   REFERENCES

Psillos, S. 1999. *Scientific Realism: How Science Tracks Truth*. London: Routledge.
Putnam, H. 1975a. "The Meaning of 'Meaning'." In *Mind, Language and Reality: Philosophical Papers*, vol. 2. Cambridge: Cambridge University Press, pp. 215–271.
Putnam, H. 1975b. "What is Mathematical Truth?" In *Mathematics, Matter, and Method: Philosophical Papers*, vol. 1. Cambridge: Cambridge University Press, pp. 60–78.
Putnam, H. 1980. "Models and Reality." *Journal of Symbolic Logic* 45, pp. 464–482.
Putnam, H. 1981. *Reason, Truth and History*. Cambridge: Cambridge University Press.
Putnam, H. 1983. "Computational Psychology and Interpretation Theory." In *Realism and Reason: Philosophical Papers*, vol. 3. Cambridge: Cambridge University Press, pp. 139–154.
Putnam, H. 1985. "A Comparison of Something with Something Else." *New Literary History* 17, pp. 61–79.
Putnam, H. 1988. *Representation and Reality*. Cambridge, MA: MIT Press.
Putnam, H. 1989. "Model Theory and the 'Factuality' of Semantics." In A. George (ed.), *Reflections on Chomsky*. Oxford: Blackwell, pp. 213–232.
Putnam, H. 1994. *Words and Life*. Cambridge, MA and London: Harvard University Press.
Pylyshyn, Z. 1980. "Cognitive Representation and the Process-Architecture Distinction." *Behavioral and Brain Science* 3, pp. 154–169.
Pylyshyn, Z. W. 1984. *Computation and Cognition: Toward a Foundation for Cognitive Science*. Cambridge, MA: MIT Press.
Quine, W. V. O. 1953. "Two Dogmas of Empiricism." In *From a Logical Point of View*. Cambridge, MA: Harvard University Press, pp. 20–46.
Quine, W. V. O. 1960. *Word and Object*. Cambridge, MA: MIT Press.
Quine, W. V. O. 1970. *Philosophy of Logic*. Englewood Cliffs, NJ: Prentice-Hall.
Raleigh, T. 2009. "Understanding How Experience 'Seems'." *European Journal of Analytic Philosophy* 5, pp. 67–78.
Ramsey, W. 1991. "Where Does the Self-Refutation Objection Take Us?" *Inquiry* 33, pp. 453–465.
Ramsey, W. 2007. *Representation Reconsidered*. Cambridge: Cambridge University Press.
Ramsey, W. 2020. "Eliminative Materialism." In E. N. Zalta (ed.), *The Stanford Encyclopedia of Philosophy* (Summer 2020 ed.), https://plato.stanford.edu/archives/sum2020/entries/materialism-eliminative/. Stanford: Stanford University.
Ramsey, W., Stich, S. P., and Garon, J. 1990. "Connectionism, Eliminativism and the Future of Folk Psychology." *Philosophical Perspectives* 4, pp. 499–533.
Recanati, F. 1994. "How Narrow Is Narrow Content?" *Dialectica* 48, pp. 209–229.
Reppert, V. 1992. "Eliminative Materialism, Cognitive Suicide, and Begging the Question." *Metaphilosophy* 23, pp. 378–392.
Rey, G. 1980. "The Formal and the Opaque." *Behavioral and Brain Science* 3, pp. 90–92.
Rey, G. 1994. "Dennett's Unrealistic Psychology." *Philosophical Topics* 22, pp. 259–289.
Rosen, G. 1997. "Who Makes the Rules Around Here?" *Philosophy and Phenomenological Research* 57, pp. 163–171.
Rosenberg, A. MS. *Eliminativism without Tears*.
Rosenthal, D. M. 1986. "Two Concepts of Consciousness." *Philosophical Studies* 49, pp. 329–359.
Rosenthal, D. M. 1993. "Thinking that One Thinks." In M. Davies and G. W. Humphreys (eds.), *Consciousness: Psychological and Philosophical Essays*. Oxford: Basil Blackwell, pp. 197–223.
Rosenthal, D. M. 2004. "Varieties of Higher-Order Theory." In R. Gennaro (ed.), *Higher-Order Theories of Consciousness*. Amsterdam: John Benjamins, pp. 17–44.
Rosenthal, D. M. 2005. *Consciousness and Mind*. Oxford: Clarendon Press.

REFERENCES   195

Rowlands, M. 2013. "Enactivism, Intentionality, and Content." *American Philosophical Quarterly* 50, pp. 303–316.

Russell, B. 1912. *The Problems of Philosophy*. New York: H. Holt and Company.

Russell, B. 1919. *An Introduction to Mathematical Philosophy*. London: George Allen and Unwin.

Russell, B. 1956. "The Philosophy of Logical Atomism." In *Logic and Knowledge*. London: Allen and Unwin, pp. 177–281.

Sacchi, E. 2022. "Is So-Called Phenomenal Intentionality Real Intentionality?" *Axiomathes* 32, pp. 687–710.

Sacchi, E. and Voltolini, A. 2017. "Consciousness and Cognition: The Cognitive Phenomenology Debate." *Phenomenology and Mind* 10, pp. 10–22.

Sainsbury, M. 2018. *Thinking about Things*. Oxford: Oxford University Press.

Schiffer, S. 1972. *Meaning*. Oxford: Clarendon Press.

Schiffer, S. 1981. "Truth and the Theory of Content." In Parret and Bouveresse (eds.), *Meaning and Understanding*. Berlin: Walter de Gruyter, pp.204–222.

Schiffer, S. 1987. *Remnants of Meaning*. Cambridge, MA: MIT Press.

Schulte, P. 2012. "How Frogs See the World: Putting Millikan's Teleosemantics to the Test." *Philosophia* 40, pp. 483–496.

Searle, J. R. 1980. "Minds, Brains, and Programs." *Behavioral and Brain Sciences* 3, pp. 417–457.

Searle, J. R. 1983. *Intentionality: An Essay in the Philosophy of Mind*. Cambridge: Cambridge University Press.

Searle, J. R. 1987. "Indeterminacy, Empiricism, and the First Person." *Journal of Philosophy* 84, pp. 123–146.

Searle, J. R. 1989. "Consciousness, Unconsciousness and Intentionality." *Philosophical Topics* 1, pp. 45–66.

Searle, J. R. 1990. "Is the Brain a Digital Computer?" *Proceedings and Addresses of the American Philosophical Association 64, pp. 21–37*.

Searle, J. R. 1992. *The Rediscovery of the Mind*. Cambridge, MA: MIT Press.

Sellars, W. 1963. *Science, Perception, and Reality*. London: Routledge.

Shagrir, O. 2001. "Content, Computation and Externalism." *Mind* 110, pp. 369–400.

Shagrir, O. 2012. "Structural Representations and the Brain." *British Journal for the Philosophy of Science* 63, pp. 519–545.

Shagrir, O. 2020. "In Defense of the Semantic View of Computation." *Synthese* 97, pp. 4083–4108.

Shagrir, O. 2022. *The Nature of Physical Computation*. Oxford: Oxford University Press.

Shea, N. 2007. "Consumers Need Information: Supplementing Teleosemantics with an Input Condition." *Philosophy and Phenomenological Research* 75, pp. 404–435.

Shea, N. 2013. "Naturalizing Representational Content." *Philosophy Compass* 8, pp. 496–509.

Shea, N. 2018. *Representation in Cognitive Science*. Oxford: Oxford University Press.

Siewert, C. 1998. *The Significance of Consciousness*. Princeton: Princeton University Press.

Siewert, C. 2004. "Phenomenality and Intentionality—Which Explains Which? Reply to Gertler." *Psyche* 10, pp. 1–8.

Simchen, O. 2017. *Semantics, Metasemantics, Aboutness*. Oxford: Oxford University Press.

Smithies, D. 2013a. "The Significance of Cognitive Phenomenology." *Philosophy Compass* 8, pp. 731–743.

Smithies, D. 2013b. "The Nature of Cognitive Phenomenology." *Philosophy Compass* 8, pp. 744–754.

Smolensky, P. 1987. "The Constituent Structure of Connectionist Mental States: A Reply to Fodor and Pylyshyn." *Southern Journal of Philosophy* (Supplement) 26, pp. 137–161.

196 REFERENCES

Smolensky, P. 1988. "On the Proper Treatment of Connectionism." *Behavioral and Brain Sciences* 11, pp. 1–23.

Sosa, E. 2007. "Experimental Philosophy and Philosophical Intuition." *Philosophical Studies* 132, pp. 99–107.

Speaks, J. 2015. *The Phenomenal and the Representational.* Oxford: Oxford University Press.

Sprevak, M. 2013. "Fictionalism about Neural Representations." *The Monist* 96, pp. 539–560.

Stalnaker, R. 1984. *Inquiry.* Cambridge, MA: MIT Press.

Stampe, D. W. 1977. "Towards a Causal Theory of Linguistic Representation." *Midwest Studies in Philosophy* 2, pp. 42–63.

Stich, S. P. 1978. "Autonomous Psychology and the Belief-Desire Thesis." *The Monist* 61, pp. 573–591.

Stich, S. P. 1983. *From Folk Psychology to Cognitive Science: The Case Against Belief.* Cambridge, MA: MIT Press.

Stich, S. P. 1990. *The Fragmentation of Reason: Preface to a Pragmatic Theory of Cognitive Evaluation.* Cambridge, MA: MIT Press.

Stich, S. P. 1991. "Narrow Content Meets Fat Syntax." In B. Loewer and G. Rey (eds.), *Meaning in Mind: Fodor and His Critics.* Oxford: Wiley-Blackwell, pp. 239–254.

Stich, S. P. 1996. *Deconstructing the Mind.* New York: Oxford University Press.

Stich, S. P. 2009. "Replies." In D. Murphy and M. Bishop (eds.), *Stich and His Critics.* Oxford: Wiley-Blackwell, pp. 190–252.

Stich, S. P. and Machery, E. 2012. "The Role of Experiment in the Philosophy of Language." In G. Russell and D. Graff Fara (eds.), *Routledge Companion to Philosophy of Language.* London: Routledge, pp. 495–512.

Strawson, G. 2010. *Mental Reality* (revised ed.). Cambridge, MA: MIT Press.

Strawson, P. F. 1950. "On Referring." *Mind* 59, pp. 320–344.

Strevens, M. 2019. *Thinking of Your Feet.* Cambridge, MA: Harvard University Press.

Sultanescu, O. 2015. "Bridging the Gap: A Reply to Hutto and Satne." *Philosophia* 43, pp. 639–649.

Swinburne, R. G. 1980. "Review of *Scientific Realism and the Plasticity of Mind*, by Paul M. Churchland." *Philosophy* 55, pp. 273–275.

Tarski, A. 1935. "Der Wahrheitsbegriff in den formalisierten Sprachen." *Studia Philosophica* 1, pp. 261–405. English translation: Woodger, J. H. (trans.), "The Concept of Truth in Formalized Languages." In Tarski, A. *Logic, Semantics, Metamathematics* (2nd ed.). Indianapolis: Hackett, 1983, pp. 152–278.

Thau, M. 2002. *Consciousness and Cognition.* Oxford: Oxford University Press.

Travis, C. 2000. *Unshadowed Thought.* Cambridge, MA: Harvard University Press.

Turing, A. 1950. "Computing Machinery and Intelligence." *Mind* 59, pp. 433–460.

Tversky, A. and Kahneman, D. 1973. "Availability: A Heuristic for Judging Frequency and Probability." *Cognitive Psychology* 5, pp. 207–232.

Tye, M. 1995. *Ten Problems of Consciousness: A Representational Theory of the Phenomenal Mind.* Cambridge, MA: MIT Press.

Tye, M. 2000. *Consciousness, Color and Content.* Cambridge, MA: MIT Press.

Tye, M. 2014. "What Is the Content of a Hallucinatory Experience?" In B. Brogaard (ed.), *Does Perception Have Content?* Oxford: Oxford University Press, pp. 291–308.

Van Gulick, R. 1995. "How Should We Understand the Relation between Intentionality and Phenomenal Consciousness?" *Philosophical Perspectives* 9, pp. 271–289.

Voltolini, A. 2022. "Troubles with Phenomenal Intentionality." *Erkenntnis* 87, pp. 237–256.

Wason, P. C. 1966. "Reasoning." In B. Foss (ed.), *New Horizons in Psychology.* Harmondsworth: Penguin, pp. 135–151.

Weinberg, J. M., Gonnerman, C., Buckner, C., and Alexander J. 2010. "Are Philosophers Expert Intuiters?" *Philosophical Psychology* 23, pp. 331–355.

White, S. 1982. "*Partial Character and the Language of Thought.*" *Pacific Philosophical Quarterly* 63, pp. 347–365.

Whiting, D. 2016. "On the Appearance and Reality of Mind." *Journal of Mind and Behavior* 37, pp. 47–70.

Williams, R. G. 2020. *The Metaphysics of Representation.* Oxford: Oxford University Press.

Williamson, T. 2004. "Philosophical 'Intuitions' and Skepticism about Judgment." *Dialectica* 58, pp. 109–153.

Williamson, T. 2005. "Armchair Philosophy, Metaphysical Modality and Counterfactual Thinking." *Proceedings of the Aristotelian Society* 105, pp. 1–23.

Williamson, T. 2007. *The Philosophy of Philosophy.* Oxford: Blackwell.

Wilson, R. A. 1994. "Wide Computationalism." *Mind* 103, pp. 351–372.

Wittgenstein, L. 1953. *Philosophical Investigations* (eds. G. Anscombe and R. Rhees). Oxford: Blackwell.

Woodfield, A. 1982. "On Specifying the Contents of Thoughts." In A. Woodfield (ed.), *Thought and Object.* Oxford: Clarendon Press, pp. 259–297.

Woodward, P. 2019. "Phenomenal Intentionality: Reductionism vs. Primitivism." *Canadian Journal of Philosophy* 49, pp. 606–627.

Wright, C. 1993. "Eliminative Materialism: Going Concern or Passing Fancy?" *Mind and Language* 8, pp. 316–326.

Yli-Vakkuri, J. and Hawthorne, J. 2018. *Narrow Content.* Oxford: Oxford University Press.

Young, J. O. 1995. *Global Anti-Realism.* Aldershot: Avebury.

Young, J. O. 2001. "A Defense of the Coherence Theory of Truth." *Journal of Philosophical Research* 26, pp. 89–101.

Young, J. O. 2018. "The Coherence Theory of Truth." In E. N. Zalta (ed.), *The Stanford Encyclopedia of Philosophy* (Fall 2018 ed.), https://plato.stanford.edu/archives/fall2018/entries/truth-coherence/. Stanford: Stanford University.

Index

For the benefit of digital users, indexed terms that span two pages (e.g., 52–53) may, on occasion, appear on only one of those pages.

Adams, Fred 5 n.10
adequacy (as substitute for truth) 120, 138, 172
Aizawa, Kenneth 5 n.10
analytic statements 139 n.37, 140 n.39, 149 n.2
ascriptivism 61–2, 123, 158 n.10
aspectual shape 18–20, 78–80, 84–5

Baker, Lynne R. 143, 148–50, 170–80
Bechtel, William 166 n.20
Blackburn, Simon 178 n.35
Block, Ned 5 n.11, 20, 22, 23 nn.40, 42, 50 n.4, 98
Boghossian, Paul 25 n.47, 112–13, 174–5
Bordini, David 63 nn.19–20
Bourget, David 5 n.10, 50 nn.3, 5, 61–2, 86
Boyd, Richard N. 150–1
Braddon-Mitchell, David 101–2, 102 n.13
Brandom, Robert M. 24–5, 112–13
Brentano, Franz C. 3–4, 7–8, 10 n.18, 11 n.21, 14–15, 169–70
Burge, Tyler 69 n.28, 122, 145 n.50, 168 n.22
Byrne, Alex 80 n.46

causal efficacy 116, 159–61
causal relevance 132, 160–1, 163
causal theory of names 31–2, 39–42, 118–21
causal-historical theory of names see causal theory of names
Chalmers, David 134
Chisholm, Roderic M. 5 n.11, 144
Chomsky, Noam 116 n.2, 166
Churchland, Patricia S. 133 n.25, 164 n.15
Churchland, Paul M. 1–2, 115–16, 143, 148, 171 n.27
Cling, Andrew 171
cognitive consciousness 50, 91 n.59
cognitive suicide 148–9, 170–80
coherence see truth as coherence
Cohnitz, Daniel 46 n.26
Collins, John 44 n.22, 165 n.17
concrete intentionality 1
content ascription, practice of 3, 33, 39, 41–2, 43 n.20, 45–7, 61–2, 83, 98 n.5, 103, 106–7, 113–14, 118–25, 139–40, 142–5, 145 n.50, 152, 154–6, 158–9, 162–3, 165, 168–9, 168 n.23, 175–6, 178 n.34, 179

content ascription, scheme of 3, 120–1, 132–3, 141–2, 179
content indeterminacy see intentional indeterminacy
content pragmatism 166, 168–9
Cosmides, Leda 136 n.32
Crane, Tim 4, 8 n.15, 132–3
cultural semantic diversity 29–33, 40, 44, 46 n.26, 123, 177 n.32
Cummins, Robert 166 n.20

Davidson, Donald 64–5, 93, 135–6
De Blanc, M. 31–2
Dennett, Daniel C. 11, 12 n.22, 52 n.8, 111 n.20, 168–9
derived intentionality 4–7, 51–2, 98–9, 144–6
descriptive theory of names 29–32, 39–42, 118–22, 131 n.22
Deutsch, Max E. 31, 38–40, 44
Devitt, Michael 31, 33, 36–7, 73 n.35, 104–11
disquotation 73–8, 152 n.5
Dretske, Fred I. 50 n.3

Earlenbaugh, Joshua 33 n.4
Egan, Frances 166–7
eliminative materialism see eliminativism
eliminativism 1–2, 116 n.2, 125, 143, 148–9, 170–1, 171 n.27, 174, 175 n.29, 177–8
Engelhardt, Paul E. 33, 44 n.22
error theory 122, 138, 175
Evans, Gareth 14 n.25
experimental philosophy 29–48
    puzzle of 44, 47
externalism, semantic 9 n.17, 22–3, 42 n.17, 59, 86 n.51, 92–3, 106–7, 122–3, 145 n.50, 155 n.8
extrinsic reduction of intentionality 49, 88–9, 96, 98–9, 117

Farkas, Katalin 62 n.18, 70, 87, 93 n.61
Field, Hartry 4 n.8, 6, 113 n.25, 141
Fischer, Eugen 33, 44 n.22
flat psychological surface 68, 70, 84–5, 91, 131–2
Fodor, Jerry A. 2 n.4, 3, 6, 22–3, 23 n.42, 49, 97–9, 115–17, 125, 144, 148
Frege, Gotllob 17–18

200 INDEX

Fricker, Elizabeth 173 n.28
functional role semantics 5 n.10, 20–5, 49 n.1,
   50 n.4, 96 n.1, 98, 101–2, 111–12, 155 n.8

Georgalis, Nicholas 71 n.33
Graham, George 5 n.10, 64–5, 92–4
Grice, Paul 5 n.11

Hales, Steven D. 35
Hannan, Barbara 143, 150 n.3
hard question of intentionality 3–4, 55, 79, 87, 93
Harman, Gilbert 8, 20–1, 63 n.19, 67–9,
   73 n.35, 74–5
Haukioja, Jussi 46 n.26
Herbelot, Aurelie 33, 44 n.22
higher-order theory of consciousness 50 n.3
Horgan, Terence 5 n.10, 54–5, 62–75, 87,
   89–90, 92–4
Horwich, Paul 176 n.30
Husserl, Edmond 4 n.9
Hutto, Daniel D. 113 n.24

intentional anti-realism, the negative
   thesis 115–18
intentional anti-realism vs intentional
   irrealism 1–3, 115–16
intentional function 9, 41–2, 73–7
intentional indeterminacy 64, 72, 76, 92–4,
   107–11, 123–4, 139–40, 154–5, 168–9
intentional inexistence 7–10, 10 n.19, 65, 85, 87
intentional instrumentalism 111 n.20, 168 n.23
intentional realism 1–3, 10 n.18, 51, 61–3, 94,
   100–1, 104–7, 106 n.15, 114 n.27, 115–18,
   122–4, 136 n.32, 137 n.33, 141–2, 144, 148,
   151–2, 154, 158–60, 165 n.16, 178 n.35
intentional stance 137 n.33, 142, 157, 165–70,
   171 n.26, 176–7
intentional suicide see cognitive suicide
intentionality as standard-object
   aboutness 16–22, 24 n.45, 25, 74–5,
   111–14, 155
intentionality, concept of 1–2, 4–5, 9, 11 n.20,
   15–17, 102, 104–7, 113–18, 155
internalism, semantic 9 n.17, 42 n.17, 62 n.18,
   145 n.50, 155 n.8
interpretivism 60 n.15, 168 n.23
intrinsic intentionality 6–7, 11–13, 51–3, 75, 77,
   77 n.40, 81–3, 95, 117–18
intrinsic reduction of intentionality 49–50,
   90–2, 117
introspection 62–78, 100, 125, 131–2, 172, 179

Jackman, Henry 46 n.26
Jackson, Frank 101–2, 160–1
James, William 68

Kahneman, Daniel 136 n.32
Kant, Immanuel 3–4, 87
Kitcher, Philip 151, 159–60
Knobe, Joshua 43–4
knowledge of content 76–7
knowledge, field of 139–43, 172, 179
Kriegel, Uriah 14–15, 24 n.43, 55–6, 63 n.19,
   82–3, 90 n.58, 97 n.2
Kripke, Saul 29–31, 38–41, 97 n.3, 116 n.2,
   118–19, 123–4, 152 n.5
   puzzle about belief 123–4
Kvart, Igal 124 n.13

Language of thought/connectionism
   dispute 131 n.22, 163–4
Lewis, David 110 n.18
Loar, Brian 10, 20, 22, 23 n.40, 24 n.46, 63 n.19,
   65–6, 68–9
Ludwig, Kirk 31, 34–6, 38

Machery, Edouard 30–3
Mallon, Ron 30–3
Martí, Genoveva 31–2
Masrour, Fred 87
McDowell, John 14 n.25, 16 n.29, 68
McGinn, Colin 78, 81–5
McLaughlin, Brian P. 133 n.25
Meinongean entities 13, 113–14
Mendelovici, Angela 9–10, 15–16, 57–62, 71
mode of presentation 17–21
Molyneux, Bernard 33 n.4
multiple realizability 128, 157, 160

narrow content 16 n.28, 22–4, 62 n.18,
   70–1, 85 n.50
narrow intentionality see narrow content
naturalistic individuation see naturalistic
   patterns
naturalistic patterns 152–9
Neander, Karen 113 n.23, 167 n.21
Nichols, Shaun 30–3, 43–4
Nimtz, Christian 33 n.4
normative inferentialism see normativity
   of content
normativity of content 24–5, 49 n.1, 97, 112–13,
   117 n.6, 119–20

Olivola, Christopher Y. 31–2
original intentionality 4–7, 51–3, 98–9, 144–5

Papineau, David 72–3, 87, 88 n.56, 95 n.63,
   101–2
Pautz, Adam 6 n.12, 51 n.6, 60 n.15, 64 n.21
Peacocke, Christopher 14 n.25
Pettit, Philip 160–1

INDEX 201

phenomenal consciousness 6–7, 49–51, 56–8,
 61–2, 64–5, 84–5, 90, 92–4, 95 n.63
phenomenal externalism 7 n.13, 51 n.7, 59,
 67 n.25, 86 n.50
Pitt, David 71 n.30
practice-dependence intentional anti
 realism 31–2, 45 n.24, 47, 106–7, 118–25,
 139–40, 143, 157, 178 n.33
pragmatism 135–6, 137 n.33, 139
Price, H. 175 n.29
primitive intentionality see primitivism,
 intentional
primitivism, intentional 6–7, 11–20, 26–7,
 42 n.17, 49, 51, 58, 60 n.15, 75, 90–1,
 113 n.24, 117
propositions 1
Psillos, Stathis 151
purport-to-refer 10–11, 13–15, 21–2,
 65–73, 89–90
Putnam, Hilary 23–4, 93, 101, 106 n.15, 110 n.19,
 122, 143 n.45, 145 n.50, 150–1
Pylyshyn, Zenon W. 133 n.25, 148, 150 n.3, 161–3

question of intentionality 3–6, 6 n.12, 11, 26,
 55–60, 66–7, 79, 89–90
Quine, W. V. O. 64, 139–40

Ramsey, William 166, 166 n.20, 174
real content see real intentionality
real intentionality 5 n.10, 52 n.8, 52–3, 82, 116 n.2
reductive naturalism (of intentionality) 12 n.22,
 21, 25, 49, 53, 55–6, 83 n.49, 89–90,
 96–114,118, 137–8, 154, 157–9, 162–3,
 165 n.16, 178 n.35
 as theory of content ascription 113–14
reference, concept of see intentionality,
 concept of
reference magnetism 110 n.18
referential diversity see cultural semantic diversity
relation in the strong sense 9–10, 87, 155
relation in the weak sense 9–11, 13–16, 22–3,
 66–7, 85, 87–92, 155 n.8, 155
relational view of intentionality 7–11, 15–16,
 66–7, 85–7, 91–2
representationalism, phenomenal 18, 50, 56–7,
 59–60, 83–5, 86 n.51, 91, 95 n.63
Rosen, Gideon 24–5, 112–13
Russell, Bertrand 3–4, 7–8, 118–19

Sacchi, Elisabetta 58 n.13
Satne, Glenda L. 113 n.24
Schiffer, Stephen 141
scientific realism 150–1
Searle, John R. 11–13, 18, 20 n.32, 52–3, 64–5,
 72, 78–81, 83–4, 134, 144, 146–7

selective scientific realism 151–2
self-ascription of content 73–7
Sellars, Wilfred 5 n.11, 21 n.35
semantic indeterminacy see intentional
 indeterminacy
semantic intuitions 29–31, 34–9, 41–7,
 63, 124–5
Shea, Nicholas 99
Siewert, Charles 60–1, 71
Simchen, Ori 110 n.19
Sosa, Ernest 33
Sterelny, Kim 73 n.35
Stich, Stephen P. 1–2, 30–3, 115–16, 118, 125,
 128–9, 132–4, 137–8, 161–2, 164 n.15, 166,
 166 n.20, 168–9
Strawson, Galen 1, 92–4
Strawson, Peter 140 n.40
success argument for intentional realism 24 n.45,
 125, 126 n.17, 133, 142 n.44, 148–54,
 159–66, 168, 170–1
Sultanescu, Olivia 113 n.24

Tarski, Alfred 135
thick logico-syntactic properties 126–131,
 135–7, 140 n.41, 146, 149–53, 156–9,
 162–3, 166–70, 172–3, 177, 179
thick logico-syntactic structures see thick
 logico-syntactic properties
thin logico-syntactic properties 126–7, 129–31,
 136, 151–4, 156
thin logico-syntactic structures see thin
 logico-syntactic properties
thought and language 4–6, 51–2, 98–9, 144–6
Tienson, John 5 n.10, 54–5, 62–73, 87, 89–90
Tooby, John 136 n.32
tracking theory 20–2, 98, 111–13
 see also reductive naturalism
 (of intentionality)
transcendence of intentionality 4, 9, 16–25,
 65–7, 69–71, 77–8, 88, 95–7, 113–14, 118
truth as coherence 120, 135–44, 146, 157,
 172–5, 177–9
Turing machine 153
Turing test 146–7
Turing, Alan 146–7
Tversky, Amos 136 n.32
Tye, Michael 50 n.3, 86 n.50

Warfield, Ted 133 n.25
Wason, Peter C. 136 n.32
Weinberg, Jonathan 37 n.10
Wilson, Robert A. 168 n.22
Wittgenstein, Ludwig 8–9
Woodfield, Andrew 24 n.46
Wright, Crispin 175 n.29